Justice and Its Surroundings

Anthony de Jasay

Justice and Its Surroundings

Anthony de Jasay

amagi

Liberty Fund

Indianapolis

Amagi books are published by Liberty Fund, Inc.,
a foundation established to encourage study of the
ideal of a society of free and responsible individuals.

The cuneiform inscription that appears in the logo and
serves as a design element in all Liberty Fund books
is the earliest-known written appearance of the word
"freedom" (*amagi*), or "liberty." It is taken from a clay
document written about 2300 B.C. in the Sumerian
city-state of Lagash.

Library of Congress Cataloging-in-Publication Data
De Jasay, Anthony, 1925–
    Justice and its surroundings / Anthony de Jasay.
        p.   cm.
    Includes bibliographical references and index.
    ISBN 0-86597-977-4 (alk. paper)
    1. Justice.   I. Title.
K240 .D4   2002
340'.11—dc21   2001050459

Frontispiece © 1998 by Lucinda Douglas-Menzies

LIBERTY FUND, INC.

8335 Allison Pointe Trail, Suite 300, Indianapolis, Indiana 46250-1684

Contents

Introduction

If "a thing is what it is, and not something else"—a safe enough proposition—we ought not to call it by something else's name or describe it by something else's defining characteristics. Wealth is wealth, and not freedom. One is a relation between persons and things; the other a relation between persons and acts. A freedom is a freedom, and not a right. The two denote fundamentally different relations between persons and acts. They need two different words to denote them, and the words are not interchangeable. Moreover, to assert a right to some freedom is to confuse a freedom with a privilege. If you needed a right to a freedom, it would not be a freedom. Rights are almost invariably represented solely in their beneficent aspect, their burdensome corollary passed over in silence. This falsifies the concept, failing to express in some way that no right can be conferred on someone without imposing an obligation on someone else; a right owing *to* somebody is owed *by* somebody else. Justice is justice, and not fairness or equality of some kind. Nor is it an all-embracing scheme of mutual insurance, and still less the terms of an agreement that might be reached under certain circumstances in an imaginary world. It is one thing to illuminate an idea by drawing parallels between it and related ones, but quite another to construct false identities that, helped by the law of adverse selection that governs much intellectual intercourse, will crowd out less-fanciful ones.

The carefree ease with which the word denoting one concept is borrowed and passed off as if it denoted another attracts little notice. Yet its gratuitousness and incongruity ought to raise eyebrows. It serves no good purpose, and it makes a curiously ill-fitting pair with the parallel tendency to dissect these concepts with the tiniest of scalpels and analyze them at painstaking, and all too often painful, length. It seems to me that by promoting clear thought, however, one would be doing a greater service to the good society than by promoting good principles.

If the reader of what follows feels that too much effort is going into the first of these objectives and not enough into the second, he now knows the reason why. I cannot prove, but am prepared to affirm, that if you take care of clarity in reasoning, most good causes will take care of themselves, while some bad ones are taken care of as a matter of course.

The title of this book tells the literal truth: the central essays, which all deal with justice, are surrounded on either side by treatments of subjects that are emphatically separate from justice, but that are never far from it, and with which it is much of the time mistakenly commingled. The state, the redistribution of income and wealth, the benefits and burdens between those who make collective choices and those who submit to them, the shaping of economic and social institutions so as to make them fit a unified ideology, and the problem of individual liberty occupy most of the areas that surround justice and sometimes encroach upon it. The essays arranged in parts 1, 2, 4, and 5 range over these fields without, of course, treating them anywhere near fully.

Although it is from these surrounding areas that claims are addressed *to* justice, it is by no means the case that all, or even most, of them are for justice to resolve. It is one of the most pervasive fallacies of contemporary political theory that, one way or another, normatively if not positively, every unfilled need, every blow of ill luck, every disparity of endowments, every case of conspicuous success or failure, and every curtailment of liberties, is a question of justice. If this were so, justice would have swallowed up the entire universe of social interactions and would have destroyed itself in the process. Called upon to set the world to rights, and to make it nice and cozy, too, justice would either act outside recognized rules or expand them indefinitely and make their system inconsistent, mutually irreconcilable. It is essential for the understanding of justice that many questions, however important to human coexistence, are irrelevant to it. Justice, to stay within a consistent set of rules laid down by just rule making, must dismiss them. If they are to be dealt with at all, it must be by principles other than the principles of justice. Securing full employment is most desirable, but that does not make it a question of justice. Lack of charity and consideration for others is reprehensible, but it is not a question of justice either.

Rival Concepts of Justice: No-Fault and Responsibility

In all reflection about what justice does and does not mean, the parting of the ways that sets the direction of all further thought comes at a very early point. One way to go, which I shall call, for want of a better word, the "no-fault" concept of injustice, is to consider states of affairs in relation to a norm, an ideal state of the world.

Actual states may be found unjust if they diverge from the ideal in certain ways. The principles guiding these findings will be the principles of justice. They can be violated without any human agency causing the violation (though it may be incumbent upon human agency to redress them if it is feasible to do so). Injustice, in short, can arise without an unjust act of man bringing it about. It is, in this essential sense, "nobody's fault."

The other way pursues fault. It is guided by an older, rival concept, where justice is inseparably united with responsibility. Redress is not called for if blame or guilt is not shown. Rules are not intended to help achieve a particular state of the world but more modestly to ensure compliance with important conventions. Chapter 10 seeks to clarify this concept, capturing its spirit in the two maxims "to each, his own" and "to each, according to . . . ." The concept, contrary to its more recent rival, does not admit that a state of affairs can be found to be unjust unless the putative injustice can be clearly imputed to an unjust act or acts. The principles of justice are those that help us tell just acts from unjust ones. If every act is ultimately the act of some person or persons rather than of such conveniently nebulous entities as history, society, or the market, personal responsibility must be pivotal to this concept of justice and decisive in distinguishing between the rival concepts and the ways their principles are derived.

Going down the no-fault way, it is perfectly consistent with the resulting principles to find that a state of affairs is unjust without attributing this to wrongdoing or unjust dealings on anyone's part. Blaming "the system" or the lack of suitable institutions is characteristic of this holistic way to justice. Obviously, a system or an institution is not responsible, or at least not in the sense relevant to acts by persons, unless, as a last resort, responsibility is traced to the acts of the persons who brought into being the system or institution in question in the first place. Thus, for instance, it could be argued that taking first possession of property was an unjust act responsible for the injustice of the capitalist system that grew out of the initial appropriation of what was previously unowned. The room that this line of reasoning secures for responsibility is likely to be made exiguous by the vagueness of the putative injustice and its remoteness in history. However, even this exiguous place is a contingent, incidental one and not an integral part of the concept. For an unjust state of the world—unjust, that is, by the yardsticks the concept generates—can come about without any man-made institution being at fault. The caprice of Nature in endowing men with different capacities and their habitat with resources is a sufficient cause and indeed the major operative one.

Perhaps the most potent force driving apart the two concepts of justice is the weight exerted on each by moral intuition. In the no-fault concept, moral intuition, and particularly the widespread, deeply felt, but inchoate feeling that most people could not and do not try to define, supports the idea that equality is essential to justice and injustice begins where equality ends. Its heavy reliance on the instinctive attraction of equality lends this concept great appeal. At the same time, the inherent woolliness of the notion of equality, and the great difficulty of clarifying it, is one source of its weakness. Its rival, the justice of responsibility, is almost leaning over backwards to allow the least-possible room for moral intuitions. Evoking our "disorderly minds" and the irredeemable inconsistencies of our moral intuitions, chapter 10 argues that a proper and solid concept of justice is composed of elements of a different and more orderly kind.

It is, in fact, the compulsive need to formulate the requirements of justice on a foundation of some, however ill-defined, ideal of equality that turns the no-fault concept into what it is. It becomes a logical necessity that it should be designed to judge states of the world rather than acts. It is morally undeserved that some people's lands should be more fertile, their climate more temperate, and their neighbors more peaceful than those of others. It is morally undeserved that one person should be born with greater (or indeed lesser) talents than another, or have more energy, application, and whatever else it takes to make himself a better life than another. Any advantage or disadvantage in achievement, welfare, or position is always imputable to differential endowments, both material and human, including the human resources of self-discipline and application. If the inventory of resource endowments is truly complete, no residual advantage remains that could be imputed to the person's own doing. He is not responsible for being ahead or behind, above or below any other person. It is not his fault or that of the other person. Nature does it all. Human injustice, reprehensible acts by individuals or groups against one another, are clearly not excluded by the no-fault scheme of things, but they are ad hoc, not integrated. Unjust states of the world would be generated by Nature even if only earthly angels inhabited it.

It is perhaps mildly amusing to find that, when each is pressed to yield its ultimate implications, both rival concepts have a strong feature in common: both have a chief culprit. For the one, the inexhaustible and principal source of injustice is Nature; for the other it is the state, or more precisely the power of collective choice to which individuals are exposed with scant ability to defend themselves. Much, if not most, such choices transgress both "to each, his own" and "to each, according to. . . ." Moreover, both of the major culprits generate injustice with complete impunity. No retribution is meted out to Nature for endowing one person with kinder and wiser parents, keener wits, and more stamina than another, and the river demons are not flogged for conjuring up the flood that spoils crops and makes thousands homeless. Nor are compensations and punitive damages exacted from the state for subjecting an individual to taxes and transfers for the benefit of other individuals favored by the majority of voters.

In a broad sense, parts 2 and 4 approach this theme from various angles, and part 1 is also relevant to it. One might continue in the same weirdly humorous, but in fact quite enlightening, vein by observing that if it were not for the complete impunity, the two major sources of injustice would perhaps not flow as copiously as they do. Failing retribution, all that is left is attempted redress. Part 2 on redistribution and part 4 on socialism, flanking the central part on justice, adumbrate some aspects of the problem of redressing the doings of Nature, arriving along diverse ways to the conclusion that these attempts are on the whole ill-advised. Part 1 poses the perhaps more radical question of whether there is really any good purpose that makes the state necessary. The received wisdom, of course, is unanimous that the state is needed for the orderly and efficient functioning of society, principally by virtue of the enforcement-dependent nature of promises and contracts. Chapters 1, 2, and particularly 3 seek to refute this, arguing that the underlying reasoning is both facile and confused. Less unanimously, much of received wisdom also holds that the state is a necessary condition of a just society. It is fairly obvious that the answer to this contention must be yes if the no-fault concept of justice is adopted and will overwhelmingly tend to no if the justice of responsibility is taken as the proper concept. On the latter basis, it is intellectually only just possible to consider the state as one of life's lesser evils, needed to ward off greater ones. More straightforward and robust arguments, though, lead one to its outright rejection.

At the beginning of this introduction, I lamented the persistent misuse of words in political philosophy, the misnaming and misidentification of concepts and the false ideas that are thus produced. The two rival concepts of justice seem more and more to be caught in this type of trap. It is facile and tempting to identify the no-fault concept with distributive justice, with the ordinary, common-and-garden name being reserved for the justice of responsibility. Such a division may make the job of intellectual map-reading easier, but it is the reading of a fairly naïve map, reminiscent of those early navigators used to draw. In fact, "distributive justice" is a pleonasm, for there is no other kind. It is of the essence of all justice that it distributes. Indeed, it does nothing else — and this is not mere verbal cleverness.

All existing distributions of benefits and burdens, rights and obligations, rewards and punishments, and all changes in these distributions are either consistent with the rules of justice, or they violate them. In the latter case, it is for justice to correct the injustice; in the former, it is for it to uphold the just distribution. Two frequently cited fallacies interfere with the understanding of this elementary truth. One is that there can be no distributive justice where nobody distributes, i.e., in a "market" economy. For here, the distribution of incomes (or other exchangeable benefits or burdens) is the wholly unintended, emergent result of countless bilateral transactions determined, in turn, by individual wants and capacities. Such exchanges are neither just nor unjust, nor are their aggregate. Where this reasoning goes astray is in overlooking that individual exchanges either are exercises of liberties (in the use of assets and the deployment of efforts and skills) and of rights—hence the overall distribution they generate is just—or are violations of these liberties and rights—which will make the distribution unjust.

The other popular fallacy is that some overall distributions are "patterned" and others are not, with "patterned" distributions being generated by "distributive" justice and others by common-and-garden variety (or, as it is even more confusingly also called, "entitlements"-based) justice. Once again, however, it is not hard to grasp that every distribution is "patterned" by something unless it is simply random. In a socialist society, the pattern may resemble some egalitarian model, though it is a safe conjecture that the resemblance will not be very convincing. In a capitalist society, the pattern will approximate what economists would predict from the pattern of factor ownership and marginal factor productivities. The capitalist "pattern" would probably differ from the socialist one; it might be more intricate and perhaps also more unequal. Each would differ from the typical hybrid that prevails in most majoritarian democracies, but all these would be equally "patterned" and equally the product of "distributive" justice.

Unsurprisingly, each of the two concepts of justice I seek to delineate and identify in this introduction has logical entailments that go beyond it and affect the way society functions; putting this another way, each concept is consistent with its own type of social surroundings. Opting for the concept that reposes on responsibility and where injustices must be imputable to unjust acts of actual persons has the stark consequence that many claims of persons or groups against one another, and many serious problems of society, are excluded from consideration within the context of justice. They are relegated to its surroundings, not because they are unimportant or invalid questions, but because they do not qualify as questions of justice.

Opting for the opposed concept, where states of affairs can be unjust without any human agency bringing about the departure from the ideal, entails that a society aspiring to be just finds itself locked in perpetual combat with the caprice of chance, blind luck, fate, the Almighty—in short, in combat against what game theory calls moves by Nature. Calamities hit innocent people, and they hit them unequally hard, with those who escape having no moral desert or claim to ending up better off. Perhaps more frustratingly to the believer in no-fault justice, Nature also treats some people better than others in giving them different genes, different abilities, and different characters. Arguably, if there were no differences between them in these respects nor in their upbringing and inherited wealth (differences they cannot be said morally to deserve), they could not expect to have either better or worse lives than any of their fellow humans. It is incumbent upon the just society either to iron out Nature's uneven work by making every life as good as every other or at least to iron out those differences that do not have, as their by-product, an improvement of the life of the least advantaged. A mutual insurance scheme, a hypothetical social contract to this effect is nothing more than the bells and whistles on the social engine that must perform this work and meet Nature's every move with the right counter-move.

Theories of justice inspired by the idea that its function is to rectify the way of the world by redistributing the good and bad things that happen to make up people's lots tend to be intellectually weak and vulnerable to the weapons of logic. For much the same reasons, however, they are emotionally attractive and appealing. They have very nearly swept the board in the latter part of the twentieth century. Chapter 9, dealing with "justice as something else," alludes to their proliferation.

Anyone who can overlook the intellectual weakness, whether knowingly or by faulty perception, finds a heroic perspective opening before him. Nature keeps shaping our social habitat, and ourselves within it, in an endless series of random moves. How inspiring it is to refuse such randomness, to keep undoing what it keeps doing, putting in the place of the accidental and morally arbitrary an order in which the principles of justice can prevail! Alas, Nature will not learn and will not mend its ways. For all its heroic ambition, this justice cannot prevail. At best, it must settle for a perpetual losing battle, effacing the work of blind chance here and there, but like in all losing battles, transforming the battleground into a depressing, messy, and sorry scene not all will greet as the scene of justice's courageous rearguard stand. No doubt the defensive struggle of no-fault justice against inequality-generating Nature will affect the distribution of welfare and indeed of all good and bad things. It may even do so massively along a broad front. Much more doubtfully, the distribution thus modified may be more egalitarian than it would otherwise have been. But unless it were hedged with implausible assumptions, a finding that the modified distribution was in fact more just would be a stand-alone, perfectly arbitrary value judgment wholly independent of any theory of justice purporting to underpin it.

Can one work wood against the grain? No doubt one can, but the result is unlikely to repay the pain. Can one make water flow upward? The proper agnostic answer is that we do not know, at least not yet. There have been examples of overcoming gravity, man has learnt to fly, and water may yet be taught to flow uphill. Most probably it will be very costly to make it do so, with much of the cost being temporarily concealed from view and surfacing in unexpected places as time passes. Attempts are continually being made to change the way societies function, to make them more predictable, impervious to chance, less subjected to the force of individual incentives and ambitions, and at least in some ways more like the ideal the no-fault idea of justice has in view. The most serious and ruthless of these attempts have already led to thoroughly shameful catastrophes for the countries concerned and have for the time being been given up. Less radical attempts, claiming to reconcile the exigency of universal welfare provision with tolerance for human nature and self-interest, continue. Some observers believe that these attempts are slowly and insidiously wrecking the societies concerned. The self-healing, self-regulating capacities, the ability to maintain useful conventions, and (let us not over-fastidiously shy away from the word) the "moral fiber" of these societies may be in danger of shriveling away. Time will tell—perhaps it is already telling it.

Collective Choice: Necessity, Convenience, and Legitimacy of the State

Individuals, groups, and classes seek to promote their conflicting interests and their competing ideals of the good life in the good society by whatever means it is prima facie rational for them to employ, given the expected benefits and the costs, material and moral, of securing them. It is natural enough that one of the means employed should be the appeal to justice. In the narrow sense, the appeal is merely a demand for adjudication, in the expectation that the recognized rules applicable to one's case will be found to be favoring one's cause. There is, however, a broader and more portentous sense of the appeal to justice. The appeal, in this broad sense, does not stop at claiming that under the rules in force, one's cause is just. It may, indeed, not try to make this claim at all and ignore the rules altogether. Instead, its appeal reverses the order of the argument altogether. It starts from the premise that one's cause is just. The rules of justice ought to be such as to bear out the truth of the premise and uphold one's just cause. Should the actual rules fail to do this, or fail to do it in an incontestable and secure enough manner, they are not proper rules of justice. They contradict the principles of justice and must be reshaped, expanded, and elaborated until the contradiction vanishes.

The ceaseless stream of attempts to shape, reshape, and bend justice and transform it into a servant of one's cause is the stuff of politics. Its effect is felt in both legislation and the execution of policies. Its instrument is collective choice (whether in its currently ascendant form of majority rule or in any other form that secures the submission of all to the choice of some). Opposed to the force of politics is the force of convention. Conventions emerge without any conscious choice on anyone's part and entail no rule of submission of minority to majority, losing coalition to winning coalition. To the extent that they are enforcement-dependent, their enforcement tends to be provided by secondary, "satellite" conventions. Obviously, we are dealing here with a notion that is far broader than the strict definition of a convention as a self-enforcing, nonconflictual coordination solution, or social norm. Important primary conventions, notably those against torts, used to be backed by secondary conventions, for example the ostracism of serious offenders against the primary convention.

These convention-enforcing conventions have lost much of their vitality as their functions have been often forcibly taken over by more formalized law enforcement by government in order to consolidate the state's monopoly of administering justice.

The basic conventions themselves, however, have very deep roots in prehistory and seem to be largely intact: their influence can be detected in the remarkable uniformity, across ages and cultures, of what most men consider acceptable conduct in their dealings with each other. It is also reflected in the broadly common understanding in most societies of what are freedoms and what are violations of rights. If people had orderly minds, never holding mutually inconsistent opinions and never being swayed by the direct day-to-day interests that proximity makes loom large, such common understanding would entail that there was only one concept of justice. Although this is only too obviously not the case, it is the case that without the foundations provided by conventions, the concept of justice would be too indeterminate to merit much attention. It would be a hollow form, capable of being filled with any content, depending on changing majorities, passing interests, and the fashions of the intellectual demimonde.

The surroundings of justice are largely dominated by two extraordinarily pervasive, and mostly opposing, forces: convention and collective choice. The former emerges spontaneously and is not embodied in any specialized institution, whereas the latter is, at least putatively, the deliberate product of a rule providing for nonunanimous rule making and is typically embodied in the state. Convention furnishes the stuffing for the justice of responsibility, whose firm but hollow forms would lack content without it. Collective choice, which imposes acquiescence by virtue of its rule of submission, is the instrument of no-fault justice. It is meant to settle the score between those who receive Nature's gifts and those who suffer from its indifference, let alone from its cruel blows. Collective choice is indispensable for evening out the inequalities that keep springing up irrepressibly from these "naturally" ordained (and perhaps also from other) causes. It would be fanciful to try and fight the battle against inequality under conditions of universal and voluntary cooperation, for on that basis the fortunate would not be willing to fight against their good fortune. A prior and irrevocable commitment to fight would be required from everyone, and such a commitment would be doubly unfeasible. It might well not be given by at least some self-interested persons who had already had some good fortune and were ahead of the game. And it might well be revoked if it were voluntary, for any self-interested person could refuse to live up to his commitment if, subsequent to making it, Nature started to favor him and he would have to fight against his own good fortune. A scheme of cooperation to combat chance, then, could not remain voluntary but would require an enforcer. The no-fault ideal, in other words, entails that a state possessing the monopoly of rule-enforcement is a necessary condition of such justice. If this justice is legitimate, the state is also legitimate.

Which of two different sets of principles of justice is really "just" is a question that, once stripped of rhetoric and ambiguity, is one of ethics. By contrast, whether the state is necessary for the very existence of a society (in the ordinary meaning of that term) is, on the face of it, an empirical question. I say "on the face of it" because it is not always evident which is the particular piece of empirical evidence that really answers the empirical question. Chapter 5, no doubt the most readable in this book, alludes to this problem. If all countries are states, does this constitute empirical evidence that countries must be states? The relevance of empirical evidence needs to be assessed in the light of the theory or theories that offer some explanation of why some observed fact should be held to support, or alternatively to falsify, a generalization. The role played here by an explanatory theory can be well illustrated by the way game theory is used to clarify the theory of the state. Such an attempt is made in chapter 3. If society is defined as requiring for its existence widespread reliance on reciprocal promises, i.e., contracts, and if contract has the incentive structure of a prisoners' dilemma, then society cannot exist because contracts would not be fulfilled. Default is rational and performance irrational for each individual. Performance would be rational for the players taken together, if there were such a thing as two parties "taken together." The problem of a collective entity, its "mind" and its "choice," is posed here and is further pursued in chapters 3 and 4. Individually irrational choice must be suppressed by collective choice. The state is necessary for society's survival.

Whether this formally correct deduction is derived from valid premises, i.e., whether it in effect is true, can be resolved empirically by investigating whether the proposition "contract is a prisoners' dilemma" is a descriptive statement of sufficiently high probability. Its probability falls drastically if there is enough evidence that performance is more and default less advantageous to each party than would appear from the face values shown in the contract. This, in turn, would be so if many or most single contracts were loosely but perceptibly tied together in a web of other contracts, present and prospective, between the same parties as well as others who are actual or potential partners of these parties. Any single contract acts as a link in a chain of contracts stretching into an uncertain future—a future, however, that will be shaped by the successive actions and reactions of the parties themselves. The rational individual seeks to maximize the present value of his gains over the whole chain. By performing as he promised in a given contract, he can expect to prolong the chain, make it sprout branches, and increase the probability that the prospective future contracts will in fact be concluded and the gains he would reap from them will in fact be realized; for by performing as he promised, he shows himself to be an acceptable contract partner. By defaulting, he would expect to produce the opposite effect, namely to shorten the chain and lose opportunities for profitable contracts. An individual contract party, by performing first, is signaling to the second performer that he is bent on "prolonging the chain" and proposes to go on performing unless stopped by the other party's default. Default, then, is no longer the dominant strategy for the latter. Contract without a contract-enforcer to whom the parties are subjected becomes credible, and all forms of social cooperation become feasible if contracts are credible. The state, then, is not necessary, whatever else it may be.

Necessity and convenience are seldom properly distinguished from one another in political theory. To say that the state is necessary for maintaining public order or reducing transactions costs, usually means that the speaker thinks it can do so more conveniently, at a lesser cost all told, than decentralized private arrangements relying on conventions could do. While something is either necessary or it is not, it may yet be convenient to some degree. Thus, the "needless state" may be convenient for some purposes for some people and not for everyone and every purpose. A case where a state is more convenient for some but less convenient for others than a stateless, ordered anarchy is, in technical jargon, a pair of Pareto-noncomparable alternatives. Objectively, there is no telling which is better. The legitimacy of sovereign authority in this case cannot be founded either on necessity or on convenience.

Redistribution: Inherent in Choosing Collectively

On examination, redistribution turns out to be the standard case, where collective choices are made by some and imposed on others, the submission of the latter being enforced by the state, which is controlled by the former. Here, the state is an instrument, not of contract enforcement to overcome the purported dominance of default over performance, but rather of the division of society into gainers and losers, free riders, and suckers by the use of taxation and the targeting of the production of unpriced, "public" goods and services to the greater benefit of some parts of society than of others. Chapter 2, discussing how taxation and the provision of "public" goods creates suckers and free riders, is placed in part 1, dealing as it does with what is the essential activity of the state. However, it already points to the intrinsic nature of redistribution, the subject of part 2. The two are hardly distinct, for neither is really conceivable without the other. The state is intrinsically redistributive. It has obvious reasons for this, but even if it did not, it would be hard to see how it could possibly contrive not to redistribute in the course of taking resources from members of society selected one way and returning goods and services to members of society selected in other ways. Whether the asymmetry is deliberate or not, redistribution occurs.

One can maintain that in this role, the state, though not necessary for social survival and not a convenience in the Pareto-superior sense that everyone would rather have it than not, is still a convenience, for without it, contested collective choices, designed to favor the winners, might be resisted by the losers. If we take it that redistribution is an ineluctable fact of social life, with stronger coalitions repeatedly exploiting weaker ones, it may be convenient to have a choice mechanism, a rule of submission enforced by the state, which ensures that the losers will submit to their fate without attempting resistance that would be futile but nevertheless require the costly use of violence by both sides before it was overcome. What the state does here might very well not be a Pareto-improvement, and we cannot really tell whether it serves the no-fault and egalitarian ideal of justice. But it does seem to be efficient in the rather simple sense that to arrive at a given result peacefully is better than arriving at it over the dead body of the losing party.

Where this argument assumes a little too much is in taking it that a given redistributive event, be it a taking, extortion, or taxation, will happen anyway, regardless of the means required to bring it about. This is mistaken reasoning, which fails to grasp the difference between a society with a rule of submission and one without. The incentive to take, extort, or tax must normally vary inversely with the probability of resistance and the cost the weaker coalition can thus impose on the stronger one, notwithstanding that by doing so it imposes a cost on itself, too. These are deep waters, and this is not the place for exploring their depths, though the moral monster they harbor can be glimpsed without much further search.

Redistribution, as its name betrays, cannot be understood without reference to some distribution that would have prevailed had it not been for some redistributive collective choice. The distribution that can serve as the reference is one on which collective choice has not impinged and that is consistent with broad compliance with conventions against torts. It is one brought about, at least ideally, by the sole exercise of individual freedoms and rights. These exercises take the form of the original appropriation of unowned property, of voluntary exchanges of goods and services produced, and the accumulation of property that results when producers abstain from consumption. This description is laborious and also inaccurate, but not markedly so. It points straight at the state of affairs that would obtain if no person involved in this distribution committed an injustice without its being redressed. By the argument of chapter 10, it is the distribution where each gets his own, the one that the individualist, responsibility-based justice requires. By the same argument, redistribution is unjust. If it is to be defended, the defense must stand on some ground other than that of justice.

The chapters in part 2 consider some such grounds. Two may merit mention in this introduction. One is the desirability of providing social insurance, protection against ill health, unemployment, disability, and old age, and doing so on a compulsory basis, covering both those who wish to be so insured and those who do not; given the cost they have to bear. The effect is redistributive, both for this subjective reason and for the objective one that some people are made to pay higher premiums than actuarially required and others lower ones. Despite some obvious perverse effects, the argument against this scheme is not simple and probably not conclusive, but it may help to see a little more clearly what is going on within compulsory insurance. The other ground, peculiar to the mature welfare state, is that a redistributive pattern, if it is time-honored, generates stable expectations of benefits that the beneficiaries come to regard as acquired "rights." What might justify continuing redistribution under these circumstances is the moral problem and the practical difficulty of discontinuing it. Chapter 8 sketches a conceivable way out that may look somewhat opportunistic or even cynical, but that at least lays bare what is perhaps the most awkward side of the problem.

Socialism: An Agent Without a Principal, a Market in Unowned Goods

Several institutions vie for the role of the Achilles heel of socialism. Ownership seems to be where socialism is most vulnerable, where the ties that some socialists, though not the classical, "scientific" ones, claim unite their doctrine to justice are the most frayed. The essence of ownership is exclusion; the owner, relying on the force of the ancient social conventions against torts, on some specialized enforcer such as the state, or on both, excludes all from the enjoyment of the good he owns, except those who obtain from him, by purchase, gift, or lease, some right of access to it. The right of the purchaser obliges the owner either to transfer to him the ownership as a whole or to allow him the use of some part or aspect of it, retaining the residuary ownership. Socialism denies that any person has the liberty to exclude another from the enjoyment of a particular good. For practical purposes, an exception is made of goods belonging to an (undefined) "private sphere." As a socialist writer on justice put it, let everybody own his toothbrush. The exception may be extended to all personal chattels, or indeed to every good that cannot directly serve as an input for the production of other goods. However far these exceptions, made in various versions of socialist theory, may extend, they remain exceptions; the general rule is nonexclusion. All good things, according to the general rule, are owned by everybody in common.

All distributions of a finite quantity of goods, just or unjust, are impossible without exclusion of some kind that rations access. The control of access may be chaotic and produce a random, unpredictable distribution, such as when a herd of hungry pigs throw themselves at a heap of maize, with some trampling down and jostling aside the others, some getting their fill and others hardly a grain. Or else it may be systematic, with orderly queuing and predetermined, if not necessarily equal, rations. Scarcity, nonexclusion, and distribution, however, are an incompatible threesome. No sooner does it abolish exclusion in the form of decentralized, personal ownership than socialism must reestablish it in some other configuration. Only in conditions of abundance, where distribution ceases to require constraint, could nonexclusion, i.e., the abolition of any form of property ownership, be achieved.

By expropriating at least the "means of production" and vesting their ownership in the state, socialism seeks, with a certain amount of tentative groping and fumbling, to accomplish two objectives. One is, broadly speaking, to assure the primacy of politics. This means a collectively chosen allocation of capital resources to various productive uses and a collectively chosen distribution of the product; the collectively chosen pattern replacing the pattern that would emerge from the interplay of voluntary exchanges under private ownership. As one socialist writer put it, the forum decides, not the market. (It is interesting to note that socialists tend to speak of the "market" as if it were a person, and a rather difficult if not downright dangerous character at that, inclined to malignant deeds. They make accusations against the "market" that they would never make against the "set of voluntary exchanges," overlooking that these two are synonyms of each other.)

A by-product of the change of ownership is that political and economic power are merged into one, vastly increasing the field over which collective choice holds sway. Many, though not all, socialists consider this, and the corollary shrinkage of the residual field left over for individual choices, as part of the objective to be accomplished.

The second, and probably less important, socialist objective is to reconcile these arrangements with the conception of justice closest to the main socialist tenets. This conception is not very well defined, in part because justice is not the primary interest of socialism. However, it never quite abandons the claim, and usually makes it quite strongly, that a socialist society is also a just society, with justice lending socialism added legitimacy, on top of the legitimacy it claims on other grounds (such as the laws of historical development and of rationality of social design). Socialism is in a delicate position with regard to exploitation and the opportunity of claiming credit for ending it; for while it can safely argue that it has stopped surplus value created by the workers being expropriated by the capitalists, it cannot easily argue that it has returned it to the workers to whom it in justice belongs. It is by emphasizing its respect for all human beings and its general humanitarian agenda that socialism makes its main claim of being a just doctrine or, more ambitiously, the doctrine of justice.

Having saddled itself with the functions of ownership, the socialist state at this point runs into one of its most unpleasant "internal contradictions." Relying as it does for allocation and distribution on a command system, it finds itself obliged to combat and if possible to suppress the ordinary incentives that induce people to evade and disobey its commands. These are the very incentives that drive a system of voluntary exchanges and generate allocations and distributions by letting everyone do the best they can for themselves. Relying willy-nilly on commands instead and finding that these are incentive-antagonistic, often positively inviting disobedience, cheating, and corrupt practices, the state must back up its planned-economy command system with a very powerful and intrusive enforcement mechanism. Plainly the harsher and more feared the enforcement, the greater the chance that commands will not be ignored or met by simulated obedience, but also the greater the contrast between it and the humanitarian face socialism wishes to wear.

In practice, despite temporary lurches into tightening followed by headlong rushes of relaxation, "real, existing" socialism tended over time toward ever weaker enforcement of ever more futile commands, until the spreading habits of sloth, theft, fraud, shirking, and pointless waste left it poised at the edge of the absurd. However, the discussion of the agency problem in chapter 13 suggests that even the best and most ruthlessly applied enforcement would have been impotent in the face of another fundamental systemic "contradiction" that must forever condemn socialism to inefficiency. In what is fondly called "social ownership," the state assumes the owner's functions in its rather poorly defined capacity of agent. It is the agent of the working class, of society, of the people, or—more disarmingly still—of historical evolution. In the capitalist system, except in the borderline case of the sole owner who is his own manager, there is a ubiquitous principal-agent problem that increases with, among other things, the remoteness and the security of tenure of the agents. Arguably, the principal-agent problem should grow to colossal dimensions under social ownership. However, the chapter in question makes the case that the problem is in fact more awesome still, because socialism effectively removes the principal from the principal-agent relation. The agent can behave as a loose cannon, a headless chicken, or a monomaniac, and all pretence to efficiency becomes a bitter joke.

Efficiency, of course, is merely one of many possible values (and only an instrumental one at that). There is no reason why it should be maximized if people are content to trade off some of it in exchange for other values. Socialism, however, lays itself bare to severe attack when it claims that there is no need to accept such trade-offs, for its system of social ownership enables efficiency to be maximized without sacrificing other values. Once experience had made this pretension untenable, there was a relatively brief flare-up of a modified doctrine that called itself market socialism. Its aspiration was to devise a system that preserved some kind of "social ownership," but made it incentive-compatible so that it would deliver efficiency like the capitalist "market" without becoming capitalistic. Chapter 14 reviews a work that sets out this aspiration. In its own right, it does not warrant attention. However, the market-socialist dream is for obvious reasons a sweet one, and it is predictable that one day soon small bands of academics and larger bands of political militants will start dreaming it again. Since the chapter is aimed not only at the book it reviews, but at some of the intrinsic features of the underlying dream that is liable to be dreamt again, it has been included in this collection. Any imaginable version of market socialism that may be proposed in the future must, to command a modicum of respect, clarify what it means by "social ownership." How does it propose to have a self-equilibrating market for consumer goods while abolishing the market in the "means of production" by abolishing their multiple ownership, and why anyone would bother to own or rent them? In addition, it must explain how it intends to secure equality of opportunity without continually sweeping away inequalities of outcomes that would arise in its system—for the opportunities within a person's reach are what they are today mostly because the outcomes he has reached yesterday were what they were.

Freedoms, Rights, and the Freedom to Trade Them

The last part of the book is devoted to some aspects of the idea of freedom. Trying to apply the maxim that each thing is what it is and not something else, there is some insistence that economic efficiency is not moral rectitude, that wealth is not liberty, and that liberties are different from rights—and that these differences have consequences which we ignore at the peril of getting mired in muddled thought. Beyond questions of clarity, however, there are others bearing on differences of conception, notably as regards the relation of liberty to justice.

If it is accepted that there is a presumption of liberty that, like certain other presumptions, can be derived mainly from epistemological considerations rather than from the intrinsic requirements of justice itself, a certain conception of liberty is discovered as a corollary. Every feasible act is deemed to be free unless a sufficient reason speaks against it. Justice has the main, if not the sole, say in deciding what are sufficient reasons. In this role, it is guided by conventions. Freedoms under this conception are a residual; they are what remains of the feasible set after unfreedoms have been identified as such by confronting them with the rules of justice and "blotted out" as inadmissible. Not all infringements of freedoms are ipso facto unjust; some, indeed perhaps the most, are really externalities reflecting facts of life. Because not all exercises of freedoms by different persons are perfectly compatible, some externalities are, so to speak, nobody's fault, and calls for their elimination are not calls of justice but of civility, mutual convenience, or norms of good taste. Conversely, infringements of freedoms by acts that are wrongful are unjust, not because they infringe a freedom, but because they violate some strong convention, most likely one against some tort. It is not that we have a "right" to freedom; it is that they (and we) have no "right" to commit wrong acts.

Opposed to this conception of liberty, which one might call "residual" if the word were a little less uninspiring and lacking in noble overtones, is one where instead of unfreedoms, it is freedoms that are specified. They add up to an itemized list that usually includes the freedom of worship, speech, and thought; the freedom to participate in collective choices; the freedom from arbitrary arrest and political and economic intimidation; as well as some vaguer "freedoms from," such as the freedom from want. Occasionally, they are called "rights" or "rights to freedoms," and are inventoried in bills of rights. Acts and types of acts not included in the itemized list have an uncertain status. Perhaps they are lesser freedoms. One authority, for instance, relegates what he calls "economic freedoms" explicitly to this lesser category. That, at least, is a recognition of their place, however lowly, in the inventory of freedoms. Perhaps acts not listed nor otherwise ranked are not freedoms at all. The suggestion is merely implicit and probably unintended, but the omission is characteristic. An itemized list of what we must be free to do will inevitably leave the major part of the universe of our feasible acts to an unspecified fate. Perhaps we will find that we are free to perform them, and perhaps we will not. One popular theory whose treatment of liberty falls within this conception affirms that liberty is actually an integral part of justice; it is nothing less than the first of its two principles. Liberty in fact means a system of "basic" liberties figuring on the itemized list. This system must be maximized for each individual, subject to the constraint that it must also be equalized as between individuals. Every application of this first principle, down to the least important, ranks ahead of every application of the second principle, up to the most important. Justice allows no trade-off between liberties and other values, no matter how little of one can be traded in exchange for how much of the other. Only a lesser liberty may be traded off against a greater one.

The principle and the instruction relating to permissible trade-offs reveal two points of great interest. The first one tells us that there is a hierarchy within the list of freedoms, since it speaks of lesser and greater ones. In the literature, this hierarchy is often illustrated by comparing the freedom of speech, a great freedom, with that of the choice between different flavors of ice cream, a superfluous frivolity. Now someone, paraphrasing a justly famous eighteenth-century author on moral sentiments, may say that man is seldom so innocently employed as when he is choosing between flavors of ice cream, whereas the same cannot be said of him when he uses his freedom of speech. But the heart of the matter is that it is nobody's business to say which freedom is greater and which lesser, nor to say that the suppression of one would be less objectionable than that of the other. The establishment of a hierarchy implies that it was established by somebody. But why was he entitled to do it and do it with an authority that bound everyone else to obey the hierarchy? One should have thought that it was up to each individual how he valued free speech and the free choice of ice cream, but the theory teaches that this is not so.

The second revelation flows from the first, but it goes further. It turns out that certain trades, notably those of "greater" for "lesser" liberties and of liberties for other things, violate the principles of justice, one of which enthrones liberty. Thus, freedom and free trade are incompatible.

A version of this thesis has been formulated in a rigorous form in a well-known "impossibility" theorem showing that under certain assumptions even minimal liberty is inconsistent with the freedom to exchange whatever one values less for whatever one values more. Minimum freedom is taken to mean that each individual is sovereign over the choice of at least one pair of free acts that are harmless to others.

He can, for instance, alone decide whether he will sleep on his back or on his belly. He would prefer to sleep on his belly, but if someone else were perversely willing to offer a pot of gold to make him sleep on his back, he would like even better to take the pot of gold. If he took the gold, he will have traded off his freedom, and if he refused it, he would have stopped both the other individual and himself from ascending to a more preferred position where he has the gold and the other fellow gets his way. The whys and wherefores of the issue are treated at some length in chapter 16.

Under "minimum liberty," the would-be sleeper is said to have at least the mastery over how to sleep. "How to sleep" is a proxy for all the freedoms that together constitute what is rather confusingly called the "private sphere" of an individual. I say confusingly, for what line, what moral, conventional, or legal border separates his freedoms that are "private" from those that are not? And if those in the private sphere have a special status and must not be violated if liberty is to prevail, what of those that fall outside the private sphere? May they be violated? The idea of two spheres, where the private one conjures up the sleeping on one's belly and the owning of one's toothbrush, is a source of muddle, mischief, or both. However, let that pass for the moment and continue talking of the freedom of choosing how to sleep, while bearing in mind that the words stand for a larger but undefined subset of the set of all freedoms.

If retaining your mastery over how you will sleep *means* that at least a minimal liberty is safeguarded (and selling your mastery *means* that it is forsaken), it becomes trivially true that minimal liberty and "Pareto-improvement" (where at least one party is made better off and no one is made worse off) cannot both be realized if the preferences of the parties are what the story says they are (which they could very well be). This is no more astonishing than to say that two mutually exclusive alternatives exclude each other. Going beyond the triviality, one must ask why safeguarding liberty entails refusing the pot of gold?

The would-be sleeper in the story has not one freedom, but two. One is to sleep on his belly or on his back. The other is to sell or not to sell to someone else his freedom to choose how to sleep. "To sell a freedom" is colloquial language for an operation where the would-be sleeper, in exchange for the pot of gold, assumes an obligation to sleep as he is told and at the same time creates a right for another to tell him how to sleep, i.e., to fulfill the obligation. A freedom is the relation of one person and one act. A right/obligation is the relation of two (or more) persons and one act. The transformation of a freedom into an obligation for oneself and a right for another is itself a freedom. In plain English, it is called the freedom of contract.

Equating a state of at least minimal liberty with a state where no individual may take a pot of gold for one of the freedoms in his "private sphere" is tantamount to subordinating the freedom of contract to any of the freedoms that fall within this sphere—a sphere, we must remember, that has no agreed or ascertainable bounds. There is no good reason why this equation should be taken as read. There is a strong reason for rejecting it, not merely as arbitrary, but as antiliberal, inimical to freedom. It purports, in the name of freedom, not only to impose a ranking among freedoms, permitting trade-offs only between lesser and greater ones, but actually to *mandate* a particular trade-off. If the liberty condition is not to be violated, the freedom of contract *must* be given up. The option of a general trade-off (any freedom against any other if they are mutually exclusive) is first replaced by a one-way option (lesser freedoms *may* be given up for greater ones) and then abolished altogether (the lesser freedom, that of trading, *must not* be exercised).

This is on the whole a harmless, albeit outlandish, pretension. As it and vaguely similar pretensions about what it takes to secure liberty trickle down to the intellectually less demanding regions of student essays and political programs, they become fuel and fodder for rhetoric against the tyranny of "the market," against which "society" must defend liberty and justice. "Society," due to the very nature of "its" choices, has at the best of times trouble enough in deciding which way is up. It is a poor outlook when those who make it their business to know better keep telling it that up is down and down is up.

Part One

The Needless State

1

Who Gave Us Order?
On Exclusion, Enforcement,
and Its Wherewithal

There is much—though never as much as we should like—that is feasible for us to do. What is feasible depends on the physical order of things and on our capabilities, enhanced by the cooperation we are given by friends and buy from strangers.

However, some acts that are feasible are not admissible. The physical order does not permit them. It imposes various kinds of costs on inadmissible acts. One is our own sense of remorse and shame, kept alive by the cultivation of a common ethical code. Another is a set of informal sanctions, yet others legal redress of torts, restitution of illicit gains, and penal sanctions. Many of these costs depend on the particular inadmissible act and the punishment effectively administered; we may thus say that the risk-adjusted consequences of inadmissible acts are intended to be negative for the actor. This seems to me as good a definition as we are likely to get without taking more trouble than it is worth.

Indirectly, this line of thought also provides a kind of definition of the social order. It is the set of institutions that singly or jointly make certain feasible acts inadmissible. Clearly, if all feasible acts are admissible, there is no social order whatever: naive ideas of freedom seem to imply such a lack, as do naive ideas of anarchy. The content and the characteristics of the zone of possible acts that are feasible-but-not-

Reprinted with permission from *Values and the Social Order,* vol. 3, *Voluntary versus Coercive Orders,* edited by Gerald Radnitzky (Aldershot, Hunts, England; Brookfield, Vt.: Avebury, 1997), 77–90.

admissible is, in any given world, in a one-to-one correspondence with the prevailing social order.

The latter may be simple or fussy, traditional or innovative, Spartan or Athenian, relying more on unspoken understandings or on explicit rules, local customs or unified legislation; which it is, what it does, and how, is no doubt closely related to the character of the society that lives by one kind of order rather than another. But whether it is the order that adapts to the character of the society, or the other way around, is a matter we can only speculate about. To what extent was socialism in the Soviet Union a product of pre-revolutionary Russia? And how far is present-day Russian society a product of seven decades of Soviet socialism?

If only because of this reciprocity, it is not a matter of indifference whether an order, or even an element in an order, emerges in the course of an "invisible hand"–type process as the largely unintended product of voluntary interactions among interested parties, or is chosen in political deliberation by some consciously directed decision mechanism. The first, by and large corresponding to what Hayek calls spontaneous order, develops gradually, is adopted voluntarily, and if it survives, it does so on its merits. The second, whatever its merits, is imposed both on those who wish to adopt it and on those who do not; it is installed and kept in being by a political process in which the winners force the losers to submit.

Consequently, whether to impose a constructed order or to stand back and let a (however imperfect) spontaneous order emerge instead, is not a "value-free" choice to be made by technocrats on consequentialist grounds, weighing economic efficiency against political feasibility. Carrying my rhetoric a little further, I have serious doubts whether we have even any moral right to *make* the decision, instead of letting spontaneity emerge, such as it will, by default.

First- and Second-Order Orders

The aspects of the social order we need more clearly to understand are common norm-like patterns of interaction in some domain of multi-person coexistence, which are useful to their adherents, hence durable and relatively predictable. Behavioral conventions are their typical example. They tend to arise and take root without anybody's conscious intent and without any organizing authority, though leadership may play a role at the origin of the convention, and in the setting of one conventional norm rather than another. Basically, these are Hayek's spontaneous social orders. Their observance helps coordinate human interactions and yields a coordination surplus, a benefit in terms of convenience, productivity, safety, reduced transactions costs, or whatever. In some cases, the coordination surplus rises continuously as adherence to the convention becomes more widespread and uniform. In other cases, there may be discontinuities, thresholds of acceptance that must be passed before any surplus materializes.

The surplus may accrue to members of the host community equally, in a biased fashion, or randomly. Everybody benefits if all speak English (or German, as the case may be, as long as all speak the same language). Everybody gains if all come to the fair on the same saint's day. Everybody is better off if all drive on the same side of the road. No matter how the benefit may be distributed among the participants, the crucial feature of such orders is that no one can deliberately increase his own benefit at the expense of his neighbor, at least not by violating the convention. These are, technically speaking, "pure coordination games" (Ullman-Margalit 1977), and their solution is a spontaneous order.

Alternatively, the order may arise from "non-pure coordination games" that contain the seeds of some conflict of interest, because they permit strategies by which the participants can improve their benefit at each other's expense. In a queue waiting to be served, everybody gains if all conform to the convention of first-come-first-served. Anyone, except the person at its head, can benefit *more* by jumping the queue as long as enough others are still willing to wait patiently. Such conflictual games may also have spontaneous orders as their solution, arising without design and conscious intent. But they are obviously more fragile. Depending on a host of variables, they may or may not be self-enforcing. In many cultures, including our own, queues usually form spontaneously and are by and large respected without explicit provision for enforcement. The same is true of countless other conventions that are intrinsically conflictual, yet implicit sanctions and the weight of breeding and custom prevent their wholesale violation. There are, however, possible combinations of conventions and their cultural surroundings that, like a rejected organ transplant, would not be viable without enforcement.

Here we have, then, a first-order spontaneous order that, in order to function, endure, and produce its benefits, requires the successful graft of a "second-order order" ensuring that the conventions of the first are sufficiently respected. This "second-order order" may itself be a spontaneous one; at any rate, the possibility cannot be prejudged and requires thought. It may also be something like the legal system of the state, for many, the obvious answer that springs to mind. However, this would be to ignore a broad spectrum of alternative possibilities. The state is at one extreme of the spectrum; a general theory, however, must encompass all other points along it, and their possible combinations. Hayek, who to my knowledge has never distinguished between pure and conflictual, self-enforcing and enforcement-dependent orders, has not addressed this issue, and has thus left open a vital flank of liberal doctrine, not so much to massed attack, but to gradual attrition.

A cornerstone of any social order, and perhaps the chief generator of inadmissibilities, is the institution of property; most of the present essay revolves around it. It is peculiar in several respects, including the fact that it bitterly divides political theory into two irreconcilable camps. Most of the other important order-producing institutions are fairly uncontroversial: no violent arguments rage about the conventions of civilized behavior, or about the most basic rules of tort or civil law. Property, however, raises passions, for much is at stake in it.

Property, for one camp, is "infrastructure." It is endogenous, practiced in all human societies from the cave-dwellers onward, and enforcement of the respect for property is also as old as humanity (or, as some students of primates have found, older). Reasonably secure property and its consequence, commerce, are for this view prior to political authority, to the state, and to a centrally enforced legal system. Oddly enough, libertarians and some classical liberals find themselves on the same side of this debate as the most orthodox spiritual heirs of Marx.

For the opposite camps, property is "superstructure" that owes its existence to an enforcement mechanism willed by society and operated by the state. The state, the legal system, the laws of contract, and other "market institutions" constitute the infrastructure upon which the superstructure of property and of the "market" are built. Property is a social privilege, its inviolability cannot be invoked against society itself, which can modify or withdraw the property rights it has granted and protected. Taking property is inadmissible for individuals, admissible for the state. This, in brief, is the theoretical basis of social-democratic and modern liberal doctrine.

It will perhaps help in assessing the "infrastructure vs. superstructure" controversy, to take a closer look at property as an enforcement-dependent convention.

Exclusion: The Enforcement of Property Rights

The paradigm of the enforcement-dependent order is the capitalist economic system. The paradigm is almost invariably presented in the context of a culture of morally unrestrained, anonymous, isolated individuals who do not seek to build and preserve a reputation for square dealing, because they hardly ever happen to deal a second time with anyone they had tricked or robbed in a first dealing. Real cultures have never been quite like this, and let us hope they never will be. In the supposed amoral and anonymous culture, the "market" (to use this somewhat sloppy term) is more dependent on some second-order enforcing order than in any other, for it is the worst of all possible worlds for capitalism. Schumpeter held that capitalism destroys pre-capitalist social virtues, and creates an amoral and anonymous setting that will, in turn, destroy capitalism. This is as it may be. Suffice it to say that, if the capitalist market survives in such a climate, by the logic of repeated interactions it can *a fortiori* survive in any other that is less anonymous and a little more moral.

Take, however, the worst-case assumptions. Under them, stealing or robbing is superior to buying, though buying is superior to not getting at all. Consequently, "spot" exchanges of adequately guarded property—a pound of sugar across the counter against cash—are self-enforcing, but contracts combining a spot delivery and a forward payment or vice versa are of course not: default on the forward half of the contract is superior to its execution, with obvious and dire implications for credit transactions. Everybody is better off if his commitments are credible to others, but he is better off still if, having been believed, he defaults on his promise. Hence no credible commitments are possible unless either default is deterred or restitution is assured. Above all, property must be physically protected, so that access to it can be made contingent on the owner's consent, which he can then sell or withhold. Interdiction of access, except by right or by the consent of the right-holder, takes care of the security of property and the fulfillment of unexecuted contracts.

In the last analysis, the problem of enforcing the spontaneous market order is reduced to one of exclusion, that is, the logical corollary of property which in turn entails the freedom of contract and the enforcement of its terms. Exclusion is the unifying principle that turns the theory of private goods (that are in the widest sense "property") and the theory of public goods into special cases of each other: goods are private when the relevant exclusion cost is incurred and public when, for whatever reason, it is not. (The exclusion cost relevant to a particular good is, of course, the cost of preventing unauthorized access to it. Arguably, there is no unauthorized access to a public good if it is intended that the entire public should have access to it.)

On a less lofty level of abstraction, a parallel generalization can be made about property in the ordinary sense, and "social," "collective," or "public" property. For the latter, exclusion cost is either not being incurred at all, or only to exclude those who stand outside the "society" or some other collective entity in question. (In strict logic, "the institution of property requires exclusion" is an analytic statement. Whether talking about any common pool ownership as "property" is a conceptual mistake and a misuse of the word—that is, whether the term "property" must imply that all equity interests in it are clearly delineated and all rights pertaining to its parts are ultimately the properly quantified rights of particular individuals—is not pertinent for our present purpose, though it is important for others. It is enough for now to note that property from which no one is excluded is a contradiction in terms. On the other hand, in a world of perfect bourgeois virtue, exclusion would be possible without the owner having to incur any exclusion cost.)

The Wherewithal for Exclusion Cost

How, and why, are the resources needed to meet exclusion cost forthcoming? If they were willingly provided by property-owners (or other beneficiaries of the capitalist system) as a matter of tacit social convention, we would have a second-order spontaneous order supporting the first-order spontaneous economic system, the "market." If, on the contrary, no resources were provided voluntarily, there would have to be a wholly "constructed" order involving the coercive taxing power of the state (or some agency that resembled it in all but name). The parable of the social contract with its attempted reconciliation of voluntariness and coercion, where coercion is by prior consent and taxation is an agreed price willingly paid in exchange for the services of the state, is of course no genuine alternative, nor has it any cognitive status. No evidence for or against it is possible, and it has no relevance for a positive theory of orders.

The all-voluntary private and the all-coercive state alternative are crude, simplified markers, standing for the two extremes of the range of conceivable solutions.

The statist, constructivist, and "post-liberal" view seems to be that failing an order inherited from past history, only the state can create one anew. But this goes against common sense, let alone strict logic. If there is no such order, there is no state to create one. In the decay or destruction of a social order, one of the first things to go is the capacity of the state to act purposefully, or at all.

The supposition that the economic system is somehow dismantled, and the state then comes to the rescue and restores property rights and creates a "market," is if possible even more outlandish. To restore property, exclusion costs have to be incurred.

However, there are no resources available for meeting exclusion costs if there is no pre-existing economic system to produce them. From this point of view, if from no other, the thesis that the state is prior to the market seems to be up against difficulties, whether its priority is meant to be temporal or logical, let alone both. There has to be some kind of economic order first, before the state can find the resource to lay the infrastructure for a new one. Perhaps, however, the old one need not be a "market" order? Yet, if it is not, can it be productive enough?

The statist solution to satisfying the enabling conditions of an economic order that is both beneficent and spontaneous, is visibly defective. A weak state, especially one with no stored-up reserves of legitimacy, lacks the wherewithal; it has little taxing power to extort it; there can be no efficient economy to extort it from, because the state has lacked the wherewithal to provide the enforcing order that could make it efficient. A strong state, supposing it is logically possible prior to an efficient economy, could find the wherewithal; but no reason is furnished why it would choose to refrain from using its strength in ways that would probably be more harmful to an efficient market than the much-dreaded Mafia. For cogent reasons, it is almost bound to invade and override property rights instead of protecting them, to impose the terms of contracts rather than to enforce those the parties would choose, to engage in ever more substantial redistribution of wealth and income—for this is the logic of the incentives under which states operate. They obey this logic to stay strong. If they do these things, though, the constructivist foundations they might lay would be inconsistent with the Hayekian spontaneously emerging market order. Can, in sum, a constructed legal order both be a pre-condition of the emergent economic one, and be inconsistent with it?

The statist, of course, is not unduly troubled by problems of consistency between the two orders, because he really wants to accouple his constructed legal framework with some Third Way, some alternative economic order that is neither "planning" nor "laisser faire." In the felicitous phrase of Mr. Václav Klaus, prime minister of the Czech Republic, the Third Way is the straightest road to the Third World; there is little else one can say in its favor, and it is not a subject that would warrant intellectual effort of analysis.

Hayek himself, rather unsatisfactorily, glosses over the problem by postulating a state that is neither too weak nor too strong but just right; a state that willingly limits itself to upholding the rule of law and to supplying the public goods "which otherwise *would not be supplied at all* because it is usually not possible to confine the benefits to those prepared to pay for them" (Hayek 1960, 222, my italics). Upholding the rule of law is, of course, itself widely thought to be such a benefit. If it is, and if this really means, as Hayek seems to believe of such benefits, that it is either supplied by the state or not at all, the state is a necessary, enabling condition of his idea of the market as spontaneous order.

No real resolution is offered by Hayek of the *quis custodiet ipsos custodes* dilemma. The substantive content of the rule of law which the state alone can uphold must, for him, be the product of spontaneous evolution, an emergent order. The state must not pervert it by constructivist legislation. Its tendency to drive out spontaneous law, to overproduce legislation (Leoni 1961), as well as public goods in general at the expense of private goods (cf., e.g., Bergman and Lane 1990), is treated by Hayek as dangerous but somehow avoidable. He has not, however, told us how.

To Grow and to Construct and the Time Each Takes

Can anything sensible be said about the opposite, all-private solution? Has the spontaneous growth of an emerging order for the enforcement of property rights sufficient internal logic and consistency? Or is it just nebulous metaphysical speculation about an utopia of arbitrary design?

As a first step, let us nail down the analytic truth that by the usual standard of instrumental rationality, it is rational for each owner to assume exclusion costs to secure his property and enforce the contracts waiting to be executed in his favor, in the same way as it is rational for him to shoulder any other cost involved in his economic activity, as long as the resulting benefit is at least equal to the cost. It pays to incur exclusion costs up to the point where marginal exclusion cost is equal, crudely speaking, to the risk-adjusted value of the marginal loss from theft and default the owner can avoid by incurring the cost. It inescapably follows that the total potential supply of wherewithal for an exclusionary order would, by and large and subject only to misjudgments of risk, always be adequate. Should it fall short, it would always pay to supply more, until the marginal equality of cost and value was achieved. (The converse is, of course, the case for an oversupply.) Exclusion cost incurred would seek the level that maximizes the excess of the total private value of enforcement over its total cost.

(I cannot deal here with the possible divergence, if any, between total private and total social value and cost.)

In a second step, let us ask why this inescapable conclusion is, as the man in the street is wont to say, "all right in theory but does not work in practice?" The answer is the standard one that it *would* work in practice if it *were* all right in theory. But it is not, given that the property owner usually has a reasonably assured option of taking a free ride. If he sees a high enough probability that "society as a whole," through the agency of the state, will look after his property and contracts along with those of everyone else (which is what Hayekian impartial and general law proposes), he need not look after it himself. The presence of the state, by holding out some more or less reliable prospect of publicly financed enforcement, unwittingly blunts the point of private efforts, if it does not render them pointless. The more reliable the prospect of effective enforcement by the state, the weaker will be the development of private efforts and the supply of their material wherewithal. Note that this effect is independent of the state's own conscious striving, visible in French and English history since about the thirteenth century and in other national histories at later stages, to elbow out private adjudication and private enforcement, seeking to gain "turf" for itself whenever it feels strong enough.

This is broadly why, to proceed to our third step, good theory could predict that real-life enforcement orders found in economies based on property, are almost always a mixture, some way along the spectrum between the extremes of the all-private and the all-state. Owners have fences, locks, alarms, dogs; buy insurance, install television monitors and electronic tagging against shoplifters; employ credit bureaus, private security agencies; have recourse to wise men and professional arbitrators. They boycott known or suspected swindlers, avoid dealings with defaulters and bankrupts, consult quality assessors before accepting deliveries, and tip off each other about the practices and habits of traders and producers. In tacit expectation of reciprocity, and sometimes also without it, they also tend to help neighbors, relatives, fellow members of clubs, friendly societies, trade associations, and other peer groups, both on matters of physical security and in the resolution of litigious issues. The habit of mutual aid, where it is efficient, may solidify into firm convention. Resources of self-help and mutual assistance are in practice supplied, not to the limit of the theoretical optimum as they should be in a purely private solution, but as a complement of the private-public mixture, a decreasing function of what the state can be relied upon to do, with greater or lesser efficiency, in these fields.

Starting from zero, on a wasteland with no history of voluntary action, the relevant private and communal skills, habits, and conventions no doubt take time to grow. But this is a truism that goes for anything that starts from zero. We may safely presume that it goes for states that are newcomers to capitalism, and propose, on a greenfield site, to "construct its legal infrastructure."

What, If Anything, Does Historical Evidence Corroborate?

Perhaps the most effective argument-stopper against the liberal hypothesis of the emergent order is that "in practice" it does not emerge. What does emerge is, at best, a quite primitive bazaar-type market and small-scale production, supposedly incapable of adopting modern technology and withstanding international competition. (Has anyone heard of the theory of comparative advantage?) What emerges at most is a severely exploitative robber capitalism ruled by the Mafia. It is claimed that only in the unique geography and history of England did capitalism emerge and flourish alongside a benign and minimal state; most historical evidence shows the primacy of the state and the dependence of the "market" on it.

It is always hard to be sure what historical evidence does or does not suggest. A good deal of evidence, however, can be cited to corroborate the hypothesis that systems of voluntary exchange arising from property and contract, favored by rules that were for the most part privately enforced, are as old as humanity and occur in a variety of societies. Whether such systems were exploitative is, of course, an undecidable question, since exploitation is in the eye of the beholder.

The law, notably tort law and the law of property based on the principle of exclusion, is historically prior to any proto-statal authority (Popisil 1971). This is borne out by the study of present-day primitive societies. Systems of voluntary exchanges of sometimes quite high degrees of sophistication, showing the essential features of capitalism, go back to classical antiquity (Love 1991). In more recognizable guises, we find them in medieval Venice and Genoa, and in their trade with the eastern Mediterranean and the Black Sea areas. They then come to flourish in the Renaissance towns of northern and central Italy, Ghent, and Bruges and the four great fair towns of Champagne (Pirenne 1925). From the fifteenth century, capitalism began to rise in England (MacFarlane 1979). English capitalism grew up in a period that, at least until 1688, was as turbulent as any in Western history, with property exposed to grave political risks. Nor did the even earlier and richer capitalist evolution of the Low Countries get much help from a settled society and the strong hand of authority. It overcame the handicaps, if handicaps they were, of the long war of independence against Spain as well as civil war and religious strife.

As far as we can tell from history, there was little or no "constructed" legal order to support the "market system" when the pace of its development was at its most vigorous (North and Thomas 1973; Jones 1981; Rosenberg and Birdzell 1986). It is as plausible to say that states hindered, undermined, and retarded markets, as that they helped them. It is significant, too, that where emigrant swarms from advanced civilizations founded new settlements, they did not seek to replicate the state authority they knew. Until organized government authority, its courts, police, and taxes caught up with them, their system of law and order was spontaneous, privately and cooperatively enforced (Anderson and Hill 1979).

There may be disagreement about the force of most historical evidence. But whatever the fragments that I have cited prove, there is one shining piece of evidence that really cannot be interpreted two ways. It is the ability of the international, footloose, stateless trading community to govern an increasingly complex system of spot and credit exchanges across and above territorial jurisdictions, by the spontaneously emerging Law Merchant, enforced mainly by peer pressure (Trakman 1983; Benson 1989). This is, as it were, the classic experiment to test what happens when states do not (because for physical reasons they cannot) impose their own organized, tax-financed order. It supports the reasonable belief that the trouble with the emergent order is not that "in practice" it does not emerge, but that for high-minded motives or for base ones, states stop them from emerging, and intrude upon them when they do emerge. (For a survey of the available evidence on the spontaneous enforcement of emergent legal orders, see Loan 1991/1992.)

Property Breeds Order

Systems of property and complex exchanges did not have to wait for states to lay their "legal infrastructure"; in many known instances, they laid their own as they went. With debatable justice, they might be called rudimentary; but is everything not rudimentary at its beginnings?

Enforcement, at all events, has no demonstrable *temporal* precedence over exchange. It seems to me, moreover, that the claim, frequently voiced regarding the travails of the ex-socialist countries, that order has a *logical* priority, is an arbitrary assertion and does not seem to follow from anything less arbitrary than itself. *If* "market institutions" really must precede the "market process" and determine the success of "market reform," it is a simple truism that they cannot be its product, and must come from somewhere else. Presumably their only source then is "constructivist legal activism." But no deductive argument or empirical evidence supports the premise about the precedence of institutions, any more than they support the claim that the chicken is prior to the egg. At best, such a claim could have the status of an expert inference from "technology": if he has neither chicken nor egg and must start somewhere, the social engineer had best start with an artificial chicken. But of course the technology is unreliable or the expert is misreading it. The artifactual chicken may be an expensive fantasy that will never lay a real egg. Starting with an artifactual egg may not help us to hatch a real chicken either. Neither project inspires much confidence.

A correspondent for an American paper, *Knickerbocker*, visiting the Soviet countryside in the early years of collectivization, once asked a *kolchos* president about their problems. "We have many great problems," he was told, "but they are all being overcome. The greatest, however, is that we have been told from above that we must dance the foxtrot in the village cultural center. This problem we have not yet overcome."

I am reminded of this anecdote when told that for "market reform" to succeed, the ex-socialist countries must have a new contract law, a bankruptcy law, stable money, a banking system, a stock exchange. In another anecdote, a totally apocryphal one, the president of the new Minsk stock exchange faxes the consultants in London: "We have licensed the brokers, put up the quotation boards, bought the computer, now what do we do?" Such institutional preoccupation is, of course, putting the cart before the horse. Real stock exchanges begin at the curb or in the coffee house, when owners have stock to trade. It does not have to be organized first: it is unstoppable. The licensing of brokers, the trading room, the tape may come in due course, but at all events not before *many* owners have *much* stock to trade. Stable money is a great help, but failing it, unrestricted barter is a more direct road to a functioning, efficiency-inducing price system than controls and repression of profiteering in an orderly legal framework. It is not the lack of bankruptcy laws and independent audits that are preventing bankruptcies and the liquidation of walking-dead enterprises, but political exigency.

There is a more fundamental sense in which the constructivist project is putting the cart before the horse. If the state is weak and its legitimacy is in shreds, it lacks the wherewithal for the construction and maintenance of a capitalist legal order out of nothing. In particular, it is too weak to protect property and ensure respect for contracts in the face of the poorer, more numerous, "socially" deserving party. In a state-made, state-directed order, wages are not bargains between employers and employees. They are a matter of politics. In such an order, the exclusion protecting property and contracts is infinitely harder to practice than in one where these are private matters privately enforced, with neither side appealing to the state except perhaps in the direst emergency. A state that has assumed responsibility for "market institutions" and depends on popular consent can hardly find the extra wherewithal, for example, to withstand pressure for insulating real wages from inflation, or for "saving jobs." The responsibilities it is assuming frustrate the emergence of an efficient economy, and prolong the agony.

Its weakness is relative, in large part due to the inordinately ambitious posture it is adopting. For it is, despite all the talk about privatization, still standing vis-à-vis society as did its socialist predecessor, both *in loco regis* and *in loco domine* both as political authority and as super-employer and super-owner. It takes all the blame attaching to both roles and cannot shift responsibility for the economic out of the political sphere. Even ruthless and practiced dictatorships have found it hard, in recent decades, to play the two roles of political lord and economic master and proprietor, all at once. But they at least had the means of their ambition until they used it all up. The ex-socialist states totally lack the means.

A spontaneous process, however its critics may scold it for being anarcho-capitalist and exploitative, generates its own wherewithal for an emergent order, which in any case is less hard to enforce. Stop stopping assets from falling, by fair processes or foul; from the hands of the state and of ownerless institutional holders, into the hands of natural persons and corporations owned by them. Let "social property" become genuine property.[1] The insistence, notably in Russia and Poland, on fairness, on preventing windfall gains and on dislodging the *nomenklatura,* are all laudable aims, but they draw the state ever further down the constructivist road and into roles that are too big for it. A tight grip, as in Hungary, holding onto voting majorities, "strategic" holdings in industries of "national interest," and selling the rest at the best possible price to Western corporations, with the proceeds flowing to the state's budget, does nothing to transfer at least one of the state's roles to a decentralized and indigenous class of property-owners. Only Prague seems, to date, to have grasped that the obvious way of transferring

---

1. Transferring a state-owned asset to the social security fund or to a bank that is really an extension of a government agency, is often said to be "privatizing" it. In effect, it is not. In terms of the argument of this paper, it is not genuine property.

state assets to the citizenry is to let each take a piece. Afterwards, they can sort out among themselves, by the ordinary processes of a nascent capital market, who shall end up owning what.

None of my argument was meant to suggest that a spontaneous order of voluntary exchanges, or a spontaneous order of their enforcement, or both, have much chance of emerging in the ex-socialist countries or anywhere else. At best, partial and fragmentary orders might spring up in the gaps, cracks, and crevices of the constructed order. It is hard to see how constructivism could fail to have the upper hand once it is assumed—an assumption governments and bureaucracies eagerly share—that the enforcing framework of order must be constructed first, what it is meant to enforce is to come afterwards. Not that it is impossible to put the cart before the horse. It is just not very practical. Nor does it prove that the horse cannot pull.

2

Taxpayers, Suckers, and Free Riders

The notion of public good presupposes a relevant "public," a set of persons who are similarly placed in some respect, such as location, language, legal status, interest, or need, and who all have free access to the good by the sole virtue of being members of the set. Publicness implies that though some or all members of the public may contribute to the cost of the good, for example by paying tax, their access to it is not "bought" by their contribution. (Public goods differ from "club goods" in that access to the latter is open to contributors only, e.g., to those who pay membership fees. However, the member may make greater use of the club good without paying more fees. Thus, while it is private intra-marginally, the "club good" is a public good at the margin in that consumption of an additional unit is virtually costless to the consumer, any increase in total cost being borne by the membership as a whole.)

The partial or total dissociation of contribution from benefit is the determining character of publicness. It is common to both the traditional theory of public goods and its emerging generalized version. In contrast to the traditional theory in which voluntary contribution by non-altruists to the cost of a public good is irrational, the contemporary approach treats the expected value of an individual's benefit from a public good as being probabilistically contingent on his own contribution and either smaller or larger than the contribution. By relaxing the traditional presupposition, the more general theory implies that if

Reprinted by permission of Sage Publications Ltd. from *Journal of Theoretical Politics* 5, no. 1 (1993): 117–25. © 1993 by Sage Publications.

the public good is valuable enough, it is potentially rational for non-altruists to contribute to it, i.e., that private provision can be perfectly consistent with free access.

The Traditional Theory

It may be held on some agreed ground (interpersonal welfare judgment, Pareto-optimality, or cost-benefit judgment) that producing a certain good is better than letting the necessary resources be used to some other purpose. If, however, the good cannot be provided for one member of the public without being provided for all others, the latter receive it as an externality. The contribution of anyone to the cost would benefit mainly the others, and the incremental benefit to the contributor would be small, typically imperceptible, and in any event smaller than the contribution. The problem is so defined as to make this the case. Hence everyone is better off if the good is provided, but for each it is better not to contribute; public provision requires compulsory contribution.

The goods in question have come to be defined by two properties, "non-rivalry" or "jointness" (greater use of the good by one user does not reduce the benefits available to the others) and non-excludability (a member of the public cannot be denied access to the good). Goods having both properties are "pure" public goods.

Traditional theory recognized that there are few or no produced goods that are "purely" public. However, it sufficed that access to the good was not or could not be made contingent upon a contribution to its cost for a problem of public finance and public welfare to arise, for left to the interplay of free choices, the good would either not be provided at all, or only in "suboptimal" quantities. The fulfillment of widely accepted optimum conditions would therefore require mutual coercion (Baumol 1952). (N.B. the prediction that the good will be "under-provided" by the market, rather than not provided at all, is open to the objection that if it is irrational to contribute to its cost, it is no less irrational to contribute a little than a lot.)

Normative Consequences

If a good is in fact in non-rivalrous joint supply, it is suboptimal to exclude anyone from access to it, since an additional beneficiary can be admitted to access without any increase in cost. Conversely, if a good is non-excludable, it must be provided in joint, non-rivalrous supply to permit non-discriminatory access by all members of the public.

How much of which public goods should be provided from resources made available under fiscal coercion? A necessary condition of optimal resource allocation is that, for every member of the public, the marginal "utility" one derives from the public good should be the same as the marginal "utility" yielded by every private good one consumes, and that no resources be left unused. This, in turn, implies that the marginal rates of transformation and of substitution between any two goods are equal to each other and to their relative prices.

However, individuals cannot normally effect substitutions between the resources they devote to private and to public goods. Their marginal rates of substitution are neither adjusted in nor revealed by market transactions. Nor do public goods have prices. A suggested solution to this conundrum was to aggregate all individual marginal rates of substitution for a public good (relative to a *numéraire* private good), as it were, "vertically," and to consider the sum of all individuals' taxes devoted to the public good as its price (Samuelson 1954).

This, however, merely yields a formal statement of the optimum in terms of unknowns which may or may not be capable of closer identification. Some may be defined by the preferences of a given individual, but the latter will have no opportunity to act upon them, and therefore cannot reveal them in the course of ordinary market transactions. Various non-market mechanisms have been suggested for inducing persons to reveal their preferences for public goods, notably by ranking alternative tax-cum-public good proposals. The basic idea is that the optimal proposal will be the one that is unanimously or near-unanimously chosen (Wicksell 1896). Taxation as voluntary exchange between the users and the provider of public goods is a common feature of these non-market mechanisms (Musgrave 1939, 1959; and Buchanan 1965, 1975).

However, intrinsic obstacles to such solutions subsist. If it is really the case that an individual benefit from a public good is not contingent on one's contribution to it, it is always best not to contribute, and not to honor any undertaking one may have given to the contrary. If revealing a preference for the good imposes a binding obligation to contribute to it accordingly, it is best to conceal (understate) one's preference. In agreements requiring (quasi)-unanimity, the incentive to sell one's veto right dearly would give rise to bargaining problems that may be intractable, or find resolution in redistributive bribes that cast doubt upon the putative merits of voluntary exchanges of the Wicksell-Lindahl type. Beyond these objections, the very meaning of Pareto-comparisons between coerced and non-coerced levels of public goods provision is open to serious doubt.

Escape Routes

Among suggested escape routes from the apparent dilemma, two have aroused wide interest. One is based on the game-theoretical finding that when a prisoners' dilemma situation is indefinitely repeated, it is payoff-maximizing for each player to contribute as long as the others do (Axelrod 1984), and this may make non-coerced provision of public goods consistent with self-interest (Taylor 1976, 1987). This argument has considerable force in contexts where the members of a non-excluded public have good visibility of each other's conduct and must count on interacting with one another in similar situations in the future. Accordingly, close-knit communities of various kinds would have good chances of providing public goods for themselves without recourse to coercion. Cases of successful voluntary cooperation and self-restraint in the use of common-pool resources (whose incentive structure resembles that of public goods) bear this out (Ostrom 1990). Large, anonymous, and amorphous groups with poor mutual visibility, however, would on this argument presumably not resolve public goods problems, however recurrent.

The other suggested escape route is the coupling of the non-excludable public good with an excludable private good, with the latter serving as a bait, as a "selective incentive" (Olson 1965). For the sake of getting the private good, a self-interested person may be induced to contribute both to it and the public good. One contribution, i.e., the price charged for the private good, must cover the cost of both goods for this solution to work. However, this is possible only if supplying the private good yields a supernormal profit, which can be devoted to subsidizing the public good. Competitors would then seek to supply the private good or its close substitutes at a lower price. A strong monopoly would be needed to defeat such attempts. How the monopoly permitting the supernormal profit could arise and persist is not clear, and the supposed role of "selective incentives" seems to contradict the logic of economizing behavior. Abandoning this logic, however, is inconsistent with the particulars that underlie the public goods problem.

Government Failure

Taking it for granted that voluntary provisions of public goods must be aborted by "market failure" due to non-excludability, traditional theory considers provision by the government, financed by taxes, as patently superior to the purported alternative of no public goods, lawlessness, and a "nasty, brutish, and short life." It seems to go without saying that since only the government *can,* it *ought to* supply public goods: "the only question which arises is whether the benefits are worth the costs" (Hayek 1960, 222). If this is the only question (and in a trivial sense there is indeed no other), it is a large one. There is no agreed way of answering it. How much of which goods are to be provided are matters decided in complex political processes. For well-known reasons explored in social choice theory, it is highly problematical to take the outcomes of these processes as the "true," credible, reliable expressions of "society's preferences." Yet, if available social choice mechanisms are not to be trusted, what other indications should one follow? On what grounds can one affirm that the benefit of a public good is (or is not) worth its cost?

Any political process offers opportunities for a winning coalition to distribute the benefits and costs of public goods asymmetrically, skewing the "product mix" to favor its own interests and tastes, and making the costs fall more heavily on the losing coalition. "The benefits are worth the cost" to the winners but perhaps not to the losers. Some or all of this redistributive effect is concealed from view, and some of it may be unintentional. Neither feature commends it.

Secondly, there is a presumption that the political process is systematically biased to overprovide the good relative to some putative Pareto-optimum. The bias may arise from "fiscal illusion"—people vote for incremental expenditure without perceiving a connection between it and their own incremental taxes—from asymmetry between those who vote for public goods and those who are made to pay for them, and from the ability of single-issue groups to press for and obtain expenditure on some special public good, of interest to the single-issue "public," by strategic voting or log-rolling. As Hayek put it, a public good must satisfy "collective wants of the community as a whole and not merely . . . of particular groups" (Hayek 1978, 111), but this merely begs the question of how we tell what "the community as a whole" wants, and how we make the political process deliver it (rather than some dubious aggregation of several particular wants).

Thirdly, there is a tendency systematically to overprovide public goods as long as their production responds to their use, consumption, or to need; for the marginal cost is imperceptible to the user, who hence has no inducement to use the good economically. A bias towards wasteful use is probably inevitable and is confirmed by experience, notably in publicly financed health-care and education.

On these and similar grounds, the provision of public goods by compulsory contributions is surrounded by "government failure" that takes the place of "market failure." However, the balance of the argument might still lean in favor of compulsory provision of at least some goods if voluntary provision were, as the traditional view used to hold, clearly non-feasible.

Generalizing the Theory

The received view of public goods is a special theory in that it rests on three particular and demanding assumptions, namely that:

(a) the goods in question are non-excludable;
(b) they are in joint supply;
(c) an individual's contribution to the cost of providing the good increases his benefit from it by less than his cost.

Each assumption can be usefully relaxed, rendering the theory capable of explaining a wider range of phenomena.

CONCERNING (A)

Excludability is not a binary, yes-or-no relation, but a matter of degree, best seen as a continuous function of the cost of excluding access to the good. This exclusion cost is, in fact, the cost of protecting (enforcing) full property rights in the good (Demsetz 1964). Part of the enforcement may itself be supplied as a public good (through the maintenance of law and order), while some of it is normally assumed by the holder of the right, the owner. By incurring the cost, the owner (typically the original producer or the reseller) ensures that access to the good is contingent on his consent, which he sells at a price. The exclusion cost can vary from the very low (e.g., measures to prevent shoplifting) to the prohibitively high. Some exclusion costs are "objective," a matter of technology and logistics, others may be subjective (e.g., the pity, shame, and social odium involved in refusing medical treatment to the indigent, or in excluding poor children from school, instead of treating such categories of people as a non-excluded public). A political decision publicly to provide a good may be due to its high "objective" exclusion cost, which would prevent profitable production for sale, or to a high imputed "subjective" cost, such as social disapproval, unrest, the risk of electoral defeat.

In principle, it seems possible to provide all goods freely to a defined community subject to a budget constraint. This is actually the case in many families where minor children get "all they want within reason," and it was meant to be the case for entire societies or the whole world under full communism. These considerations help us to see all goods as public, with private goods as a special case, or vice versa. A good is treated as a special case according to its exclusion cost. The differential advantage of publicly providing a good can be taken as the saving of this cost. This is trivially true if exclusion cost is defined all-inclusively. In a non-trivial sense, there is a balance of advantages and disadvantages. Among the latter is the encouragement of wasteful use.

There is some evidence that exclusion cost is sometimes ill-judged and over-estimated, deterring otherwise feasible private provision and militating for publicness. The for-profit provision of intellectual property, broadcasting, adjudication, contract compliance, public safety are among those suspect areas where exclusion costs may be lower than generally thought. In these and perhaps other areas, publicness may not be indispensable and for-profit production may be feasible. A notorious case is the lighthouse; it has long been cited as a paradigmatic non-excludable good, yet it turns out that English for-profit lighthouse operators, from the seventeenth century to their nationalization, were perfectly able to collect lighthouse dues from shipping. In fact, ship-owners petitioned for operators to be granted the right to erect lighthouses and collect dues (Coase 1974).

CONCERNING (B)

Non-rivalry or jointness is a special case where the supply of a good is abundant enough relative to its "relevant public" for every member to consume it, or otherwise benefit from it, at least up to some culturally conditioned standard which may but need not imply satiety, and where adding one more member to the public does not make the good less abundant. In the general case, supply may fall short of this level or exceed it, varying from inadequate to redundant. However, except for rare instances confined mainly to non-produced goods (e.g., daylight, language) as supply is decreased or as the public is increased, the benefit to the representative member of the public sooner or later declines perceptibly. Access to the good becomes "crowded" and sets off some process of non-price allocation. The latter may be wholly informal (the cheekiest consumer with the sharpest elbow gets the greatest benefit and the shy one gets none) or formalized, as in queues, lotteries, rationing, etc. Arguably, there will be some threshold degree of crowdedness, hence a threshold quantity of the good, past which the benefit yielded by the good is so impaired that it no longer satisfies the criteria, notably *free access* to some standard of benefit, that qualify it as a public good.

If this is the case, the good is discrete, "lumpy," indivisible up to the threshold. Some goods are, of course, "lumpy" intrinsically, regardless of the size of the public they are destined to serve; a road bridge has a minimum length set by the breadth of the river and a minimum width set by a single carriage-way. But even technically divisible, continuous goods may take on a discrete "lumpy" character when provided publicly, because they must be tailored to a given public with given customs, standards, and expectations. Unlike private goods, the supply of public goods and the size of their public are not reconciled by prices. That public goods have an *inherent scale aspect* determined by the scale of their public has an important consequence for the thesis, crucial for the traditional theory, that an individual's benefit is not (or virtually not) contingent on his contribution [cf. (c) below].

CONCERNING (C)

An individual's contribution to the total cost of providing a public good may, but by no means must, increase his expected benefit from it by less than his cost. It is perfectly possible that it will increase it by more. The question cannot be prejudged. The contrary supposition in traditional theory is rooted in the idea that the effect of a marginal contribution to total cost is a marginal increase in total benefit; this benefit is heavily diluted among all members of the public, most of it accruing as an externality to its other members, the part accruing to the individual contributor being (except in freak cases) imperceptibly small. However, for this to be the case, the total benefit from the good must be a continuous function of the total cost devoted to it, each small increment of the latter producing a small increment in the former. If, on the contrary, the good is discrete, "lumpy," the benefit from it will vary discontinuously at some threshold or thresholds. (Actual supply may be inadequate or redundant relative to the threshold size that matches the relevant public.) Marginal benefit may be nil (if the good is redundant) or equal to the total benefit (if without the marginal contributions the critical threshold supply would not be forthcoming). There may indeed be several critical levels corresponding to successive "lumps" of the good, or the good may be "lumpy" up to some level and continuous beyond it (Hampton 1987).

In general, therefore, the individual's valuation of the (uncertain) benefit he thinks he would get from contributing some sum of money or effort to the cost of a public good depends, in addition to the advantage of the public good over private ones, on his subjective estimate of the probability that the total benefit (or a "lump" of it) is contingent on his own contribution.

The traditional theory can be viewed as a special case of this general theory, namely the case where for all (or virtually all) members of the public this probability is small enough. But there is no a priori reason why this case should predominate. If no fewer than k members of an N-member public must make some predetermined contribution in order to secure some threshold supply of the public good, it may be reasonable for members to assume that the probability of their own contribution being required to secure such supply is k/N—though of course there may be particular grounds for forming a higher or lower probability estimate. This quotient, combined with the advantage of having a good provided publicly rather than devoting the resources in question to private substitutes, determines whether the expected value of the benefit from one's own contribution is greater or less than its cost.

Spontaneous Cooperation to Produce Public Goods

The provision of public goods cannot be analyzed properly without some use of game-theoretical tools, for an individual's best course of action depends on what others choose to do, and in the absence of coercion or self-enforcing mutual promises (either of which would remove the kernel of the public goods problem) the actions of others can at best be anticipated, surmised, inferred from what may seem best for them to do. The special assumptions of the traditional theory give rise to a game of prisoners' dilemma. It is best for each not to contribute regardless of what the others may choose to do. In a more general theory, there may be no such clear and simple imperative. If the differential advantage of having some public good is sufficient, the expected (probability-weighted) value of the benefit derived from one's own contribution may exceed its cost. The relevant "game," then, is no longer a prisoners' dilemma, for out of four possible stylized outcomes, non-contribution will then produce either the best or the worst (instead of the third-best), while contribution will produce either the second-best or the third-best (instead of the worst).

In the face of this payoff structure, a rational non-altruist has no dominant strategy. Contribution involves paying for oneself and for the free riders who chose not to pay and got the good all the same; the unfairness of playing "sucker" and missing out on the chance of a free ride argue against it. Non-contribution may yield a free ride, but it involves the risk of foregoing the benefit of the public good (or of a "lump" of it) if too many others also choose to bet on the uncertain chance of a free ride, and contributions fall short of the threshold level. Each individual's subjectively best strategy depends in some manner on the probability one attaches to others taking or not taking this risk. In fact, the choice of strategy is the choice between two risks: of finding oneself in the role of "sucker"; and that of losing all or a large lump of the benefit of the public good for lack of contributions.

Taking either risk to avoid the other is perfectly rational, and one is not a priori "more rational" than the other. The relevant subjective probability judgments and public goods preferences may vary widely from one person to another. Expectations of each others' behavior, therefore, need not be mutually consistent; it would indeed be surprising if they were. Logically there is, then, room for schemes of voluntary cooperation for the provision of a public good, with or without "political entrepreneurs" organizing them. In such schemes, "sucker" and "free rider" roles would be adopted spontaneously according to risk-choices, instead of being allotted by the government, that is, imposed by a politically stronger coalition on the weaker one.

3

Prisoners' Dilemma and the Theory of the State

Collective choice, reached by a recognized choice mechanism ("the king in his council," or "majority vote") preempts, or overrides, individual choice. It can do so by virtue of the authority of the state, enforced in the last resort by its monopoly of armed force. Theories of the state seek to explain why this has come to be the case, or why it is right that it is so. They must account either for the subjects' acquiescence or for their consent. In an acquiescence-based, Humean theory the origin of the state is exogenous; in consent-based, contractarian theories it is endogenous. In this essay we shall be concerned with consent-based theory, though acquiescence will obtrude before we shall have concluded.

Consent to the state's authority is weak or strong, roughly according as the subject is thought to regard it as a convenience on balance, or as a necessity without which life in civil society would be inconceivable. Weak and strong consent bear no relation to the distinction between limited (Lockean) and absolute (Hobbesian) government. Both weak and strong consent imply acceptance of the state's monopoly of enforcement, albeit for different reasons. Limited government cannot be enforced against the monopolist of enforcement. It is unintelligible to consent to the latter but not to consent to absolute government. If limited government exists, it does so as a vow is kept, unenforceably. Weak consent is rational if the anticipated benefits generated by the state

From *The New Palgrave Dictionary of Economics and the Law,* edited by Peter Newman (London: Macmillan Reference Limited, 1998), 3: 95–103; reproduced with permission of Palgrave.

exceed the anticipated costs, in the spirit of Leo Strauss's (1953) "political hedonism." Such consent can be solicited by references to the supposed increasing-returns character of producing defence, the protection of rights or dispute resolution; to reduced transactions costs; or to the efficiency or welfare gains from what Karl Popper (1963) called "piecemeal social engineering." Strong consent is forthcoming not as a result of any fine calculus, but because alternatives to the state are held to be unthinkable, contradicting as they are understood to do the iron logic of the non-cooperative "game" that in manifold social interactions corrupts human conduct, the prisoners' dilemma. Since Hobbes first injected it into political theory with the "Invader" of another's property, and Rousseau with the hunters who fail to catch the stag, this type of dilemma has been decisive in explaining why individual choice will rationally yield to collective choice, and why citizen-principals transfer power to an agent-state.

To overcome the dilemma, credible commitments are required: and they seem to presuppose a sole, unchallengeable enforcing agent. If such an agent did not exist or lacked the monopoly capacity of coercion, rational people would invent it, and endow it with power by disarming themselves.

Underlying the strong consent-type theory is the recognition that, unlike Robinson Crusoe, man in society can enjoy benefits, including positive externalities, whose costs he has not borne. The possibility of making gains by imposing losses on others, including future generations (as is the case with private or government dissaving, and the abuse of common-pool resources), renders social life fragile. From this springs the belief that, but for virtue, a stateless society would self-destruct. Virtue, to be sure, is not dead. We know it when we see it. But in the large group, among faceless men, it may or may not be there, and reliance on it would be reckless. Minimal prudence requires a state to overcome the dilemma and to protect society against itself.

It is possible to hold this belief too strongly. The logic of the stark, abstract statement of the prisoners' dilemma helps make it deceptively compelling.

Perform or Default: The Setting

In the general social dilemma, stated as a prisoners' dilemma, two players (who can be persons or groups, coalitions operating by a collective choice mechanism), interacting in some endeavor, have two available strategies. One is to do one's part, to perform as you would wish the other player to perform, to fulfil the intrinsic purpose of the interaction, to discharge the obligation at least implicitly undertaken by entering into the interaction in question, or *P* for "perform." The other is to shirk, to fail to do as you would wish the other player to do, to default on obligations, or *D* for "default." The four possible combinations of the two players' chosen strategies provide four possible game solutions. Each solution generates a game sum divided into two payoffs, one for each player (see Figure 1). Players generally choose strategies according to their preferences (though depending on the way payoffs are defined, they may be allowed a little leeway to choose counter-preferentially). They can prefer solutions, or payoffs. Solutions are relevant to collectively rational choice, payoffs to individually rational choice. Throughout, I shall take players to obey the requirement of individual rationality.

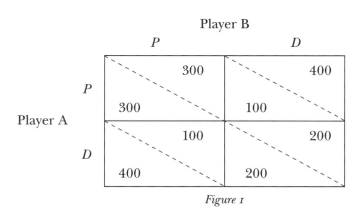

Figure 1

Are the payoffs to be understood as "subjective" utilities, or as observable goods having an "objective" identity? If they are utilities, there is yet another parting of the ways. Utility may mean "that which motivates choice," the rational person's *maximand,* including virtue if he is, and prefers being, virtuous. Or it may be confined to a narrower class, such as is supposed to move *homo oeconomicus.* If the former, the larger payoff is always chosen. If the latter, it is possible that the Nash equilibrium is never chosen; explicit room is left here for altruism, pride, shame, or sheer mental laziness. Whichever kind of utility were considered, its incommensurability as between persons would render the idea of a game sum, and collective rationality, moot.

If payoffs are made "objective," visible, the inconveniences of the concept of utility are avoided. Wealth creation and redistribution are as straightforward as utility creation and redistribution are not. Admittedly, in the face of wealth payoffs, one cannot treat payoff maximization as a corollary of rational choice. However, for integrating an informal game model into social theory, the balance of advantage seems to tilt in favor of talking of visible, material payoffs such as wealth. (An index-number problem in measuring wealth will speak against this alternative, but no other seems unblemished.)

Suppose now that players move in sequence to execute their chosen strategy. With Player A moving first, Player B second, the four game solutions can be written as DP, PP, DD and PD. PP and DD provide symmetrical payoffs of 300 each and 200 each respectively. With DP, A gets the free-rider payoff of 400 and B the sucker payoff of 100, and *vice versa* with PD. The individually rational solution is DD, for it maximizes either player's payoffs whatever the other player may do. The game sum, then, is 400. It is beaten by the mutually cooperative PP solution with its game sum of 600, and even by the asymmetrical DP and PD solutions, where a free rider and a sucker jointly collect 500. (The latter result can be avoided by squeezing the free-rider and sucker payoffs until they sum to less than DD, but the former cannot without abandoning the prisoners' dilemma assumptions).

The game entails a conflict between collective and individual rationality that justifies the state as the means for having collective rationality prevail. By the same token, it suggests a conflict between free choice and Pareto-optimality; for if the players could not freely choose D and were coerced to P, both would be richer. The alleged impossibility of the Paretian Liberal, where the exercise of a liberty by one person in a matter about which a second person has a stronger preference than the first, is incompatible with Pareto-optimality, owes its existence to an implicit prisoners' dilemma that prevents the two persons from contracting to mutual advantage (Sen 1970b). It is only fair to point out that for A. K. Sen, the originator of this impossibility theorem, the first person would not, could not, or ought not to trade his liberty to another person against a consideration he preferred to exercising the liberty, even if a contract to this effect embodied credible mutual commitments, i.e., if there were no prisoners' dilemma standing in the way (Sen 1983, 23–8).

As it stands, the prisoners' dilemma model of social interaction merely speaks of a payoff-difference between *PP*, mutual performance, and *DD*, all-round default. A mere payoff difference may elicit consent to the state that can, by enforcing commitments, move society from *DD* to *PP*. But this need be no more than weak consent, which may not be forthcoming if the payoff improvement was judged too modest compared with the coercion it costs to achieve it. However, the grand tradition of political philosophy, which meanders from Hobbes through Rousseau to modern contractarianism, is not to weigh the improvement on any fine scales. Its sense of the payoff difference is a descent from the thinkable to the unthinkable, the lawless war of all against all, the frustration of the General Will, the chaotic lack of secure property, and (in some versions of social contract theory) distributive injustice.

Is the Default Strategy Dominant?

One can challenge the logic of the dilemma—does it really mean what it appears, and is generally understood, to mean?—or its relevance—do any important social interactions really resemble it?

The former type of challenge boils down to arguing that the prisoners' dilemma, ostensibly a statement that, coupled with a maximization assumption, has the dominance of the default strategy as its analytic consequence, does not in fact entail a dominant strategy. Gauthier (1986) has proposed the thesis that practical reason counsels players to abandon straightforward, and adopt constrained, maximization that regards the interest of both players, maximizes the game sum as well as the individual player's payoff *ex post*, provided—and this of course is the *punctum saliens*—the other player is also a constrained maximizer.

This means that in sequential play, if the first player performs, the second player does not exploit him by responding with default. This is achieved by developing a moral disposition to repay performance with performance. The disposition is visible, and can be detected in advance of play, so that the first player can have foreknowledge of whether his performance would or would not be reciprocated. Obviously, players with a moral disposition would seek to play with others of a like disposition, and would do collectively and individually better than people lacking the disposition. Gauthier (1986, 169) stresses that his conclusion does not depend on iteration of the game, but applies with equal force to the one-shot prisoners' dilemma.

There are weighty objections to constrained maximization. The only rational disposition is to act rationally. No disposition to deviate from rationality can be rational. To assume a disposition to maximize would seem redundant. So does one to constrained-maximize, if constrained maximization is in effect the successful version of maximization as opposed to the self-defeating straightforward version. However, constrained maximization is only successful under the peculiar assumption of mutual clairvoyance by the players, credible foreknowledge taking the place of credible commitment and having the same effect.

The disposition to perform, then, in order to transform *PP* into an equilibrium and to break the dominance of default, boils down, not to a bias to act one way, rather than on the balance of advantage, but to a capacity to read the opposing player's mind; and it is this capacity that must be detected by the other player in order to remove any temptation to default. Under these conditions, the prisoners' dilemma is the equivalent of Newcomb's Paradox. A big prize may or may not have been placed in a closed box; next to it, in an open box, there is a small prize, a sure thing ready for the taking. If you take the sure thing of the small prize, the closed box will prove to have been empty; if you decline the sure thing, you will find the big prize in the closed box. The prisoners' dilemma is in essence a Newcomb's Paradox, with a pair of boxes for each player. Whether default is dominant hinges on the probability each of two players attaches to both players reading each other's minds and correctly predicting what the other will do. David Lewis (1979) has shown that if the big prize is *very* big relative to the small prize, a *very* small probability will suffice to justify declining the sure thing. It would then be, so to speak, rational to play irrationally (see Nozick 1993). Orthodox ("causal") rational choice theory would quite properly object that there is no cause for assuming that the probability of mind-reading foreknowledge should be anything but zero. It has been argued (Heiner 1996) that signal detection theory provides clues to a player's intentions that may serve as a substitute for supernatural clairvoyance. Apart from their extravagance, both the clairvoyance and the signals detection approaches amount to adding to the prisoners' dilemma a vital information content that would simply transform it into a cooperative game by making commitments credible. In its absence, the mutual default solution is the Nash equilibrium; it is dominant and Pareto-inferior.

The Repeated Game, and Hobbes's "Foole"

The grim logic of the one-shot prisoners' dilemma does indeed seem unshakeable; but does that matter much? For it is pertinent to ask whether, in a social setting, the one-shot variety can often arise. It is quite plausible to hold that it can occur only with difficulty, as a special case.

Axiomatically, today's worth of employing a strategy today is the present value of the effect (if any) on all payoffs present and future, accruing to the player. Obviously, today's strategy may make a difference not only to today's payoff, but also to the future payoffs that could be expected from alternative future strategies in games with both the same and other players who had access to the same network of stochastic information. Informally, this would amount to some chance of information reaching them by the "grapevine." The maximizing strategy to be chosen today is one whose effect is the greatest among all presently available members of the strategy set. Maximizing the present value of the effect on all payoffs, present and future, collapses into maximizing the immediate payoff if at least one of two conditions, independence or irrelevance, holds true.

INDEPENDENCE

The specifications of any future game where the player participates remain unaffected by the solution of the present game.

This condition in effect says that by playing "default," a player does not reduce the probability of having any player he meets in a future game play "perform." By the same token, it also says that by playing "perform," the player cannot improve the probability of his future partner also playing "perform." There is, notably, no scope for what we may call a strategic choice of strategy, designed to influence the strategy choice of a future player, including his choice between playing and not playing.

What the independence condition reveals is that whether a game is repeated or not is not or not only a matter of exogenous circumstance, but a product of the players' maximizing calculation. Maximizing the present value of expected payoffs means, among other things, that if games have only positive payoffs, it is better to play, even if the payoff is low, than not to play at all. Failure to get anyone to play with you is then a foregone gain, and the refusal of a prospective partner to play with you is tantamount to a punishment if the supply of available players is finite, or if finding them involves search costs. This is true even if the game is a prisoners' dilemma with mutual default as its solution, for in that game both players still get what game theory calls their "security-level" payoff. The "security level" is to the mutual performance payoffs as catching the hare is to killing the stag in Rousseau's Hunting Party. A more tragic conception would interpret mutual default as a negative sum—for example, the two players killing each other. In this conception both mutual default *DD* and unilateral performance *PD* would yield death as the payoff, but at least in *DD* the player would have the satisfaction of taking the other player with him.

With mutual default being a negative sum solution the "security level" would be found in "no play," in becoming a hermit. The punishment of being left out is harsher if the missed game would have yielded a payoff above the "security level." Any consistent punishment, however, such that the default strategy involves a sufficiently large foregone gain, "switches on" the well-known Folk Theorem (Sabourian 1989), by which the mutual performance strategy is an equilibrium, as is every other mutual strategy (if any such exists) that lifts the present value of both players' payoffs above the "security level."

Let this theorem be applied to a social situation of many potential players, each of whom has a "budget constraint" in terms of capacity to perform, take on employment, deliver a product or fulfil a task, obtain credit or commit capital—in short, a finite "stake" to play with, therefore, a finite number or scale of games to engage in. Finding the best games, whose payoffs promise the greatest excess over the "security level," then becomes an integral part of maximizing the present value of payoffs. Finding the best games is, *cet. par.*, the same as inducing the best partners to play with you. Pairs of players who are deemed each other's "best" partners (employers, employees, customers, suppliers— or, indeed, friends, comrades-in-arms, and spouses), at least within the confines of their opportunity set or search budget, will maximize the present value of the cumulative payoffs from their limited capacity to play, by *building* repeated games with mutual performance. In pure game theory, the players find a game of given initial specifications and adjust their strategies to the estimated probability of its repetitions. In social life, this probability itself is manifestly a function of their own strategy. They can *make* the probability increase by performing and decrease by defaulting. (Default reveals either that a player is not nice to play with, or that he holds a set of expectations that would probably make him default the next time round, too. Only the second reason is relevant among rational players.)

The bearing of this on the cost that it is worth incurring to build a reputation is evident. Reputation is perhaps the strongest single factor in making a player appear as a desirable partner, hence in enlarging the field from which he can easily select desirable partners.

It could be argued that reputations are like dispositions, in that rational choice allows no influence to either. Unless virtue is its own reward (i.e., it has "utility" for whoever practices it), it is irrational to have a virtuous disposition, or indeed any other except, truistically, the disposition to be rational. Likewise, it is irrational to act in conformity with your reputation unless, again truistically, this merely means conformity to a reputation for always choosing rationally. But this apparent analogy with a disposition is false. For what Player *A* must establish is a reputation, not for always performing as a dumb machine that does not know any better, but for always recognizing the reasons for doing so, due to his superior understanding of human psychology, his far-sightedness, his stakes in parallel games that may be affected by how he conducts himself, etc. This has a credibility in Player B's eyes that a gratuitous propensity to perform for no apparent reason, on a par with a gratuitous disposition, a "taste" for performing, cannot have side by side with the half-frightening, half-reassuring assumption by B that A is rational. It is best if B believes that what keeps A honest is his justified calculation that honesty is the best policy.

Can the independence condition stated above, namely that choosing a particular strategy today has no effect on future payoffs, be rescued from the perspective of strategy choices as choices among the present values of the expected streams of payoffs that these strategies generate? In any given game, can we say both that default is the dominant strategy (i.e., the game *is* a one-shot prisoners' dilemma), *and* that the expected punishment meted out to default makes of the mutual "perform" strategy a static equilibrium that repeats itself indefinitely until some relevant parameter changes? Plainly, if we say the latter, we are in the realm of cooperative games. This is, paradoxically, true of each single one-shot game, since the relevant payoff from a single interaction is the present value of the difference that that particular interaction makes to the stream of payoffs that a player can rationally expect to be forthcoming from a future lifetime of games. The explanation of the paradox is that continuing social life is *eo ipso* repetitive.

Default in today's game remains consistent with maximizing the present value of all future payoffs if it jeopardizes neither the finding of desirable partners for future games, nor the likelihood of the latter adopting a "perform" strategy. This will be the case if (though perhaps not only if) the fact of the player's default remains undetected for long enough by a large enough segment of his potential game partners— which is best achieved not by concealing the default, but by the defaulter being unidentifiable, or anonymous.

The first line of defence of strong consent, in fact, is the claim that, whatever may have been true of human conduct in the tribal, face-to-face society, the *Gemeinschaft,* has ceased to be so in the "large group," the "Great Society," the *Gesellschaft,* as well as the mass market favored by the economies of scale, and other forces thought to be similarly inexorable. In complex society the individual is said to have ample opportunity for interacting with others anonymously, hence irresponsibly. He can default with relative impunity, collecting the free-rider payoff without thereby having any influence on the strategies others will choose in future games where he participates—if indeed he is given a chance to participate at all. Hence in the Great Society and the mass market the Independence condition is allegedly satisfied, the default strategy is restored to dominance. The general proposition that the one-shot game is a special case of the repeated game remains true; but with Independence, the present value of all payoffs, present and future, is maximized by simply always maximizing the payoff in the present. The present casts no shadow over the future.

IRRELEVANCE

Next to Independence, Irrelevance is the other sufficient condition of the social relevance of one-shot prisoners' dilemmas. The future is irrelevant if it casts no shadow over the present. For one, the discount rate may be very high, so that the player might as well ignore what his defaulting in today's game will do to his payoffs in future games. A *very* high discount rate is, of course, a valid condition, but is unlikely to play much of a role in a world where most players save and invest, lend and borrow at humdrum single-digit rates. Another factor making for Irrelevance of the future, however, is less implausible. We might call it the Last Game factor. Plainly, if the present game is the last in which a player will participate, he should play it as he would a one-shot game; if it is widely known that his nth game will be the last game, by backward induction he must play every intervening game as if it were the last game. If the end of the world had been announced, all should do this. If the world went on but the player knew that he was not going to, he might do best for himself by making a last "killing."

Less dramatic cases, however, tell us more about how Irrelevance works. One such is the fly-by-night operator who lacks resources, competence, staying power. He plays a one-shot prisoners' dilemma, i.e., chooses default, because he could not really perform at the level expected in the game. He will do a sloppy job, furnish a defective product, and move on. Another is the Transient Tourist, whose every dealing with the locals has default as the dominant strategy for both sides, because both he and the locals know that he will not be back to deal again. Finally, there is the somewhat sad case of the Man Without Qualities and of no substance. Unlike the fly-by-night operator, he does not take the money and run. He is given no opportunity to take the money. He can offer so little to other players by way of performance that they will also hold out little prospect of a rewarding payoff to him. Mutual performance may here amount to no more than a lowly casual job for poor pay. Mutual default, absenteeism, shirking, ill-treatment, or no pay and no job might all amount to much of a muchness, making little difference to payoffs present or future.

While irrelevance-of-the-future cases do correspond to one-shot prisoners' dilemmas, they do not seem to have the weight to come anywhere near justifying strong consent by the representative rational individual. Does the independence-of-the-future argument weigh enough? If anonymous players are not identified with the strategies they employ, their future payoffs may well be independent of their present conduct; they can default with impunity, and, being rational, they will. Consequently, anarchy must be unsustainable and the state as ultimate enforcer of formal or informal commitments indispensable.

In fact, if anarchy is unsustainable, the best rational choice explanation seems to lie in the strong attraction of coercing one player into unilateral performance, with the other player enjoying free-rider advantages. Conquest from within (the Capetians in France) or from without (the Normans in England), historically the typical genesis of the state as a monopoly of using force, is a response to this attraction.

The fallacy of the anonymity argument lies in an almost trivial feature of the prisoners' dilemma that tends to be overlooked. In order for "performance" to be met by "default," the players' strategies must be hidden from each other or the game must be sequential. If two players execute their respective strategies simultaneously, and can to some minimal extent monitor each other, only symmetrical interactions make sense; much as I should love to default while you performed, you will not perform if you do not see me perform too. This game has only two symmetrical solutions, *PP* and *DD,* both equilibria. Simultaneity of execution transforms it from a prisoners' dilemma into an assurance game. Its counterpart in social life is the "spot" exchange, the cash transaction: it is "delivery against payment," whether the exchange is material or moral. This kind of protocol does admit anonymity, though certain simple safeguards may lend it additional comfort. There *is* no free-ride option; only the gains from a completed trade are on offer. Hence there is no need for a contract-enforcing authority. The game *is* cooperative because the underlying contract is self-enforcing.

By sharp contrast, a protocol with sequential, non-simultaneous execution of strategies does not admit anonymity in social interaction. The first player must perform before he sees the second player do so. This is tantamount to a credit transaction, in legal parlance a (partly) executory contract. Such a contract, however informal or even metaphorical it may be, must have named parties; the first performer, under everyday circumstances and *compos mentis,* will not deliver value on credit to a party he cannot identify (or whom a trustworthy intermediary has not identified on his behalf). Anonymity is tolerated by simultaneous, but is inconsistent with sequential, play—which, unsurprisingly, spoils much of the charm of the default strategy.

Nothing in the passage from few to many players, from the subsistence economy to the "global market," can alter this common-sense truth. The safeguards, aids, and comforts designed to mitigate transactions costs with non-simultaneous performance, the specialist agencies that assess quality and credit risk, and the ones that assure against it, that develop with the extension of a market, do more to confirm this central conclusion than to fray its edges. The reputed death of the community at the hands of what we loosely call modernity, and the rise of the anonymous individual, have implications that are indisputably momentous. But they impinge on the role of virtue rather than on narrow utility maximization, on the influence of moral precepts rather than the logic of Nash equilibrium, on the ear we lend to Aristotle and Kant rather than the one that listens to Hobbes.

In two key passages of Leviathan (Hobbes [1651] 1968, 203, 205) the Foole tells himself that, as "there is no such thing as Justice" and "every man's conservation, and contentment (is) committed to his own care," . . . "there is no reason why every man might not . . . keep or not keep Covenants." He then finds to his dismay that if justice does not demand the keeping of covenants, expediency does: for if he breaches his covenant, he "cannot be received into any Society" and, in the terminology of this essay, will not get to play in future positive-sum games "but for the errour of them that receive him." It takes a Foole to rely on "errour" and collective foolishness to let him get away with it. Foolishness is surely an inadequate source from which to draw the imperative need for an enforcer of covenants.

Yet such are the workings of the "sociology of knowledge" that public consciousness does not retain the Foole, but does retain the bowdlerized War of All Against All. The theory of the state, with strong consent to its authority, continues to be reproduced on the basis of a prisoners' dilemma whose social significance seems to shrink remarkably under an analytical stare.

The Public Goods Problem

There is something of the Indian rope-trick about the prisoners' dilemma. It reveals itself to be a single instance of a chain, or network, of repeated games, whose relevant payoffs turn out to be the present values of the future payoff-streams that the player expects to earn thanks to, or despite, his choice of present strategy. The Rope Trick shows an equilibrium solution of mutual performance, making commitments to perform credible. They are self-enforcing as the rope in the Indian rope-trick is self-supporting.

The game, in other words, generates the "keeping of Covenants," the very element whose lack makes for non-cooperative games and whose presence suffices to make them cooperative. Once the Indian Rope Trick has been displayed, the show is really over and the audience might as well go home. The basic social interaction is exchange. Except in special circumstances, completion of the exchange is a Nash equilibrium; subject to the same proviso, contracts of exchange are normally self-enforcing; by and large society plays a cooperative game and needs no subjection to an enforcer.

However, this show ends too soon and the audience may feel cheated. The program has bypassed what is widely considered the *pièce de résistance* in the modern theory of the state, the problem of non-coerced "collective action," more precisely the public-goods problem. "Collective action" as such, *pace* the eponymous title of several influential books, presents no problems, let alone a dilemma. Collective action is only a problem if it is onerous (rather than enjoyable), and if its benefits are not reserved for those who have assumed its burden — i.e., if it is a public good.

Public goods are usually defined as "non-excludable," meaning that access to them cannot be reserved only for those who pay their cost. However, every good is excludable at *some* cost. The cost of exclusion is incurred for private, not incurred for public, goods, perhaps because it is very high, perhaps for other reasons. Voluntary contribution to the provision of a public good is widely accepted to be inconsistent with narrow utility or wealth maximization, the incentive structure in question replicating that of a prisoners' dilemma with non-contribution as the dominant strategy.

However, if the inherently continuous nature of social interactions will, so to speak, dehorn the dilemma, why should voluntary contribution to public goods be problematical and why should taxation to exact contributions be a function that the state must fulfil, and only the state can fulfil? In fact, it makes perfect sense to define public goods so as to encompass everything man-made that is collectively, rather than individually, chosen. Defense against foreign aggression, the maintenance of a legal order, and the redistribution of resources to achieve a collectively chosen norm of social justice, can formally all pass for public goods along with lighthouses and traffic-lights. The effect is to make "public-goods provision" and "enforcement of collective choices" identically equal to each other. Understanding the state as the provider of public goods is, then, to understand it fully, leaving no residue.

By backtracking a little way to the real-life prisoners' dilemma as a repeated game with mutual performance as its Nash equilibrium and with the one-shot variety as a special case, one can rapidly grasp why, in the public-goods interaction, the game is not seen to be generating its own transformation from non-cooperative to cooperative play by creating credible commitments. As long as the putative dilemma concerns the division of labor and the exchange of its fruits as the basic building-block of social cooperation, the relation of the players is essentially a contract relation. The intrinsic purpose of the game is to complete the exchange. By the very act of entering the game a player signifies an intention, whether sincere or not, to complete his side of the informal contract. He who defaults first is frustrating the intrinsic purpose of the game. Unspoken as the covenant may have been, he breaches it. The ensuing sanction applied against him by potential players, above all that he will not be invited into the most desirable games in the future, is simply a reflection of his lower value as a game partner. It is the effect on the discounted value of his expected payoffs that keeps him honest and renders his commitment credible.

If, however, he is making no commitment, nothing can render it credible. Contrary to the basic contract-of-exchange situation, the player in the public goods' interaction makes no implicit promise. He invites no trust and betrays none. By consuming a public good he is admittedly enjoying a benefit to whose cost he has not contributed. But ought he to have done so?

Defensible arguments abound on either side of the question. If the good was a "pure" public good (i.e., "non-rivalrous"), his consumption of it did not deprive anyone else of any potential consumption; it had no opportunity cost. However, some goods may be non-rivalrous over some range, becoming progressively more rivalrous, "crowded" as that range is passed either because the number of consumers increases or the scale of provision decreases. Be that as it may, the claim of harmless, costless consumption does not stand up to the "what if everybody did the same?" objection. It may also be said, without violating this Kantian precept of universality, that benefiting from a public good is morally the same as accepting an unsolicited gift: the recipient owes neither payment nor a gift in return. An opposing view invokes the ontology of a club: if you are a member, and enjoy the facilities, it is literally meaningless separately to ask whether you owe the club dues or not (McPherson 1967, 64). If this analogy could be sustained, consuming a public good would indeed morally entail a tacit expression of a commitment to contribute to producing it. But the analogy is easy to reject: people choose to join clubs, but most of them have not chosen to be members of a society. It would be an unwarranted imposition to require them to emigrate if they did not volunteer to pay for the public goods that they found on offer. It is of course possible to argue, as Herbert Hart does (1983, 119), that this is a breach of the duty of fairness. However, nothing entitled the providers of the public good to understand that the consumers would, by consuming, feel duty bound, and be committed to bear the cost of provision.

A shorter way of putting all this is that public-goods provision *is not exchange*. On the contrary, it is its *negation*. Publicness entails a break in the *nexus* between value received and value provided, benefit and cost, performance against performance. For any given individual, there is no such *nexus*. It is only at the level of the "public," typically though not necessarily the entire population of a body politic, that beneficiaries and contributors are all in the same set and benefits for the set as a whole match contributions by the set. The setting of the public-goods interaction, unlike the exchange interaction, fails to provide any incentive to honor commitments.

Non-Exclusion: Do Public Goods Pose a Dilemma?

The realm of exchange is populated by goods that are private because access to them for use or consumption is prevented by exclusion, whose cost is borne by or for the benefit of the owner who grants access only against adequate consideration. Incurring exclusion cost allows exchange, i.e., that any benefit derived from the good should be matched by a corresponding contribution to its cost. Some goods have low, others high or very high, exclusion costs. Public goods are the special case of private goods where exclusion cost is not being incurred, either because it appears collectively rational (in some normative sense welfare-enhancing) to save it, or because it is deemed unjust, or morally objectionable, to make access to the good dependent on payment. If it were the case that incurring exclusion cost just "did not pay," the good could not be supplied privately, *nor publicly*, unless the above reasons for public provision obtained. Collective choice, then, decides that a good shall be publicly provided. It is that choice that makes the good a public good. The public goods interaction is an *n*-person game with two strategies: to contribute or not to contribute to the good's cost. All *n* members of the set of players may consume it; a subset (the "suckers") contribute, the corresponding complement (the "free riders") do not. (The complement may be empty.) The standard view is that this is a prisoners' dilemma, where voluntary contribution is irrational.

This view, which has common-sense appeal, rests on the (usually unstated) assumption that the total benefit from a public good is a continuously increasing function of the total contribution to it (Olson 1965: 9–15). A single contribution by a player produces a marginal benefit that is spread evenly among the n players. Only the fraction $1/n$ accrues to the contributor. In the neighborhood of the social optimum, marginal benefit and marginal contribution are roughly equal, hence if $n > 1$ the fraction of marginal benefit accruing to the individual contributor is always smaller than his contribution. It is usual to blame the "large-group problem" for the failure of voluntary provision, but in strict logic any group (i.e., more than a single individual who gets what he pays for) is too large.

The implication is that non-contribution is dominant. Hence, if collective choice wills that there shall be public goods, it must also will that at least some members of the beneficiary public be forced to make contributions to meet the "need," i.e., the intended scale of public provision of the good. How large this contributor subset shall be and how large the free-rider complement, i.e., to what extent the provision of the good should be redistributive, raises well-rehearsed questions of fairness, welfare, and justice. The collective choices adjudicating these questions will be the by-products of the collective choice regarding public goods. In this way, the whole theory of the state is wrapped up, in the most compact manner possible, in the purportedly unique public, fair, and welfare-enhancing solution of the public-goods dilemma. It is true that the dilemma has horns only because, and to the extent that, individual benefit and contribution are disconnected. It is also true that no law of nature disconnects them. A collective decision to avoid exclusion and its attendant costs does it. Yet if it is really the case that exclusion is sometimes unbearable, or its cost unconscionably high, strong consent to the state gets at least *prima facie* support from instrumental rationality.

Public Goods As a Hawk-and-Dove Game

A good deal has been written to show that it is feasible privately to produce "public" goods, or rather goods we tend to think of as public (Demsetz 1970; Friedman 1978; Benson 1990; Ellickson 1991). In many cases, exclusion cost proves less prohibitive than tends to be assumed, or innovative exclusion mechanisms or common decency on the part of consumers reduce exclusion cost and enable the good to be traded in ordinary market exchange. There is also a strain of political thought that rejects arguments for non-exclusion, i.e., for providing certain goods and services to a chosen public for free or under cost, on grounds of welfare maximization or social justice. By questioning that such non-Paretian categories as aggregate welfare and social justice can have intersubjective meaning, and that collective choice can have a consequentialist justification, this strain of thought attacks the root of the theory of the state by challenging the *raison d'être* it derives from public goods.

A philosophically less fundamental, but technically perhaps interesting, challenge aims at the incentive structure of the public-goods interaction. In brief, it points out that the premises that make the interaction a prisoners' dilemma are not universal truths. Different assumptions, equally defensible, give rise to an incentive structure that is not a prisoners' dilemma, but a game of hawk-and-dove. The defence of these assumptions rests on a probability and utility calculus that induces the players to value the "sucker" payoff from an "unfair" contribution more highly than the payoff from mutual non-contribution (i.e., non-provision of the public good). Vigorous objections to this calculus have been made by Kliemt and Lahno (1992) and Sugden (1991/2). The continuity of the function relating total benefits from a public good to total contribution may well not hold. "Lumpy" public goods, for one, are inconsistent with the continuity assumption (Hampton 1987). To produce a "lump," a corresponding lump of contributions must be made by a sufficiency of contributors. If one fails, the whole lump fails, i.e., the good is not produced. The marginal product is in that case equal to the whole "lump." Consequently, the proposition that the effect of one's own contribution on one's own benefit is always smaller than the cost of contributing, which holds when incremental benefits accrue continuously, ceases to be true when they come in lumps, let alone when they have a binary, all-or-none character. Arguably, public goods do have this character by virtue of their dimensionality, being destined for a non-excluded public of a given size with given "wants," and having no price that would adjust "wants" to the supply of the good.

Unlike the prisoners' dilemma, the payoff structure in such an interaction can have mutual non-contribution (failure to produce the public good at all) in worst place, while the "sucker" payoff (contributing and giving others a free ride) moves up from worst to third-best. As a result, two pure strategies, the "hawk" and the "dove," would both be equilibria. The hawks take the chance on a free ride, assuming enough doves will come forth to produce the good, and doves contribute unilaterally rather than take the risk of the good failing to get produced. Hawk and dove roles would be assumed by individual choice. The game would remain strictly non-cooperative, with no mutual commitment to give it an exchange-like character. Some goods would be publicly provided from voluntarily offered taxes, recalling the Wicksellian solution of optimal taxation (Wicksell 1896) without any attendant preference-concealment incentives. How this schema seems in effect to have worked for a quintessential public good, the lighthouse, is admirably set out by Coase (1974, 1988).

The Principal-Agent Problem

We have seen why theories of the state that stay within the rational-choice tradition tend at least implicitly to rely on the prisoners' dilemma to furnish the reason for individuals to surrender their autonomy to a collective-choice mechanism, and endow the state with the powers to enforce the resulting collective choices against any challengers, including those who would have preferred different choices. This puts a great weight on the prisoners' dilemma. Its capacity to carry it off, so impressive when seen as an abstract construction, proves questionable when examined in real social interactions. In the most basic and essential form of social cooperation, namely exchange, the game is a contract that the continuity of social relations invests with self-enforcing properties. The state is logically not "prior to the market." In the public-goods interaction, the prisoners' dilemma logic is less unconvincing, though still somewhat inconclusive. Derivation of the need for the state from public goods rather than from exchange, however, suffers from a weakness. While exchange is undoubtedly a constituent element of society, it is not evident that public goods are. Arguing from public goods for collective choice raises a distinct whiff of circularity. Collective choice having justified public goods, can public goods then justify collective choice?

Vanquishing the prisoners' dilemma, then, may or may not warrant strong consent to the state. Whether it does is likely to remain an evergreen, unanswerable question. However, its very formulation is grossly incomplete without incorporating within it the principal-agent problem that must be lived with and consented to together with the state.

It is a problem that has waxed and waned ever since states can be said to exist, from time to time assuming monstrous proportions with gruesome consequences. Though unlikely, it is possible that state power in the hands of paranoiac tyrants, glory-seeking dictators, and obsessive social engineers is a thing of the past. If so, we are still left with a sober and dull kind of irreducible principal-agent problem that is the logical corollary of imperfect control by the principal of the actions of the agent and of asymmetric incentives. The standard objection to apprehensions about the agent's self-serving use of his discretion is that, wherever there is democracy, there is no discretion by the agent, since abusive governments are revoked at the next election (Hampton 1990). Thanks are due even for small mercies, but this mercy is small indeed; for while governments can be revoked, the state and its monopoly power cannot be, any more than the genie can be put back in the bottle. At the very lowest, its various institutions, and the bureaucracies that live in and off them, have a continuing existence and permanent interests independent of governments that come and go. At its highest, the very nature of the state, *any* state, however constitutional or democratic, gives rise to a deeper principal-agent problem that goes beyond alienated bureaucracies or corrupt politicians. Since there is an agent that will duly enforce whatever decision is produced by the collective choice mechanism, powerful free-rider incentives are created for using the mechanism in ways that would be simply uneconomic if enforcement were not available as a "public good"; too many free rides would cease to be free. The everyday manifestations of this phenomenon, with interest groups and "rent-seekers" exploiting the general public through policies enforced at the latter's own expense, are well known from the Public Choice literature. A more general and more abstract statement of the case would be that the availability of the agent-state *ipso facto* sets up a "game" in which some principals will, in an unstable solution, always form an alliance with the agent at the expense of other principals.

Collusion and Acquiescence

In contractarian theories of the state, one or both of two contracts play a part. In one contract, principals seeking to organize their passage from the state of nature into civil society agree to a collective-choice mechanism. They undertake mutually to abide by the decisions the mechanism produces, and give a mandate to the state to enforce this undertaking against themselves. The state is not a contracting party. Alternatively, a contract among principals creates the agent-state, and a second contract between the principals and the agent defines the latter's mandate. Both types of construction suggest an intent by the parties that the agent should serve the principals (the General Will, the Common Good) rather than itself, and that it should serve them impartially (equality before the law, equal protection). Virtue can transform such intent into a credible commitment. Without enough virtue, no part of it is credible, because neither contract has a self-enforcing structure: principals can, by recourse to the collective-choice mechanism, secure higher payoffs by forcing other principals to make do with lower ones. The prisoners' dilemma, as it were, comes back with a vengeance. Combined with an enforcing agent, it has an asymmetrical equilibrium, i.e., redistribution.

Enforcement of mutual performance under the social contract might in turn be contracted for between the interested parties on the one hand and an enforcer on the other. However, unless *that* contract is self-enforcing, it too must be enforced in its turn. The first-order enforcement problem is resolved only to create a second-order one, and so on indefinitely. The third-, fourth-, or nth-order contract, as far as we can grasp them, are no less enforcement-dependent than the first-order social contract itself.

Whatever else the prisoners' dilemma "paradigm" may tell us, it tells clearly that enforcement-dependence involves an infinite regress, that can only be stopped if at some stage in the regress an enforcement contract proves to be self-enforcing and a cooperative "game" is created. It is difficult to reject this logic, and to assert in the same breath *both* that men need the state because contracts of mutual performance are undermined by the prisoners' dilemma, *and* that the social contract is not so undermined.

Default by one set of "players," forced performance by another as the solution of the social contract "game," can be interpreted in two ways. The agent-state either has a personality and is a player in its own right, or it is a purely impersonal instrument. Given the former conception, a three-person game would emerge, with the set of principals dividing into two, and one subset forming an alliance with the agent to exploit the rest. Two players would share the free-rider payoff (in terms of Figure 1, they would share 400) with the third reduced to the sucker payoff (100). The game sum would be 500, compared with the 600 with mutual performance of the social contract. Taking the alternative conception of the state as a pure instrument, a winning coalition of principals would capture it and force the losing coalition to accept the sucker payoff. The game sum would be suboptimal just as in the former case. In both cases, the equilibrium would be unstable. It is perhaps tempting to see in the former conception an analogy with the autocratic, in the latter with the democratic state, but at this level of abstraction it would be foolish to push the analogy at all far. Any real-life redistributive state can be seen as an approximation, an empirical match of either conception.

Since there are built-in incentives for collusion between some minimally sufficient subset of principals and the agent, or for such a subset to gain control of the agent, it is not surprising that the idea of consent as a decision, or state of mind, common to all rational individuals who are unanimous in their desire to secure the precondition of social cooperation, looks to be ill-fitting to real societies. At best, weak consent, contingent on a variable balance of reasons, may prevail. However, if any really universal ground can be imputed to all rational persons on which they cannot but accept the principle of collective choice and its enforcement, it is acquiescence in accomplished facts that are too difficult to undo.

4

Is National Rational?

Ruminating on the causes and consequences of ethnic strife, I was reminded of a young woman who at one time used to type my manuscripts. Before she learned to read my handwriting, she kept mistaking my *r* for *n*, so that when I wrote "rational" she would type "national," and vice versa. The results were sometimes quite surprising. The mistake suggests an association of ideas and a potentially serious question. Can national be rational?

Most people of liberal leanings tend to regard (and to deplore or despise) nationalism, along with the feelings that feed it, as a gut instinct, and not the most creditable one at that. It stands outside the purview of critical reason, rather like a taste we do not dispute, an ultimate preference, a Humean "passion" that can explain human conduct but that neither need nor can be explained in terms of other, more final, more basic preferences or ends.

Although I sympathize with that position, I think it gives unduly short shrift to the issue. Nationalism, whether despicable, deplorable, or not, is dangerous, potent, and important; it calls for closer consideration. One way of doing justice to the phenomenon of nationalism is to treat it counterfactually. Even if in fact it springs from sentiment fueled by historical accidents, it may be worthwhile to try to see whether nationalism could possibly be the product of rational choice. If it is, we should be able to find a theory that can explain the phe-

Reprinted with permission of the publisher from *The Independent Review: A Journal of Political Economy* 3, no. 1 (summer 1998): 77–89. © 1998 The Independent Institute.

nomena of nationalism *as if* they were appropriate, perhaps even the best available responses utility-maximizing individuals could make to the similarly utility-maximizing strategies of others. For present purposes, I use "utility-maximizing" in a loose sense that is almost tautological but has the merit of encompassing everything an individual thinks he should do, given his means and the information at his disposal, to get the best possible combination of all the things he values, whether they be tangible or intangible, moral or material.

If we could construct such a theory, nationalism and its principal institution, the nation-state, could be represented as instrumental, serving a purpose, comprehensible in terms of methodological individualism. We could inquire into the efficacy of nationalism in promoting the aims (maximizing the utility) of those who embrace it and subject themselves to its disciplines. In the present article I engage in an elementary thought-experiment. I seek to find a plausible theory that, running in terms of broadly conceived cost and benefit, could furnish elements of an answer to the question, Is national rational?

The Differential Advantage of Group Action

For nationalism to make any sort of maximizing sense, there must exist important situations ("games") of human interaction in which the best response to the expected utility-maximizing actions of others is a group response. Impossible for any lone individual, such a response is available only to a group of individuals acting uniformly. They must form a group and then reach and submit to group decisions. In return they reap the differential advantage that, according to the hypothesis, such action can yield.

The advantage, if any, depends on at least two variables. One is group size and composition: who is in the group and who is left outside? The larger the group, the stronger it is, but perhaps the less cohesive; and the larger it is, the smaller the world outside it that group action can exploit for its own advantage. The other variable is the appropriateness of the group decision to which its members conform. How is it reached? Is the process, to use simplistic categories, democratic or autocratic? How does it allocate costs within the group, and what mechanism preserves it from stupid mistakes? Needless to say, both variables go to the heart of the problem of separate nations with their processes of collective choice and enforcement.

Bargaining and Taking

For present purposes, let us divide all possible interactions into four jointly exhaustive classes. One is pure cooperation. I help you, perhaps you also help me, or we both harness ourselves to a common endeavor. We are both better off as a result, but I am not trying to be even better off by haggling or pushing to make you a little less well off. The second is the kind of exchange whose ideal type is perfect competition. We engage in division of labor, we both gain; perhaps we would each like to gain more by making the other party gain less, but we are ex hypothesi "price-takers"—the terms of exchange do not depend on us and cannot be changed by any strategy. In these two types of interaction, there is no conflict: an individual's utility-maximizing behavior would not be any different if his choices were made collectively for him and all others.

The opposite is the case in the other two types of interaction, where strategy influences the gain each makes. Here it is not implausible (though it is certainly not demonstrably true) that individuals can do better by submitting to collective choice and acting as a group. One such case is any exchange that is not perfectly competitive and whose terms are bargained. The other comprises all takings by force, intimidation, or fraud. Instead of exchange, it offers gains from robbery, enslavement, blackmail, and conquest. Defense against robbery, enslavement, blackmail, and conquest is of course the integral complement of these interactions. Even if it is not—or is not always—the case that in these "games" individuals adopting a unified course of action collectively do better than if each chose his strategy for himself, the conventional wisdom supposes that group action is more efficient. Because the conventional wisdom cannot really be falsified, it is accorded near-universal credit.

Nations and What They Cost

To capture the differential gain, groups must be formed and maintained. Their size, shape, cohesion, and modus operandi are bound to matter both for their efficiency in producing gains and for the cost of forming and maintaining them.

Historically, the dominant form of the collectively acting group has been the linguistic community, which fulfilled the most basic of group functions—including some and excluding others—by means of a common tongue separate from other tongues. Whether the historical dominance of language, rather than clan, tribe, race, class, or religion, as the crucial feature of group demarcation corresponds to the requirements of greatest efficiency (or least cost) is a matter of conjecture. Believers in sociobiological selection who regard the survival of a social institution as a test of its efficiency (which tends to be confused with "survival as a test of the capacity to survive") tend to think it does correspond. In any event, until comparatively recently *nation* meant a linguistic community, and only since the late eighteenth century has the word taken on a clear political connotation.

Apart from language, the group typically demarcates itself from others by means of conventions, customs, shared legends about its own history, loyalty to a center, and some degree of territorial exclusivity. All these demarcating features are costly to bring forth, live with, and uphold. The cost is probably higher the greater is the required degree of group cohesion. As a general rule, there is a cost involved in requiring conformity and forgoing the advantage of diversity *within* the group as well as in requiring diversity *between* groups that would otherwise drift toward a shared conformity.

From Nation to Nation-State

Maximizing the putative differential advantage of group over individual action by incurring the costs of group formation and maintenance, up to the point at which marginal group gain ceases to exceed marginal group cost, is ex hypothesi collectively rational: it is the course of action that secures the greatest possible total advantage, hence also the greatest average advantage for each of the group's members. Any one member, however, can do better than the group average if he does not contribute to costs while others do. In other words, it is individually rational to take the free-rider option if it is available. If all or even most members of the group do so, costs will not be met, and individual rationality will frustrate the collectively rational outcome — the standard outcome of the inherent prisoners' dilemma that is supposed to characterize all public-good situations.

The same dilemma-generating incentive structure characterizes a nation acting as a discriminatory group that favors its members over nonmembers. Suppression of the free-rider option is thought to require the enforcing capacity of an agent placed above individuals. Hence it is rational for the nation to transform itself into a nation-state. (How individuals are induced to make the joint effort to bring about this transformation, which is no less a public-good problem than the one it is called upon to resolve, is a question I must leave in limbo. It is not specific to the nation-state but common to all proposed cooperative solutions of a prisoners' dilemma that depend on the cooperative solution of a prior prisoners' dilemma.)

The task of the nation-state is easier and the cost of its enforcing action lower, the weaker is the free-rider temptation. Weakening it, covering it with shame and guilt, is the function of patriotism in its many forms, a sentiment that it is collectively rational to foster. Hostility to and suspicion of foreigners and foreign ways, and love of one's own kind, function *as if* they were deliberately chosen means of helping to overcome the dilemma that what is collectively rational is individually irrational. It would be a functionalist fallacy, however, to conclude that the virulent and unpleasant nationalism we see around us, which is so much more vigorous than class hatred and class solidarity, is due to nationalism's capacity to help resolve a fundamental social dilemma. Nonetheless it seems that if nationalism did not exist, it would pay the nation-state to invent it.

From Public Choices to "Public Choice"

The nation-state, like every other kind of state though perhaps more effectively and ruthlessly, facilitates the making of public choices for a whole group that impose losses on one part of the group and bring gains to another part. Unlike ordinary conflict outcomes in which one party gains and another loses because might makes right, the public choices effected through a nation-state's political process are generally alleged to make some net contribution to the "common good" or the "national interest." The claim is justified one way in democratic regimes, another way in autocratic or intermediate ones, but its basis is always the gratuitous assertion that, notwithstanding the redistribution, the choice generates a positive net balance of utility, welfare, or national strength. As a rule these assertions are either unfalsifiable (when they depend on interpersonal comparisons of utility) or demonstrably false, as in the case of wealth-reducing protectionist measures and most other restrictions of the freedom of contract. Public-choice theory has established beyond reasonable doubt not only that such measures are wasteful in terms of forgone wealth but more significantly that they are not accidental aberrations; on the contrary, they are the irrepressible corollaries of the individually rational, maximizing use of politics, where "politics" means simply recourse to a binding social-choice mechanism.

One possible aspect of redistributive politics peculiar to some nation-states without being uniformly true of all is a propensity to redistribute liberties, rights, and privileges from heterogeneous minorities to the dominant nationality within the state. Present-day liberal opinion considers such policies, which oppress ethnic or religious minorities, as morally more wicked than the routine redistribution of material resources from dominated to dominant subgroups. The collectively irrational, wealth-wasting effect of redistributing material resources has been well established by economic research, whereas the loss inflicted on an entire collectivity by the persecution of internal minorities is more conjectural. It is probably fair to suggest, though, that short of exterminating them, organized discrimination against minorities is collectively irrational, though individually rational, at least prospectively, for members of the dominant group.

These redistributive public choices, remote as they may seem from one another, all share the basic feature of a prisoners' dilemma, namely, that the strategy it is rational for individuals to adopt is in fact suboptimal. (In an *n*-person game where *n* is large, the solution may not be suboptimal for *all* players; but the total and the average pay-off will be less than they might have been. That result qualifies it as collectively irrational.)

The Costly Stalemate

Indecisive, fruitless conflict is, I believe, the best understood of the dilemmas that entrap nationalism in collective irrationality. This hackneyed theme deserves only a brief recapitulation. The differential advantage of group action works against individuals; but if this suffices to make them form a group that ends up as a nation-state, then no individuals will be left in the types of interactions in which they could suffer differential disadvantage. All will shelter in groups of a similar type; nation-state will face nation-state.

If all adopt the same strategy, none gains from it but none can afford to abandon it. This statement will be true of individuals as well as nation-states. Individuals must seek the protection of their nation-state to preserve their liberties, property, and "identity" from other nation-states. But no additional gain can be had from doing so; indeed, some might say that entrusting one's liberty or property to the protection of the state is foolhardy, a sure way of losing some of it. Yet in the face of foreign nation-states, one risks grave losses by not doing so, too.

"Disarmament," figuratively and literally, in cultural and economic matters as well as in terms of guns and rockets, is best for all if all states do it, but irrational for any individual state both if the others disarm and if they don't. Such is the logic, purportedly (but inaccurately) derived from Hobbes, that is supposed to govern international relations among nation-states and that stops most of them from becoming anything else but nation-states—organized vehicles of wary and jealous nationalism.

It is easy to overstate this case. The logic at its base is far from being as watertight as it may look. Nevertheless, there are enough historical examples where it has worked "by the book," as Hobbes is supposed to have said that it must. The bestiality of Hutus and Serbs against their unprotected, ethnically different fellow countrymen warns us that there are even worse solutions than nation-states facing off against other nation-states in balance-of-power stalemates that, happily, neither side has the stomach to test.

Two of Everything

Individually rational choice provides incentives for ethnic groups of imperfectly defined identity—incipient, underdeveloped, or nascent nations—to invent themselves a history, claim mature nation status, and seek to establish themselves as sovereign political entities. That project involves secession from an existing nation-state or multinational state. If the attempt at secession is resisted, a separatist movement, often with an illegal wing employing violent means, will maintain a situation of simmering conflict. If the attempt at secession succeeds, two states and two governments will exist where only one did before.

In many cases the separatist movement has genuine grievances, normally arising from the failure of tax-financed state education, state-controlled mass media, courts, and government offices to foster preservation of its language. This failure, a vice of omission, is sometimes hard to distinguish from a vice of commission, a deliberate centralizing, unifying policy to impose a single national majority language and cause the minority tongue to shrivel up and die. It is not altogether clear what the duties of a state are with regard to the preservation of several languages and cultures within its territory, nor what a colonial power owes to a colonized people to help it maintain its native "identity." The question is less obvious than it looks, and answering it would be a good deal simpler if the educational and other influences affecting the survival of language and ethnicity were not tax-financed products of collective choices, that is, if the state itself played a lesser or no role in shaping them. Nor is it clear when a separatist grievance is genuine and grave enough to justify secession and to brand resistance to it as tyrannical. These hard or undecidable cases all enter into the complex rights and wrongs of self-determination, which I shall confront later.

For our immediate purposes, the interesting thing to wonder at is the nature of the incentive to secede, to put two governments in the place of one, when there is no genuine grievance, in the accepted meaning of the term, when ethnic minorities are recognized by neutral observers as having equal liberties, equal rights, and "equal opportunities," whatever the latter is supposed to mean. (The neutrality of an observer who finds that an ethnic minority enjoys the same liberties, rights, and opportunities as the majority will almost certainly be contested by the advocates of the minority in question—it would take angelic fairness to accept that judgment. For the minority, just being in the minority means that its "rights" and "opportunities" are not equal to those of the majority. It is for this reason above all that the claim that Slavs were not oppressed in the Austro-Hungarian empire or that Germans and Hungarians were not unfairly treated in interwar Czechoslovakia is so contested and contestable.)

Let us, therefore, take the (perhaps somewhat idealized, perhaps actually counterfactual) case in which an ethnic group living in a state dominated by another ethnic group has no grievance other than its minority status. Why, then, does sheer "otherness" alone generate conflict? Let us even assume that the state in question is of optimal size, so that the relation of its intrinsic costs to the benefits it can procure by having individuals act collectively is as good as possible. In this case, arguably it would be collectively rational for the minority group not to secede. However, for at least some members of that group it would still be individually rational to mount a separatist movement, because of what we might label the "Paris cultural attaché" syndrome. The label looks facetious, but it is revealing.

Each government has a cultural attaché in Paris, an ambassador to the Court of St. James, a chief delegate to the United Nations, a minister of this and a minister of that at home, and so forth. The separatist movement can attract a disproportionately large number of local patriots, frustrated teachers, poets in the vernacular, and young people troubled by a mismatch between their ambitions and their abilities, all of whom harbor the fond hope of becoming their future government's cultural attaché in Paris or somebody equally enviable. It is well known that people tend to overvalue very small chances of large prizes, in the sense of betting on them at shorter odds than the true actuarial odds that would make the bet a fair one; this tendency is what makes bookmakers rich. Such behavior is perfectly consistent with (subjective) rationality as the maximization of expected utility, if the bettor either misjudges the true odds or attaches a more than proportionate increase in utility to a large increase in his wealth. (His action would be irrational if his betting in the face of known actuarial odds were inconsistent with any continuous and positively sloped utility function.) The separatist who overestimates his chances of becoming his country's cultural attaché in Paris or who attaches immense value to such glamor is presumably quite rational in militating for secession at great cost to his ethnic group, and thousands of militant separatists may all be rational even if all but one must fail to get appointed to the dream post in Paris.

The upshot, however, would be collectively irrational for all separatists taken together, and even more so for the whole ethnic group, on whose behalf the separatists militate but which contains nonseparatists as well as separatists. The horrors suffered by many if not most African peoples under vicious, corrupt, and irremediably incompetent post-colonial native governments provide a telling example of the price a liberation movement imposes on a whole collectivity for the satisfaction of the ambitions of a very few.

Evidently, not every secession produces fabulously bad government on the African model. For the horns of the dilemma between individual ambition and collective well-being to hurt, nationalism need not cause a proliferation of bad governments. A proliferation of governments is itself a wasteful phenomenon, making room for the growth of parasitism, even if the governments are just the average, indifferent sort. That the multiplication of states should give rise to two good governments where only a bad or indifferent one existed before, is of course possible, but it is hard to see on what grounds one should expect such an outcome.

How to Determine the Self?

Whenever the group organized under one sovereign political authority is heterogeneous in any major respect, so that the interests and preferences of its subgroups differ, conflict arises, which governments may or may not resolve by the ordinary political processes for making public choices. I am not suggesting that the democratic process is likely to generate "good" solutions and the autocratic process "bad" ones. Everywhere in the range between the two extremes, the political process produces outcomes that reflect the might of the opposing forces in being. When, however, the heterogeneity is ethnic in nature, the resulting conflict is—or at least since World War I has been widely considered to be—subject to resolution not by the ordinary political process but by invocation and exercise of the right of self-determination: Might must yield to right.

"Right," if the word is used properly, implies that the rightholder exercises it by requiring another party to perform or suffer some act defined by the right and that the party in question has the obligation to perform or submit accordingly. The act is favorable (beneficial) to the rightholder and unfavorable (onerous) to the obligor. By exercising the right of self-determination, the "self" requires some national government to release it from that government's authority and prerogatives. Moreover, that government must release not only the person or persons who possess the right but also some part of the national territory, loosely defined as the part in which the "self" in question resides. But who is the "self"?

At a glance, one can count no less than four ambiguities in the right of self-determination, each adding to its obscurity.

The first arises from the jointness of some person or persons as the rightholder and some territory that the rightholder is entitled to take out of the territory over which the obligor (the state of the dominant ethnic group) is sovereign. Jointness means that the "self" who exercised the right to secede can hardly be a single person, for what would be the territory he was entitled to take out of the obligor country? Nor, for the same obvious reason, can the "self" be a very small number of persons. If entitlement to territory goes with residence, the smallest "self" that determines where it and its territory belong must be either large enough to populate a territory that can either make another country, with what that implies in terms of geographically and economically sensible new frontiers, or contiguous to another country to which it wishes to be joined. Some gerrymandering can ease the problem of secession, but is gerrymandering in its favor a right of the minority and consequently an obligation of the majority?

Hence arises the second major ambiguity. An ethnic group living in another ethnic group's state and large enough to claim a division of territory is seldom homogenous. Within the territory it claims, it may be dominant, have a plurality, or even constitute an overwhelming majority. Nevertheless, minorities may live in its midst; do they also have the right of self-determination? Anglophone Canada has a francophone minority, which constitutes the majority in Quebec alongside an anglophone minority. Who in Canada is the "self" that holds the right of "self-determination"? Who in Quebec? And who in a particular area, county, or town within Quebec? The glib answer is "the majority," but why is the francophone majority in Quebec entitled to take the province out of Canada if an anglophone or just anti-separatist majority in Montreal is not entitled to take the city out of Quebec? Protestant Ulstermen formed a minority in prepartition Ireland, but they constitute a majority in Northern Ireland and a minority in many areas of that territory. Similar ambiguities abound in Transylvania, the Vojvodina, Catalonia, and elsewhere. When does a minority of those living in a large territory start to enjoy the status of a majority of those living on a smaller territory, entitled to exercise a right to detach it?

A third ambiguity of self-determination is bound up with the second. If the political map is not to become a mosaic of small pieces, the "selves" who can determine themselves must be sizable multiperson ones even if, luckily, they are homogenous and not multiethnic. However, if the rightholder is a multiperson entity, who exercises its right? Societies, communities, and groups do not decide. They have decisions made for them by some formal or informal mechanism actuated by individual decisions. It is far from evident what this mechanism should be for the right to be validly exercised. What role is to be given to "freedom fighters," militant separatists, qualified or simple voting majorities? The decision to exercise the right, to hold it in reserve, or to renounce it may change the life of generations. It is invidious for some to decide for all, whether the decision is to go or to stay. Nonunanimity is one of the great potential vices of any collective right and any collective obligation. The vice is more serious than most in the case of the right of national self-determination.

The final ambiguity is too obvious to need elaboration. Where the obligor is sovereign, enforcement of the obligation is absent by definition, a contradiction in terms; if self-determination were enforceable, the state would not be a sovereign entity. For a nation-state comprising a majority (or otherwise dominant) group and a minority, it may be collectively rational to accept self-determination as a right and to honor the corresponding obligation; likewise it may be collectively rational for the minority to retain but not to exercise the right. But it may be impracticable to share the advantages of either alternative between majority and minority in a manner that would put both in a preferred position, compared to the third alternative, which is an attempt to exercise the right and a failure to honor it, that is, unresolved conflict. Hence it may be rational for the minority to agitate for secession and for the majority not to yield.

The Need for War

All dilemmas that involve individually rational conduct leading to collectively suboptimal results can be overcome by appropriate rules. This statement is obviously true of open conflicts, whether arising from rival nationalisms or not, that either fester and remain unresolved or are resolved in a fight, with escalating recourse to force by attacker and defender, in which the parties taken together incur a joint cost that leaves both victor and vanquished worse off than no solution, let alone a nonviolent bargained solution. The bargained solution, though Pareto superior to the conflict, often cannot be reached for the same prisoners'-dilemma-type reason that opposes individual to collective rationality. I use "prisoners'-dilemma-type" loosely, to indicate an incentive structure in which a player can rationally expect to do better by being uncooperative, nasty, obstructive, and unduly demanding both when he expects the other player to be cooperative and undemanding and when he expects him to be uncooperative and demanding.

Of course, appropriate rules can always ensure a peaceful and Pareto-optimal solution—a hackneyed conclusion ceaselessly repeated in "internationalist" Wilsonian exhortations.

But if recognition of the potential benefit of rules were always sufficient to make the parties concerned adopt and obey them, then rules would hardly be needed in the first place. Right incentives would elicit right choices spontaneously. Rules that aim to neutralize the "wrong" sort of incentive structure, however, are not self-enforcing. The individually rational strategy may well be to disobey them. Making them binding requires enforcement; but nation-states live in the "state of nature," where rules are not enforced by a third party, a specialized enforcer, a world government mandated to punish transgressors. Technically, the situation is one of anarchy of *some* degree of orderliness, with occasional breaches of order.

One measure of the orderliness of international anarchy is the predominance of peaceful, negotiated solutions of conflicts between nations, as opposed to recourse to war. "War" in this context may mean a shooting war or a trade war if trade is important enough to the party refusing to yield in bargaining. War, whether economic or military, waged by a state differs from one waged by individuals in that the latter directly accept or decline the costs they would incur as a result of their choice of war or peace. In wars waged by states, costs fall on individuals who cannot decide to bear or to escape them.

However, paradoxical as it may sound, the total exclusion of war by universal military and economic disarmament would logically make negotiated solutions hard if not impossible to reach. If war were "outlawed" and the outlawing were enforced, a party to an international conflict would never gain by making any concession that would leave it worse off than its initial situation from which the bargaining started. Conflicts, therefore, could be peacefully resolved only if the initial situation was Pareto inferior, that is, if both parties could gain by moving away from it. For less benign conflicts to have a bargaining solution, it is logically necessary to introduce a dynamic factor that makes the initial situation progressively worse for the holdout party refusing to make the bargaining concession. That factor is the growing risk of war as long as the negotiation remains deadlocked. The more failure to agree looks like failure to avert war, the more the bargaining solution, with one party making the concession, resembles a move by both parties to a Pareto-superior position.

However, only the sporadic occurrence of war—that it remains, albeit distant in space or time, an event well within human experience—makes credible the risk of war that renders the failure to agree Pareto inferior. If war were either unknown or known but by some miraculous means "outlawed" or considered unthinkable in our present world, its threat could never serve to render concession in bargaining a rational strategy. Paradoxically, in a world of sovereign states, the possibility of war and its occasional occurrence are probably necessary to motivate parties to move from conflict to accommodation.

This conclusion is not cheerful, but it is a corollary of a system of groups—typically, nations organized in states whose vocation is to promote group interests. It is difficult to see how the conclusion can be avoided or attenuated, allowing peace to prevail without getting help from war, unless the institution of the state itself is avoided or attenuated.

Breaking the Link between Costs and Benefits

The sprawling argument must now be rounded up and forced into the straitjacket of a conclusion of sorts, with some pretension to generality.

Nationalism is a set of beliefs and behavioral norms designed to foster ethnic separateness and survival. By "designed" I do not mean to imply conscious calculation but rather consistency with what calculating individuals might have rationally chosen. Nationalism is a powerful aid in capturing some advantages available for group but not for individual action.

The organized agent of nationalism is the nation-state. Its essential function is to replace individual by collective choices in any domain (over any pair of alternatives) that collective choice itself—or, as some theorists prefer to express it, collective meta-choice "at the constitutional level"—decides to preempt. On the face of it, the nation-state is a means capable of producing collectively rational outcomes that would be out of the reach of individuals acting rationally; sovereignty over individual actions must therefore rest not with individuals but with the organized collectivity. Nationalism is, among other things, a conviction that this condition is proper.

Perversely, however, the very machinery intended to impose collective rationality may produce the opposite effect. The state suppresses the basic dilemma in which individuals choose the free-rider option, evade the bearing of group costs, and as a result have no group benefits to share in, nothing to "ride free" on. But although this dilemma is suppressed, others crop up.

The stronger and more irresistible the machinery for imposing collective choices, the greater the temptation to manipulate and exploit it to individual advantage. The very ease of imposing public choices gives rise to a complex web of redistributive maneuvers within the nation-state: fiscal, regulatory, and protectionist measures, most of them wasteful and lacking the transparency that would allow them to be seen for what they are.

Moreover, although the nation-state, as initially justified, is a tool to enable an ethnic group to prevail over outsiders, its advantage disappears when the outsiders obey the same rationality and organize themselves into nation-states. The dilemma then arises that although it is individually rational for each nation to seek strength in unity and armed protection behind national frontiers, it would be collectively rational for all to dismantle the frontiers, both military and economic, and disarm.

A further dilemma appears when each ethnic subgroup aspires to be a nation and each nation seeks to have its own sovereign nation-state. There is a putative disadvantage in not having one when others have theirs. Control of the means to impose collective decisions on all is intrinsically attractive. One machinery for a large group made up of two subgroups may be the efficient solution, but it is individually rational for both subgroups to have their own governments, both sovereign, harboring two parasitic teams of office-holders where one would do. Separatist movements as well as the resistance they face, whatever their real causes, could be rationally explained by this dilemma alone. Finally, again paradoxically, the sovereignty of nationally distinct groups makes war a necessary condition of the peaceful resolution of international conflicts.

In the last analysis, these dilemmas and perverse unwelcome solutions probably have a single root cause. The making of collective choices that are binding for all, to which nationalism calls for dutiful submission, loosens if it does not break the link between benefits enjoyed and costs borne by any given individual. Then it becomes individually rational for some people to make everyone pay for something that benefits them alone; to make only some pay for the putative "common good" of all; and even to send some people to die in war, often for the good of nobody except those few whose vanity is served.

In sum, collective choice inspired by nationalism fails in its own purpose and gets entrapped in irrationality. Though not strictly within the scope of an analysis of nationalism, a plainer, blunter conclusion also imposes itself; that never mind any test of rationality or efficiency, collective choice—no matter how inspired—would have a hard time withstanding the test of morality.

5

Empirical Evidence

Throughout its history, humanity has permanently displayed a physical condition classified in ordinary language as "illness" or "disease." There has always been what Hume would call a "constant conjunction" between human life and illness.

The Hobbesian hypothesis that illness is a necessary condition of the survival of the human species has strong empirical support. It has never been falsified.

Throughout its history, humanity has permanently displayed a social condition classified in ordinary language as "the state" or "government." There has always been what Hume would call a "constant conjunction" between human society and government.

The Hobbesian hypothesis that government is a necessary condition of social life has strong empirical support. It has never been falsified.

Arguments in favor of the prevention or eradication of disease are evidently misguided and may be dangerous. They are often put forward by naïve persons with little understanding of reality.

Arguments in favor of fostering society's capacity to evolve anarchic orders and live with less or no government are evidently misguided and may be dangerous. They are often put forward by naïve persons with little understanding of reality.

This piece is previously unpublished in book form.

Part Two

Redistribution

6

A Stocktaking
of Perversities

Why, despite its recognized perverse effects, do societies opt for an expanding welfare state? Public choice theory accounts for this in terms of the prevailing choice rule, "majoritarian" democracy. This contractarian perspective holds that other, more benign choice rules could be adopted. The reviewer disputes this view on the ground that if the public choice approach is generalized, the choice rule must be seen to be the product of the same influences as the choices within the rule. "Majoritarian" democracy maximizes the scope for redistributive legislation, hence also the expected gains from politics; it will be "chosen" in preference to more benign rules.

Anti-poverty programs prolong poverty. Minimum wage legislation reduces employment and does not noticeably raise the earnings of those who do find jobs despite it. Universal educational opportunity leads to the massive erosion of standards of literacy and numeracy. Aid to families with dependent children helps to break up families and promotes childbearing by unwed teenage girls. Social Security stimulates consumption at the expense of saving, eating into the capital stock that would be called upon to help honor pension promises. Paying people when ill encourages malingering, paying them when out of a job en-

Reprinted with permission from *Critical Review* (fall 1990): 537–44. © 1990 Center for Independent Thought.

courages them to wait for an "acceptable" job to turn up. Rent control induces maldistribution of the available housing, penalizes the homeless, and in due course reduces the housing stock altogether. Compulsory insurance provokes more frequent occurrence of the event people are made to insure against. A redistributive fiscal system churns income flows among social groups "horizontally" but does little to redirect them "vertically" to fulfill its ostensible goal, greater equality.

For the benefit of those for whom this kind of sad litany is still news, Richard E. Wagner's *To Promote the General Welfare: Market Processes vs. Political Transfers* (San Francisco: Pacific Research Institute, 1989) proceeds to a workmanlike stocktaking of the perversities of the welfare state, showing in the process that these are mostly predictable effects of a single common cause, the unrestricted power of democratic decision making.

Most of us are individually straight if not downright square, yet collectively we are nothing if not perverse. The costly failures of welfarist redistribution and their corrosive effect on the fibers of society are not seriously in dispute. Nor are many left who still believe that if a policy proves to have too many unpleasant by-products, a better one can be found that will bring only pure bliss. Yet there is little sign of any contemporary society really trying to kick the welfare habit—at best, there are periodic good resolutions to cut down on the fixes. Why is this so?—and must it be the case?

Many answers are floating about in the public consciousness. Some are on the comic strip level: "Surely You Don't Want Jones Back?," "Market Socialism Is the Best of Both Worlds," and "We Can't Have a Darwinist Free-For All." These are not amenable to critical scrutiny. Others are less simple but just as simplistic. However, three are, to my mind, worth discussing.

Welfare Relativism

The first is the answer sophisticated American liberals and European social democrats would give under pressure. They do not seriously contest that welfarism does, in roundabout ways, call forth a shabby catalogue of perverse effects (though they do not despair that reason backed by research can in due course deal with them). Other effects of the welfare state, however, they consider indubitably positive. They tell you that good and bad effects of different kinds and affecting different people are incommensurable and cannot be balanced against one another in some logico-mathematical operation. "The welfare state is a millstone around society's neck" and "the welfare state is the best instrument of social justice we have" are not descriptive statements, but expressions of preference, and one is no more "valid" than the other. Welfare relativism does not argue about the "right" tradeoffs between justice and efficiency, liberty and equality, and so forth, that a rational society *ought* to have chosen, nor does it claim that individual wishes, once fed into the political sausage machine, somehow come out in the form of the "wrong" collective choice. It accepts that the policy society does choose, perverse effects and all, is what it wants—for the allegation that it "really" wanted a different one is meaningless.

The second answer, which I would label Hayekian liberal, is that it is right and proper to stretch out a social safety net to catch those who fall, as long as this is not done in the name of social justice and with an egalitarian intent. Hayek agrees that "the amount of relief now given in a comparatively wealthy society should be more than is absolutely necessary to keep alive and in health,"[1] and he accepts that the availability of such relief will induce people to let themselves go and rely on it, as well as that the state should compel all to insure against life's hazards and should develop some institutional framework of administering welfare. "Up to this point the justification for the whole apparatus of 'social security' can probably be accepted by the most consistent defenders of liberty."[2] What Hayek finds unacceptable is that the apparatus should have redistribution as its avowed aim,[3] though it is not obvious why it matters so much whether welfare policies are meant to be, or just are, redistributive. It seems, however, that it is redistributive intent that vitiates welfarism and should lead to its rejection if collective choice were not perverse.

1. F. A. Hayek, *The Constitution of Liberty* (Chicago: University of Chicago Press, 1960), 285.
2. *Ibid.,* 286.
3. *Ibid.,* 289.

Wagner parts company with Hayekian and indeed all classical liberalism when he admits arguments for the legitimacy of intentional redistribution: for example, when individual charitable giving is conditional on enough others giving, too, so that charity functions as a public good the state can Pareto-optimally provide; when people are "risk-averse" and actually like progressive taxation as a form of insurance that even those who never collect from the policy are willing to buy; or when redistribution is the price all agree to pay to secure acceptance of the existing order by those who do least well under it. Here, Wagner stands squarely in the contractarian tradition, as befits a disciple of James Buchanan and a co-editor of *Constitutional Economics.* The notion that redistribution is good (Pareto-superior) for both gainers and losers because it is a necessary cost of producing civil society, however, has two versions. Buchanan's shows how redistribution may be a condition of preventing our relapse from social cooperation to pre-contract lawlessness. Rawls's affirms that redistribution in conformity with his "difference principle" leads to *willing* social cooperation as distinct from social cooperation *tout court.* The former version is as it may be, but to believe in the latter is to believe anything. Wagner wisely keeps a safe distance from Rawls's contractarianism.[4]

The Charms of Churning

The third kind of answer as to why we collectively opt for the welfare state, even if individually we disapprove of its works, emerges from public choice theory, a body of doctrine that has become part of orthodoxy in political economy. Wagner's book is a lucid illustration of many of its themes, largely free from the suffocating jargon of so much current writing in the social sciences. His focus is "constitutional" in that it bears upon causal relations between decision rules and the decisions

---

4. In particular, Wagner (34–35) is rightly unimpressed by the maximin strategy that Rawls, in order to get his result, needs to pass off as the dominant one in the pre-contract position—i.e., unanimous agreement by the parties that the "difference principle" shall govern distribution among them.

they help to produce. So does a large part of the literature, from the study of elections and public utility regulation to game theory. However, according to his preface, this focus makes his book "unique," a case of academic hard sell that devalues an otherwise sober piece of work.

Summarily, public choice theory shows how a given set of social decision rules, such as "majoritarian democracy," has as its corollary a system of incentives, such as the potential payoffs that can be won by particular voting coalitions, to which the participants in the political process respond in predictable ways. With the insights of public choice theory, it is easy to grasp how, for instance, even minority groups can obtain overt or covert transfers that, by accepted modes of reckoning, confer smaller benefits on them than the cost they impose on the community. Publicly provided goods mostly enjoyed by a particular segment of society but paid for out of general taxation are, of course, analogous to transfers in their redistributive effects. Potentially, majority rule allows everybody to profit under some heading as a member of some minority, while paying for every other minority benefit as a member of the majority; it is theoretically possible for literally each and every voter to be worse off thanks to the welfare state that each nevertheless keeps voting for. What is more appalling still, each is perfectly rational to do so.

One characteristic of public choice theory is that it gets its results by having everybody, including the politicians, play the game by the rules to his best advantage, reacting to incentives, uncontaminated by ideology and metaphysical beliefs. Classical liberals, in diagnosing the perverse ailments of the body politic, used to blame the gullibility of the electorate, the fatal conceit of social engineers, and the dishonesty of demagogues. An approach that does not need recourse to such human weaknesses is presumably better theory, though one suspects it may inspire worse historiography. This, however, is just my self-indulgent speculation, the pursuit of which would loosen our grip on the subject in hand. Back, therefore, to rules, actions, and payoffs.

The Sanctity or Profanity of Rules

What is strange in Wagner's work, and not only in his, is the juxtaposition on the same plane of the "welfare state" and the "contractarian state" as two interchangeable possibilities that could be chosen, rather like celibacy or marriage, rail or road, sea or dry land, town or country. From this treatment comes the cohabitation, under the same intellectual structure, of the positive study of public choice and the normative precepts of "constitutionalism." The ability to have them as bedfellows is due, as far as I can judge, to a crucial maneuver around the genesis of rules and their immutability.

In public choice, winning groups get the best available payoffs and impose worse ones on the losers. However, for some reason or other, this ceases to be true where the payoffs are indirect and take the form of alternative constitutional rules, which are but gates giving access to direct payoffs. Redistributive direct payoffs depend on collective decisions, and constitutions are systems of rules for making them. One can identify these rules as, in effect, indirect payoffs. Some rules hinder redistributive decisions, others help them. Hence some constitutions are a manifest source of better direct payoffs for the prospective beneficiaries of public largess than others. The contractarian-cum-public-choice school appears to hold that these persons and their respective groupings respond to incentives and maximize payoffs when shaping legislation and imposing policies, but not when shaping the constitution that is a determinant, both of what policies may be imposed and who is entitled to impose them.

In actual life, for ad hoc reasons there happen to be defective constitutions which are not neutral, but loaded in the sense of facilitating collective choices that are contrary to the Lockean ideal or to some notion of natural right. By the contractarian logic, however, these are avoidable aberrations, for there is, in a society with the usual divergent interests, a place to be filled by a constitution that *could have been* unanimously agreed upon in an original contract, if the occasion to propose one had arisen. Its terms are at worst indifferent, at best benign, in that they hold no bias and threaten no adverse consequences for any person, group, or class, and promise benefits at least to some. Such a contract is concluded, as it were, in a state of innocence, before original sin, that is to say before there can be generalized collective choice, including contested choice where the winners can carry the day over the opposition of the losers. For, as contractarians might explain, winning coalitions can impose their will on the losers once there are rules for telling who has won, but not before. Consequently, in the choice of rules there can be no imposition, but only quasi-unanimous consent, and this is the fundamental reason why the *choice of the rules* is invested with an aura of sanctity, as opposed to the profanity of contested *choices within those rules*.

An obvious down-to-earth objection to this is that momentous choices can and since time immemorial have been imposed by some people on others without benefit of agreed, formal rules. Let it be the case, however, that there is a benign constitution to begin with and the greedy gremlins who swarm around public choices had no hand in its making. Since, however, they know no taboos and are led by interest, what is to stop them from profanely starting to reshape the constitution the moment it provides them with the rule system for engineering agreement to non-unanimous choices?

Article 5 of the U.S. Constitution, providing for the manner in which "rules for choosing" may be altered, erects obstacles to constitutional change which make it more difficult to *amend* the rules than to *apply* them in ordinary legislation. But such difficulties exert their "constitutional drag" essentially through augmenting the size of the winning coalition required for carrying the rule change; a broader coalition must be in favor than is needed for passing ordinary laws. Public choice theory, if it were not imbued with the contractarian dream of redeeming the republic through prescription, would in good logic have to predict that an impartial constitution will first be changed to suit the broad winning coalition, and then be changed again to let progressively narrower coalitions despoil ever larger minorities, until the rule system finds its final resting place—the "End of History" of media gurus—in unlimited bare-majority democracy. At this "End of History," *no minority right or privilege can subsist without* (at least tacit) *majority consent* and no potential winning coalition that could carry the day under the existing rules can hope to augment its redistributive spoils by getting agreement to change the rules any further.

Generalized Public Choice

In reality, things work more insidiously than this. Constitutional change need not pass through the straight and narrow gate of some Article 5. The transformation of the U.S. Constitution from a rule system classical liberals used to admire, into one where modern American liberalism has all the elbow room it may desire for its redistributive exercises (even though the Rehnquist Court cramps its style in other respects), took place in more diffuse and unobtrusive ways.

Statute law, even when it ranks as constitutional law, is never simply "applied"; we would need no judges nor advocates, but only bailiffs and jailers if it were. In marginal cases, the courts have to make or re-make law before applying it, but in all cases they must interpret it to some degree,[5] and it is flying in the face of experience to suppose that judicial interpretation—be it informed by the best in legal scholarship and honesty—can for long dissociate itself from the political climate, the pressure of society's demands, and, most potent of all, the trend of articulate opinion.

This is how the very Fifth and Fourteenth Amendments, once seen as the cornerstones of private property rights and the freedom of contract, have since been discovered to be no obstacle at all to the elaborate regulation of business, the broad advance of eminent domain, extensive legislative intervention in the distribution of incomes, "positive" discrimination, the shift of power from state to federal authorities, and so forth. Without significant recourse to any "rule for changing rules" that the original Constitutional contract may have pro-

---

5. Any law (no matter how fussy or "special" in the pejorative sense) is more general than any case to which it might apply. The judicial decision that a class of cases in fact includes a given case, involves the cognitive operation of identifying each in terms of the other. "Substantive due process," itself an interpretation of the Fifth and Fourteenth Amendments, rules out as unconstitutional a class of legislative acts that would "deprive any person of life, liberty or property without due process of law." Whether the fixing of minimum hours of work in bakeries or minimum wages for women fall within this class or outside it is patently a matter of interpretation, and the interpretation has undergone enormous change in the present century. However, the change was fully to be expected on "public choice" grounds.

vided for, enough of the essentials have changed *de facto* to transform American politics from "constitutional" to "majoritarian" democracy. A generalized public choice theory that did not confine its scope to the special case of "choices within given rules," but exposed all political alternatives, including the rules for choosing among them, to the maximizing hypothesis that has proved fruitful in the study of the pork barrel, the growth and tenacity of bureaucracies, the deficit, and the essential perversities of the "promotion of the general welfare," could have predicted this outcome, too.

Putting it at its simplest, majorities choose legislation that maximizes their gains from politics, and they learn to choose a constitution that maximizes the scope for such legislation. The second part of this double proposition follows from the same premises as the first, though the relevant maximizing processes may not be equally rapid and straightforward. Public choice theory, once it relegates the happy vision of a "rights-based," rights-conserving, and liberty-securing constitution to its proper place alongside all of the other good things we cannot have, is well enough set up to digest both.

7

On Redistribution

The principle of gravitation is no more certain than the tendency of such laws to change wealth and power into misery and weakness. (David Ricardo 1817)

There are three distinct prima facie cases against redistribution. All three are still lingering in the back of the public mind, though they are getting fainter as time passes. Two of them invoke final values: the inviolability of duly acquired rights, and the preservation of liberties. The third is instrumental, having to do with economic efficiency in a broad sense.

The first case, at its most basic, posits that either income is earned under the provisions of valid contracts and assets are held under good title, or not. Thus, the distribution of income and wealth is either lawful according to the property and contract laws in force, or it is not. If it is not, the distribution must be redressed; but if it is, there is some uncomfortable discord between political authority's duty to uphold lawful titles and its mandate forcibly to redistribute them. The duty is constitutive of the state and, it may be felt, is anterior and superior to the mandate; the mandate is contingent on which part of society succeeds to impose its will on the rest. The duty and the mandate contradict each other.

The second case is less clear-cut, yet is not devoid of plausibility. Its theme is that the more a redistributive state solicits an electoral man-

Reprinted from *Advances in Austrian Economics* 2A (1995): 153–78, with permission from Elsevier Science.

date to protect some of its citizens against want, misfortune, and life's many other risks at the expense of other citizens, the more it fails to shield them from its own power, enhanced as it is by the very mandate to redistribute.[1]

The third case is quite pedestrian in that it does not appeal to any final value, but merely to instrumental rationality of the "*if* you want this, do not do *that*" kind. It claims that redistribution is counter-productive, frustrating what it seeks to achieve. Production and distribution, in an economy governed by voluntary exchanges, are jointly determined: *pace* J. S. Mill and the cohorts of his followers, there is no reason to expect that distribution can be changed by a political decision, however arrived at, without production changing, too. This is the case, among other reasons because factor inputs, factor proportions and outputs, are dependent on factor rewards and vice versa. There is a presumption, founded on general equilibrium theory, that redistribution reduces the probability of a Pareto-efficient factor allocation being achieved. *How much* this matters is an empirical question; some would tend to shrug it off as a very affordable cost, others judge that it shrinks the cake, and its future growth, severely enough to defeat the very purpose of redistribution. Theory can make some deductive attempt at predicting the gravity or otherwise of the problem. Section III of the present paper sketches such an attempt. The main instrumental case against redistribution is economic, but it spawns auxiliary cases that are primarily ethical, or sociological: improvidence, shirking, moral hazard, dependency, and the disintegration of the traditional family are the most frequently invoked.

Whatever their intrinsic merit, these cases have insufficient persuasive force, if one judges by the little effective weight they carry in modern times. Redistribution, it is argued with some justification, is ubiquitous and commonplace the world over just as breaches of the sixth commandment are ubiquitous and commonplace. Few priests, and fewer wise ones, deem it opportune actively to fight a universal practice as long as it is done in moderation, and is not flaunted; it is

---

1. ". . . the state protects the people against every disaster except those it inflicts on them itself" (Walzer 1983, 83). Walzer aims his barb at the "people's democracies," but he scores upon every kind of state to some degree.

then just a venial sin, a peccadillo, not to say a *péché mignon*. Likewise, few of the now extant political moralists and economic purists refuse to condone a degree of redistribution, though they accept it more easily if it does not flaunt egalitarian aims, but comes instead as a corollary of the alleviation of poverty, the assurance against ill luck, or the provision of public goods.

This accommodating stance is not, as one might easily have suspected, blatantly pragmatic and cynical. There are bone fide moral and instrumental arguments bolstering it up, arguments that manage to stay within the broad conservative and classical liberal traditions. Staying within these traditions, they do not concede much to egalitarianism. They do not agree, as other traditions would do, that a distribution of some widely desired aggregate, such as income, wealth, knowledge, or opportunity, is ethically more praiseworthy, and socially preferred, if it is more equal; yet they condone the attendant policies, or seem to ignore their redistributive character. The intellectual tolerance of redistribution, even in quarters where one would expect it to meet with severe condemnation, is a phenomenon worth closer analysis. It yields what I believe are interesting insights.

I

Absolution is routinely given for moderate redistribution in pursuit of noncontroversial aims. Hayek, who evidently appreciated as well as anybody the several prima facie cases against redistribution, has on many occasions set them out in summary versions, yet condoned and indeed positively commended the practice. His is the paradigmatic example of unexpected tolerance:

[Limiting the mandate of government] to the maintenance of law and order cannot be justified by the principle of liberty. Only the coercive measures of government need be strictly limited. We have already seen (in chap. XV) that there is undeniably a wide field for non-coercive activities of government and that there is a clear need for financing them by taxation. (Hayek 1960, 257)

Hayek, in making this singular distinction between coercive and noncoercive government actions, appears to be classifying taxation itself as noncoercive, a judgment that has an obvious bearing on his position regarding redistribution. Thus, he goes on:

> as we grow richer, that minimum of sustenance which the community has always provided for those not able to look after themselves, and which can be provided outside the market, will gradually rise . . . government may, usefully and without doing any harm, assist or even lead in such endeavors. There is little reason why the government should not also play some role, or even take the initiative, in such areas as social insurance. (Hayek 1960, 257–58)

However, it is one thing for the state to assure an irreducible equal minimum for all, but it is another to guarantee whatever vested interest each happens to have or thinks he deserves:

> an important distinction has to be drawn between two conceptions of security: a limited security which can be achieved for all and which is, therefore, no privilege, and absolute security, which in a free society cannot be achieved for all. The first of these is security against severe physical privation, the assurance of a given minimum of sustenance for all; and the second is the assurance of a given standard of life, which is determined by comparing the standard enjoyed by a person or group with that of others. The distinction, then, is that between the security of an equal minimum income for all and the security of a particular income that a person is thought to deserve. (Hayek 1960, 259)

The latter is redistribution Hayek rejects, the former is redistribution he finds both inevitable and acceptable, in some cases indeed commendable. For an antiegalitarian, it is noteworthy that his approval goes to the assurance of an *equal* minimum to everyone, while he disapproves of the claim for absolute security because it cannot be achieved for *all*. Would he support the claim if it *could* be? Nearly twenty years later, he lists, among the legitimate functions of government "the assurance of a certain minimum income for everyone" (Hayek 1973–1979, 3: 55). Moreover the minimum income in question is not some absolute floor of subsistence, determined by the physical requirements of human survival and reproduction, but a social or political variable. Some critics of the welfare state have attempted to contain redistribution within bounds just consistent with, and not exceeding, the dictates of charity, compassion, and social solidarity. The bounds thus set were meant to stop the proliferation of "welfare rights" giving rise to a spread of entitlements, and their seemingly endless ratcheting upwards. The argument which, if it prevailed, would fix the "socially" assured minimum income at some absolute level, and do away with "relative deprivation," appeals to the satiability of basic needs (Raz 1986, 235–44; Gray 1992). Whatever one may think of the force of the "basic" and "satiable" needs argument for producing agreement on the guaranteed minimum level of well-being, or of resources, to be fixed (how palatable must be the portion of food containing just enough calories for survival? — how far should medical resources be stretched to treat a given complaint? — what is the kind of shelter every family should be able to fall back on? — how long is a piece of string?) Hayek clearly, and wisely, does not seek to shut off the claims of relative standards, comparative well-being, and an inflatable minimum. He accepts, as a fact of political life, that:

> the amount of relief now given in a comparatively wealthy society should be more than is absolutely necessary to keep alive and in health. We must also expect that the availability of this assistance will induce some to neglect such provision against emergencies. (Hayek 1960, 285)

In a fine illustration of how one thing leads to another in a chain whose end, if it has one, we do not even dimly discern, this observation moves him to endorse the raison d'être of compulsory social insurance:

> . . . it seems an obvious corollary to compel them to insure (or otherwise provide) against those common hazards of life. The justification in this case is not that people should be coerced to do what is in their individual interest but that, by neglecting to make provision, they would become a charge to the public.

Finally, once the state requires everybody to make provisions of a kind which only some had made before, it seems reasonable enough that the state should also assist in the development of appropriate institutions.

Up to this point the justification for the whole apparatus of social security can probably be accepted by the most consistent defenders of liberty. (Hayek 1960, 286)

Little by little, from egg to tadpole to bloated-to-bursting frog, the shape of the fully grown welfare state emerges from an argument that starts with the "noncoercive" provision of minimum subsistence. Reaching this point, Hayek delivers himself of a number of puzzling reflections on a par with his description of government activities financed by taxation, that is, the forcible diversion of resources from one owner and one use to another, as "noncoercive." Basically he seeks to separate compulsory insurance, and for that matter the provision of welfare in general, from redistribution, as if the first were logically conceivable, and practically possible, without the second:

Though redistribution of incomes was never the avowed initial purpose of the apparatus of social security, it has now become the actual and admitted aim everywhere. No system of monopolistic compulsory insurance has resisted this transformation into something quite different, an instrument for the compulsory redistribution of income.

It is essential that we become clearly aware of the line that separates a state of affairs in which the community accepts the duty of preventing destitution and of providing a minimum level of welfare from that in which it assumes the power to determine the "just" position of everybody and allocates to each what it thinks he deserves. (Hayek 1960, 289)

Clearly, awarding to each an entitlement to some minimum income is empirically indistinguishable from awarding to each an entitlement to what "the community thinks" he deserves. The motivation may be different: regard to need in the first case, regard for deserts in the second. It may be conceded, too, that while the first award gives full satisfaction to need or what is taken to be such, the second does only partial justice to desert: each beneficiary deserves *at least* the common minimum, and that is all that will be awarded. While none deserves less, the community may well "think" that some deserve more, without making it its business to see to it that they do in fact get more.[2] These distinctions exist, as it were, inside the "community's" head without finding any reflection in its legislative decisions, hence in what is taken from some and given to others. However, diverting resources from their owners to those who would not otherwise enjoy them, *is* redistribution, no matter for what deep motive it is undertaken, and no matter whether it is need or justice that it is meant to satisfy.

Believing that compulsory social insurance is at least potentially non-redistributive, that in its pristine form it *was* non-redistributive, and that it was only politics that deformed it into a generator of redistribution, is to miss essential features of it. It is a truism that in any insurance pool the premiums of some are "redistributed" to pay the claims of others. Yet there is a strong presumption that if the participants in the pool have freely agreed to pay the premium, they must have valued the insurance at least as highly as its cost. Though it may be unscientific to affirm that they "revealed a preference" for being insured, it is surely right at least to take their voluntary act as weighty evidence of it. Both classes of insured—those who did and those who did not claim for losses—made a Pareto-improving bargain. "Subjectively"—and how else can the matter be evaluated?—no redistribution from one to the other has taken place.

Compulsory insurance, however, where everyone exposed to a type of damaging event must be covered whatever his own assessment of the probability of damage and of its importance (i.e., whatever its Bayesian expected value, henceforth "subjective loss expectation"), whatever the statistical probability (henceforth, "actuarial loss expectation"), and whoever pays the premia and the claims, is inevitably redistributive. Since such considerations will enter into an argument I will be putting forward in Section III, I shall attempt to clarify some welfare aspects of insurance with some care.

2. A political community is apt to worry more about seeing that everybody gets "no less than." At best, it is prepared to leave it to private, decentralized exchange mechanisms to allocate more to those who deserve more. At worst, it deems that such mechanisms allocate rather more than the more deserving in fact deserve, and proceeds to claw back what the "blind forces of the market" have "overallocated."

In a regime of voluntary exchanges, the demand for insurance is an increasing function, among other things, of the subjective loss expectation, and its supply a decreasing function of the actuarial loss expectation. Let all other things be parameters for the present purpose. The efficient premium in a competitive insurance market (assuming no administrative costs, no investment income, and break-even operation taking good years with bad), is set at the level where it and the two kinds of marginal loss expectations (the subjective and the actuarial) are mutually equal. At the efficient premium a proportion of risks will typically be left uninsured. If, instead of uniform pricing, discrimination is practiced and the market is segmented into categories according to risk quality (moral hazard being deterred by experience-based penal premiums), the proportion left uninsured will be smaller, but the principle remains the same: the actuarial loss expectation is no higher, and the subjective loss expectation is no lower, than the premium.

Under compulsory insurance, these selection mechanisms are not allowed to operate and the efficiency condition would, as a rule, not be met. Everybody who is exposed is insured whatever he, and whatever the insurer, may think of his exposure. Two solutions are possible. If a uniform premium is set at the average of the actuarial loss expectations,[3] there will be redistribution from "good" risks to "bad," that is, from those whose premium is more than the actuarial loss expectation relevant to their particular case, to those whose premium is less. This can be attenuated by discriminatory pricing. In addition, there will also be redistribution for a different reason that cannot be attenuated: in a typical compulsorily insured population, there will be a proportion of people whose subjective loss expectation is lower than the premium, and if they are made to pay the premium all the same, these people are in effect making a forced transfer to those of whom the opposite is true.

The other possible solution is to abandon the idea of a self-financing insurance pool (or pools) where members of an exposed population mutually guarantee each other against their exposure, without any par-

---

3. With discriminatory pricing, the premium ensuring breakeven in a given market segment (risk quality) will be the average of the actuarial loss expectations for that segment. The argument in the text will apply *mutatis mutandis*.

ticipation by the non-exposed part of society. If this constraint is lifted, the premium (or the spectrum of premia) can be fixed at any level, from zero to very high. With a zero or very low premium, the non-exposed must make good the actuarial deficit, and with a very high premium they get the surplus. The scheme, in short, is in this case redistributive both *within* the insured population and *between* the insured and the uninsured. It is not evident why anyone should, as Hayek patently did, choose to regard only the latter of the two streams as redistributive.

Obviously, the uninsured against one type of risk are often insured in other pools, other schemes of social insurance against other types of risk. Wearing one hat, they subsidize others; wearing various other hats, they are subsidized. One of these hats is that of the general taxpayer, who subsidizes social insurance schemes that are in deficit. Another such hat is that of the employer who subsidizes employees if premia are deemed[4] to be paid by payroll taxes.

In the limiting case where premia are zero, social insurance loses the last vestiges of an (albeit subsidized) pool of those, but only of those, who are at risk, and appears as a pure redistributive measure where "society" simply compensates the victims of various kinds of adversity, from ill health or unemployment to old age. The entitlement to compensation is the consequence, not (nor even in part) of the compulsory purchase of insurance, but solely of the victim's membership of a defined class, in much the same way as in the case of the guaranteed minimum income. This case can be seen as a unified multi-risk pool with universal participation, that one way or another collects from its members whatever it pays out on claims, but what it collects from a particular member ceases to bear any relation, however exiguous, to the actuarial risk the member in question presents to the pool.

The more diverse and developed the institution of "social" insurance and the more types of damaging event it is intended to compensate for, the harder it becomes to tell even the proximate (let alone the ultimate) net beneficiaries from the net contributors, and to quan-

---

4. I say "deemed" advisedly. Given the epistemological handicaps of the social sciences, we cannot tell who "really" pays the payroll tax, the employer, the employee, or either in his capacity of consumer or supplier.

tify the redistributive effects. That the net benefit from being insured against an event that does not take place within a period, or ever, is wholly subjective and under compulsory insurance remains "unrevealed" by any transaction, is only one of the many causes of our unavoidable ignorance about who really gets what from whom. All we can discern with anything approaching certainty is that a great deal of churning of taxes and compensations is going on, often to and from the same person, class, or income category.

We know that, except for the cost of "churning" them back and forth, money benefits and money contributions cancel out[5] for society as a whole. We can also surmise, on the deductive grounds surveyed in this section, that except in some freak case, they are very unlikely to cancel out for smaller subsets of society. Why Hayek thinks that it is only due to the corruption of politics that these compulsory schemes degenerate into redistributive ploys is hard to understand. Maybe he feels that redistribution is not redistribution unless it redistributes a lot, and modern social insurance schemes forged in the heat of the struggle for electoral survival redistribute more than the early models conceived in pre-democratic political calm.

Besides awarding a minimum income and instituting compulsory social insurance (which the propensity to improvidence, induced by the assured minimum income, renders necessary), Hayek attributes one more legitimate function to the state. It is one that, while going beyond the enforcement of "general rules of just conduct," yet presents "no threat to liberty" and "involves no coercion except for the raising of the means by taxation" (Hayek 1978, 144, cf. 111). This function is the production of public goods.[6] Taking the orthodox position of dividing public from private goods by the criterion of non-excludability, he requires government to supply:

5. Needless to say, this is not intended to mean that utility gains and losses also cancel out. There is nothing we can say descriptively about the "balance" of utilities. Normative judgments are of course always possible. But there is no intelligible test of "validating" such judgments.

6. Hayek treats law and order, not as any other public good, but as a separate category. The same separation is maintained by Buchanan's distinction between the "protective" and the "productive" state, the former producing law and order, the latter (other) public goods.

. . . services which otherwise would not be supplied at all (usually because it is not possible to confine the benefits to those prepared to pay for them). (Hayek 1960, 222)

The state's mandate appears perfectly straightforward:

. . . the only question which arises is whether the benefits are worth the cost. (p. 351)

Indeed, *tout est là,* and what is to be done is quite clear once we have defined and calibrated costs and benefits as both commensurate and properly measurable. It only remains to see which is greater. Before this pleasant formality can be accomplished, however, many other questions must be answered first, and while they are hard to answer in every language, in the language of methodological individualism they are absurd and have no answers worth making. Striking a balance between the individual benefits and the individually borne costs of public goods presupposes one of two kinds of commensurability, one strong, one weaker but still extraordinarily demanding. Whatever is taken to be the motive of choice between two states of affairs — whether it is plans, preferences, utility, or happiness — it must either be cardinally measurable on a scale unique from the origin up to a linear transformation, or it must be at least be amenable to interpersonal difference-comparisons. In the former strong case, everybody's preference-satisfactions or utilities before and after the production of the public good can be added up, and the two sums compared.

In the latter, weak case, we must perform, for a population of n, $n-1$ interpersonal difference-comparisons of the form: A's benefit from the public good exceeds his share of the cost by more than B's benefit falls short of the cost he bears, and this surplus benefit, a sort of interim subtotal, is greater than the amount by which C's benefit falls short of his cost, and so on. The resulting net balance[7] has at least as many de-

---

7. This balance is intelligible if it is not claimed to be an empirical, descriptive statement, but the outcome of pairwise normative judgments. It makes perfect sense for the judge to say that A's gain adds more to society's contentment, is a greater moral good, improves a state of affairs by more, and so on, than B's loss deducts from society's contentment, and so on. No harm is done as long as all

grees of freedom as the number of judges judging it, and there are as many judges as people affected by the benefit and the cost. This holds true not only for the absolute magnitude of the balance, but even for its sign. There is some sense, not at all easy to pin down, in which redistribution can be said to be taking place; if all costs and benefits were money sums, we might find redistribution of money income or wealth. Public goods, however, are unpriced and translating the benefits they yield to individuals into money sums is dubious, to say the least. It is neither necessary nor profitable to delve any further into the mare's nest of a cost-benefit calculus for public goods, except to wonder at Hayek's apparent fearlessness in treading on this terrain.

However, he absolves public goods from the sin of redistribution, perhaps because he thinks it is a merely venial one, to be shrugged off. He is prepared to believe that public goods can be supplied in a non-redistributive manner if

> . . . the wants satisfied are collective wants of the community as a whole and not merely collective wants of particular groups. (Hayek 1978, 111)

and (truistically) if the taxation they necessitate is not used for the redistribution of income (Hayek 1978). Of the latter condition, Hayek believes that it is satisfied if taxation as a whole (including both direct and indirect taxes) is not progressive (Hayek 1960, 307). He correctly notes that even proportional taxation is redistributive if the matching expenditure benefits some people more than others. To his mind, however, this need not generally be the case; implicit in his notion of "the wants of the community as a whole" is the suggestion that when expenditure is devoted to satisfying such wants, all benefit equally (by equal absolute amounts?—or in the same proportion as they contributed to the expenditure?—or by some other formula of proportional equality?). Adopting this optimistic view about the possibility of distributionally neutral state expenditure, he proceeds to find distributionally neutral state income in proportional taxation. Combining the two

---

accept that another judge need not agree, that we are all judges, and that there is no intersubjectively applicable test to resolve disagreements.

allows him to approve even high taxation if it is to finance government functions he would approve on independent grounds.

All this raises the suspicion that one way for Hayek to excuse the redistributive features of a social institution or rule he accepts, is to deny that it is redistributive. There is always some plausible distributive criterion that is violated by a given pattern of taxation. By the criterion of discretionary income, for instance, a proportional tax is liable to undo the pattern of pretax distribution; it is precisely the progressive tax, if progressing at the rate suited to the pretax distribution, that is apt to leave every taxpayer's *relative* discretionary income little changed. By the criterion of "real income" or "utility," in turn, just about anything can be safely affirmed about relative distribution pretax and posttax, since these terms refer to what goes on in people's heads, often unrevealed by their actions and undiscovered otherwise.

II

It is no doubt self-delusion to suppose that a society governed by a self-chosen social choice rule[8] can avoid redistribution, or rather keep it from rising above the threshold of visibility and becoming the central subject of politics. To the extent that redistribution is recognized as the focus of political conflict, reconciling belief in its legitimacy with belief in the rule of law and in the worth of efficiency requires an apology. Redistribution must be shown to offer favorable trade-offs to appease the consequentialist. (The deontologist, depending on what deontic

8. By "self-chosen" I mean a rule with a self-referential feature that permits the rule to be employed for its own amendment. A formal example is a constitution providing for a procedure that, if it is followed, results in constitutional change. In reality, society always chooses its own social choice rule, in the sense that it has some intrinsic capacity to reject (make unworkable, undermine, corrupt, and in the limit, overthrow) any rule it would not choose if given the chance, or could not amend in conformity with the rule itself. The proposition applies to social choice rules that are constitutions (requiring a good deal of willing respect and cooperation to work); it may not apply to a rule that is tantamount to dictatorship.

rules he commits himself to, either cannot be appeased, or does not need to be.)

It does not suffice to deny, as Hayek seeks to do, that public resource use and involuntary transfers from individuals to the government cannot be distributionally neutral, but will always favor some at the expense of others, at least relatively. Nor is it good enough to dismiss the redistribution generated by modern politics as a fact of life that the wise will turn a blind eye to. A blind eye is the less excusable the more one finds, on looking at contemporary evidence, that if it ever was, redistribution is no longer the unsought-after side-effect of government executing its various laudable tasks, but rather the reason why some of these tasks have been assumed by it; redistribution is the reward winning coalitions earn for entrusting power to a particular government.

Apart from the egalitarian argument which ascribes value, and in some of its versions overriding value, to certain equalities,[9] or posits

9. Valuing "certain equalities" is of course different from valuing "all equalities" or simply "equality." Egalitarians do not value every or any Aristotlean, "proportional" equality. The sufficient condition of an Aristotlean equality is that some benefit accruing to a member of a class bears the same relation to a variable characteristic common to all members of the class, as the benefit of every other member. Classic examples are "to each according to his need," "to each according to his merit," or "to each according to the marginal product of his work." The equi-proportionality condition is evidently consistent with a very "unequal" distribution, some members of a class getting more benefit than others according to how much of the qualifying variable—need, merit, marginal product, and so forth—they successfully claim.

Serious egalitarians do not admit that a benefit should be a dependent variable. To get equality among a class of persons regardless of their variable characteristics, they make the benefit depend on a constant common to the class. A common constant of the class "workers" is, of course, that they work; equality requires that they all get the same wage regardless of their variable effort, or effectiveness. Under this equality condition, nonworkers may or may not get anything, and it is irrelevant what they get. However, the abandonment of proportionate equality is the first step to serious, universal egalitarianism (where, e.g., workers and nonworkers get the same thing).

The second step is to constrain the choice of class within which equality is to be sought. If we choose to divide a universe into any number of distributionally relevant classes, even non-proportional, absolute equality within each class them as deontological imperatives, redistribution can also be defended on instrumental grounds. I propose to bypass egalitarianism as a doctrine. It is neither wholly uninteresting nor a wholly fatuous attempt at legitimizing redistribution, but I have had my say about it at other junctures; on the present occasion, I intend to consider only the instrumental (or consequentialist) defence. Three principal trade-offs of the form "redistribution may do some bad, but it manifestly does more good than bad" provide its backbone.

1. THE "SUPPRESSION OF FREE RIDING" TRADE-OFF

The argument is that we are, taken together, rich enough to look after the less fortunate in the community. (Whether the community is defined as the extended family, the parish, the country, or all humanity, has some effect on the strength of the argument: the larger the community the stronger is thought to be the case for coerced charity.) The archetypal Victorian mill owner was supposed to grind the face of the workers in the dust, but as he grew rich, he devoted part of his profits to good works in the mill town, lifting them, or their widows and orphans, up again. Most of us have some propensity to do likewise. However, the propensity is greatly curbed by the temptation to take a free ride on the propensity of others, or alternatively by our indignant perception that others are succumbing to the same temptation, leaving us to carry an "unfair" share of the load. Along standard prisoners' dilemma lines, each relatively well-to-do person would prefer to see poverty relieved without his personally having to contribute to its relief, but each would prefer to contribute if all others did, rather than see poverty go unrelieved. Consequently, all would rather have a

---

will permit any number of inequalities within the universe. Hence the striving to make the relevant classes as large as possible and, in the limit, all-encompassing, universal. In the limit, there is only one class, it includes everybody, and everybody gets the same measure of the benefit to be distributed. *Absolute* equality for a *universal* class is the logical terminus of egalitarianism.

For a different basis of reasoning leading to a fairly comparable result, cf. Raz 1986, pp. 225–27.

situation where all are forced to contribute than one where all charity is voluntary.[10]

Charity being subject to a prisoners' dilemma and hence requiring coerced contribution is a thesis that shares the weakness common to all orthodox public goods theory, namely the assumption (usually unstated) that the probability of a benefit (e.g., the relief of poverty) being contingent on a given contribution (e.g., that I give, or my club or trade association gives for charity) is nil or at best imperceptibly small. For this to be a coherent assumption, other conditions must also hold: above all, the public good must be continuously divisible. This is not the place for a full critique of the standard public goods thesis, the less so as there is yet another side where the defenses of the redistributionist case are equally vulnerable.

Let us for the moment admit that there is, in fact, a trade-off between coercive redistribution and poverty relief. Consider next the analogy with the apocryphal Victorian mill owner. He grinds the face of the poor; this describes his approach to his business, his profit-and-loss account. He can afford, and wishes, to relieve poverty; this desire is reflected in his appropriation account. How he appropriates his profit to reserves, to his personal consumption and to good works is posterior to his decision about price, output, technique, and so forth. These decisions do, while the appropriation of the result does not, affect the efficiency of resource allocation which requires that, subject to the usual provisos about competition and externalities, he should maximize profit.[11]

10. "The argument that charity has some characteristics of a public good . . . amounts to the prediction, perhaps untestable, that a parliament of donors would agree to contribute more to charity, than would be forthcoming in a competitive market" (Wagner 1989, 172). Wagner himself is commendably skeptical about the force of this argument. Cf. the investigations of Karl-Heinz Paqué of the effect of taxation on private charity (Paqué 1986).

11. A word about the "socially responsible" business enterprise is in order here. Corporate management is asked, by theorists of "business ethics," to balance the interests of the owners against those of the other "stakeholders," including employees, suppliers, customers, the local community, the disadvantaged, and so forth. Taking some account of some of these interests may, for all we know,

However, society's conduct differs essentially from that of the individual mill owner. Society's involuntary contribution to charity is unlike the voluntary appropriation by the mill owner in that, like every other tax (except the legendary, rather Yeti-like lump-sum tax) it affects rewards and costs at the margin. It is avoidable if the relevant economic activity is avoided. It acts, as it were, on people's profit-and-loss account, rather than on the appropriation of what they have earned. It is hardly possible to sustain the claim (if it were made) that in the face of a rise in taxes on factor incomes, or for that matter in other taxes, allocative efficiency is generally preserved. Consequently, deducing a favorable trade-off—wanting to suppress free riding implies that people actually prefer to be forced to give, hence the bad is absolved, while the good of poverty relief remains—is telling only half the story. The untold half may brutally tip the balance the other way.

2. THE "COMMUTATIVE VERSUS DISTRIBUTIVE JUSTICE" TRADE-OFF

Protecting everyone's lawful property in assets and income is a demand of commutative justice; redistribution amounts to overriding its demand.

Advocates of redistribution counter this by claiming that it misstates the demand of commutative and ignores the demand of distributive justice. The relevant argument relies heavily on the ideas of an unowned pool of wealth emitting bountiful positive externalities.

Current income produced and enjoyed by the members of society is said in a large measure to be attributable to an accumulated pool of tangible and intangible wealth. It is no more yours than mine. It em-

------

be sound business practice and calls for no special exhortation. The "balancing" that social responsibility is supposed to entail does not instruct management to adopt sound business practice. Doing that is management's duty anyway. Rather, it instructs management to *depart* from that practice, to do *less* than its duty to the owners for the sake of doing something *more* for other parties. This is a call both for the misuse of the mandate management receives from the owners, and for a deliberate departure from allocative efficiency. Heeding the call is neither ethical nor useful.

bodies the lasting results of social cooperation since the dawn of history. Individual productivity owes as much or more to this pool than to the efforts of the producer (Feinberg 1984, 16).[12] This view is seductively plausible and lends itself to eloquent formulations:

> . . . products are no longer just my doing, or even yours, mine, his and hers in identifiable proportions. Society now makes its own important contribution; so does tradition. Not even the products of thought retain much purity. A medical researcher might make a discovery of great commercial value. He might have worked terribly hard to bring it off. But even so, who trained him? Who moved the subject to the point where the discovery became possible? Who built the lab in which he worked? Who runs it? Who pays for it? Who is responsible for the enduring social institutions that present the commercial opportunities? One who cleverly exploits the social framework has both his cleverness and the framework to thank. (Griffin 1986, 288)

This line of reasoning is meant strongly to suggest that commutative justice does not properly vest ownership of the product in the producer. Given the vast role of the "pool of wealth," the argument goes to show that the rule of commutative justice that suffers in the tradeoff is, in fact, ill-founded and ill-fitting, not worth shedding tears over. We may not precisely know what part of current production we owe to the opportunity costs incurred by its producers and what part is to be ascribed to general social and economic conditions, metaphorically incorporated in the "pool of wealth." Very likely the respective parts cannot be "known," but must be adjudicated by the political process that administers distributive justice.

I am unaware of any author putting forward the whole of this argu-

---

12. It is preoccupying to see Feinberg, a modern legal philosopher of the very first rank, fall in with this same confused view of the claims of ownership. Marx, too, used to muddy his own waters with it, for he left us wondering whether it was the worker alone who created value, or whether it was he and a string of mostly defunct savants, inventors, lawgivers, and gendarmes, and there is no telling who added how much? To our days such woolly accounting remains the stock-in-trade of middlebrow social theorizing.

ment in defence of redistribution. Many, however, use diverse facets of it. Doing so at least implicitly facilitates conclusions that would otherwise be very difficult to sustain. These are some of the best examples:

- Expropriation without compensation is not, but taxation is, perfectly consistent with respect for property rights.
- Property rights are not absolute, but limited by all the other interests society chooses to foster. It is society that maintains law and order and enforces property rights, which is tantamount to such rights actually being *conferred* by society; calling for their enforcement *against* society itself is an absurdity.[13]
- Distributive justice must start from a baseline that is unencumbered by morally arbitrary ownership claims purporting to arise from original endowments and subsequent contractual acquisitions.
- The distributive outcomes of processes of voluntary exchange are illegitimate by virtue of the notorious failure of markets to internalize externalities.

The last of these derivatives of the idea of an unowned pool of wealth reaches to the heart of the matter. The others are mainly gratuitous affirmations or empty verbiage, but the externality argument looks as if it had some hard substance, amenable to analysis. It is through it that the entire pool-of-wealth line of defense is best tackled.

As a starting point, I take an externality to be a (good or bad) consequence accruing to a third party upon the execution of a contract by two parties (or, less typically, upon a unilateral act of one). Voluntariness of the contract, suitably defined, implies that each contract party receives what he considers sufficient consideration for executing his side of the contract. The good or bad of the third party is not part of the incentives or deterrents that motivate the contract and its exe-

---

13. Cf. Judge Posner's account of how, on a certain reading of their opinions, Legal Realists and Critical Legal Scholars regard public power over private action: "When I eat a potato chip I am actually eating the government's potato chip with its permission, since it is the government that created, recognizes and protects my property right in the chip" (Posner 1993, 569).

cution. The parties would do exactly the same thing if there were no good or bad consequences for any third party. It is this restriction that renders the name "externality" apposite.

The adequacy of the consideration, that is that each contract party gives sufficient value for value received, has crucial importance. By the principle of *ne bis in idem*,[14] the third-party recipient of a positive externality is under no obligation to reward or compensate its originators in any shape or form. If "society," or past generations, have created that positive externality, its recipients owe nothing for it to "society" or to contemporary heirs of past generations. Whoever created it *has already been paid in full.*

Second, I understand the "unowned pool" apology for redistribution to refer not to one, but really to two different, purportedly redistributable pools. One is the positive "sum" of genuine unintended externalities that are generated by such useful processes of cooperation as the production of goods, of knowledge, and of the conventions that in turn further facilitate the social cooperation that generated them. The other pool is the "sum" of government (or para-statal) services, a material public infrastructure, law and contract enforcement, and (contingently) "social" insurance, health, and education services. Metaphorically, these things are provided in execution of a virtual contract between the state and the taxpayers. If the metaphor were true to reality, the beneficial effects of these services *over and above* the benefit the taxpayers "bought" for themselves, could pass for a positive externality received by the nontaxpayers. Invoking *ne bis in idem* again, the taxpayers would have no claim for redistributive compensation from the nontaxpayers. Why anyone should think that compensation might well be due the other way, *from* the taxpayers who provide the beneficial externality *to* the nontaxpayers who receive it (which is the usual direction of most redistributive proposals) is a puzzle I leave the gentle reader to contemplate for himself.

If, on the other hand, the metaphor of the state contracting with the taxpayers to furnish services is not accepted as an explanation of how the social framework has come to be paid for, *ne bis in idem* is not applicable either. It may be, though we cannot really tell for sure, that the

14. Roughly: not twice for the same thing; no double jeopardy.

taxpayers have been badly done by. For if there was no voluntary contract, but instead compulsion to buy government services, they may have been made to overpay. Some of the tax they paid for their own benefit, some for the benefit that spills over and accrues to the non-taxpayers. Then compensation is due to the taxpayers from the non-taxpayers—broadly speaking, from the poor to the rich. We may safely take it that this proposition, too, would be disowned and vigorously rejected by the protagonists of the "pool of wealth," who would swiftly turn their backs on the regressive redistribution this would entail.

The upshot, then, is that if analytically there seem to be two "pools"—one resulting from voluntary exchanges, the other from the exercise of political power—for the purposes of the argument they can be amalgamated. The single common pool we are left with is unowned. Ordinary private goods come into being with property rights attached to them. Externalities, by contrast, are not acquired by individual factor-owners as and when they are generated. "Society" no more owns the putative pool of them than do particular individuals.

However, the latter wittingly or unwittingly dip into the pool in the course of their income-earning endeavors. When the externality that helps enhance an individual's income or, more broadly, his overall well-being, is (to use public goods language) "uncrowded," there is a close analogy with the Lockean idea of just original appropriation: there is "enough, and as good left in common for others" (or at any rate for the next person, which is what matters here).

The use of knowledge found in the public domain is a purer illustration of the principle of the "uncrowded" public good than Locke's occupation of virgin land. If you go and look up a piece of useful information in the public library, you do not reduce the amount of useful information anyone can find by taking the like trouble. (It may limit its usefulness if the condition of "uncrowdedness" does *not* hold, i.e., if your benefiting from the information reduces the benefit the next person can derive from it.) Satisfaction of the Lockean proviso comforts the egalitarian preconception that privileged status is due to outcomes where no one gains more than anyone else, because the first-comer leaves enough and as good to the second-comer. But the proviso does not do anything else. It becomes a requirement of justice only *by virtue of this egalitarian demand being first agreed,* and there is no compelling reason why it should be.[15]

If it is not, what holds for "uncrowded" externalities holds for them no less as and when they become "crowded." The only ground on which anyone ("society?") can vindicate a right to stop the early bird from getting the worm (or the fattest of several worms), to prevent the first-comer to gain the most, to outlaw the consequences of alertness and above all of luck, is the question-begging one that unequal benefits need some particular justification to be tolerated, failing which they should be undone, redistributed. Not everybody would concede this right and submit to the corollary obligation to give up unequal gains, and many in fact do not. Until all do and the Lockean proviso is accepted as a self-evident first principle—which is neither very likely nor, I think, at all desirable—appropriation of unowned goods can only be governed, as it always was, by the immemorial social convention of first-come-first-served. It is the *suspension* of this principle that must be justified by particular reasons (an emergency, the dire need of the latecomer), not its application. In the absence of such suspensive reasons, finders are keepers regardless of whether enough and as good is left to other seekers and, indeed, to non-seekers. Even if the "pool of wealth" *were* diminished by people helping themselves to it, nothing about an externality *being* an externality would make redistribution of the benefit, once it was internalized by the finder, any more legitimate.

It so happens that under the hypothesis of an accumulated pool of agreeable externalities, the very processes of production and exchange that are enriched by people helping themselves to the pool, and by so doing depleting it so that less is left for latecomers, must be supposed by the same token to be replenishing the pool by the agreeable externalities *they* generate. For if *past* social cooperation has left over externalities that enrich the present, why should we not assume that *present* social cooperation will likewise enrich the future?—though room may

15. Of course if a strict egalitarian moral axiom is first accepted, redistribution becomes mandatory if benefits are unequal to start with, *for whatever reason.* The argument from unowned and unearned externalities becomes quite unnecessary.

always be left for the second-order question about the present doing *enough* for the future.

I do not, in any event, think that one should consider *this* the clinching argument. The decisive argument is surely that good externalities are, in strict justice, not owed to anyone because the activities that have generated them had already been fully rewarded, and do not call for reward a second time. This is no more and no less true if we cannot identify the unwitting benefactors. Externalities that cannot be, as it were, traced to somebody's particular act do not, for that reason, put us in debt to "society" any more than do the externalities we *could* impute to particular persons put us in debt to *those* persons. Wherever they come from, they first belong to somebody when they are internalized. The rightful owners are those who, by no matter what combination of luck and desert, manage to internalize them. Yet it is perhaps comforting to reflect that first-come-first-served need not, and probably does not, imply that second-comers find only a dried-out pool.

3. THE TRADE-OFF BETWEEN "CAPITALIST PROPERTY RIGHTS AND SOCIAL PEACE"

It is a remarkably widespread supposition, going back to Marx, but held nowadays mostly by non-Marxists, that redistribution from rich to poor helps the rich. They give up some of what they have and, with that, buy themselves safer possession and enjoyment of the rest. Notoriously, Marx took this supposed trade-off so seriously that he came to consider revisionist socialists and all promoters of "social reform" as the worst "objective" enemies of the working class; for such success as they had must "necessarily" retard the total expropriation of capital by the proletariat (though, happily, it could not altogether prevent it). Capitalists, taken individually, are incapable of acting on the trade-off no matter how much they would profit from it. Marx nebulously, and later Marxists more clearly, saw the "fallacy of composition" one commits when one supposes that individual capitalists will normally act in the interest of their class. However, a redistributive state that takes some of their money and gives it to the workers, coerces them for their own good. It is quite plausible to see Bismarck's "social" legislation as the state acting out the role assigned to it in Marxist lore;

the charm of this particular chapter of history is that even if "objectively" Bismarck served it, in his own mind the capitalist interest was among the least of his concerns.

In a non-Marxian vein, some form of the hypothesis that surrender of part of their state-of-nature advantages by the better-placed can purchase some favorable behavior-change on the part of the worst off, underlies much of modern social contract theory (though not the Hobbesian original). In Buchanan's (1975) version, a redistributive bargain is the equilibrium solution of a game that dominates other solutions yielding inferior payoffs to both rich and poor due to the excess cost of protecting very unequally distributed property. It is possible to read, though I am not sure one should read, into Gauthier's version (Gauthier 1986; Gauthier and Sugden 1993), notably into the idea of the "minimax relative concession," a comparable redistributive bargain. Rawls, of course, obtains a certain just distribution by agreement among persons oblivious of any relevant differences between them. This is consequently not a bargain between rich and poor, because the distribution is decided by them when neither knows that he is or is likely to become rich or poor. Nevertheless, the belief that satisfying the requirements of distributive justice generates "willing" social cooperation permeates the less formal parts of his text. It is true that once his difference principle is put into effect, the less privileged have nothing more to gain *from* the more privileged, but then presumably both gain some more from nature because they all cooperate more "willingly," in ways we can only imagine.

No one has, to my knowledge, explained *why* redistribution stopping well short of strict, universal equality should appease the less privileged if they were not appeased to start with. If history teaches anything, it is the opposite. More often than not, concessions have only incited the recipients, sensing that the other party was on the run, to demand more concessions. If this were not so, concessions would not almost invariably turn out to be "too little, too late." Complete breakdowns in bargaining, ranging from deadlock to revolution, are usually proceeded (can we say "brought about") not by unyielding resistance from the outset, but by a series of piecemeal concessions coming eventually to a halt. What little we know of revolutions does not suggest that distributional conflict and class conflict can be best understood in terms of commercial bargaining, as depicted by the economist's apparatus of a Pareto-superior contract curve of mutual advantage.[16]

High theory, suitably watered down, has duly percolated to the depths of popular sociology and political advocacy. It is now the received wisdom that sometime between the two world wars capitalism was saved by government asserting novel powers to regulate it, novel rules to curb the freedom of contract, novel knowledge to keep the economy on a smoother path and to avoid the "wild swings" of free enterprise. Capitalism was saved a second time, even more decisively, by government increasingly shaping the distribution of wealth and income in keeping with the notions of justice democratic majorities have come to profess. This has at last begun to give the propertyless the material security capitalist economics, for all its recognized efficiency, has failed to assure. The putative rescue that turned capitalism, despite itself, away from the road to self-destruction was planned by the Keynes, Laskis, Beveridges, and Attlees of post-Depression Britain, by the New Dealers, by the social democrats of German-speaking and Scandinavian Europe, by unionists and intellectuals the world over who saved capitalism not only despite itself, but despite *themselves*. It is now de rigueur to hold that the society they fashioned is "pluralist," reflects a balance of all legitimate interests instead of giving free rein to just one, protects the weak, tempers envy and resentment, and upholds principles of justice and solidarity when these principles risk being swamped by the "blind forces of the market." By doing all this and more, "postindustrial" society is supposed to be moving toward

16. The basic reason why applying the theory of commercial bargaining to redistribution can produce such gross errors is that in the former, the parties bargain in secure possession of the property they may choose to exchange. Bargaining is about the terms of exchange, and either party can desist from dealing, returning to a safe baseline. Class conflict is about the very existence of the property rights of the rich, not about the terms on which both parties might be ready to exchange rights. The rich cannot desist; there is no safe baseline. They cannot just say to the poor that they would just as soon keep their riches. The poor have some ability, by peaceful political or violent means, to take it away from them. Nor is there any good and permanent reason why once a bargain is reached that gives the poor some riches in return for their promise not to covet and contest the rest, the poor should keep this bargain. However, these are deep waters and cannot be explored now.

the grand compromise between efficiency and equity. A system that maximized efficiency would collapse under the weight of the social discontent it could not help to provoke. Some sacrifice of efficiency buys its survival.[17]

The German theory of *soziale Marktwirtschaft* goes in one respect even further than any of the "social contract cum redistributive trade-off" theories surveyed earlier. What the theory really states is not easy to pin down. Ludwig Erhard considered that there was, in fact, no such theory (and no such thing); joining the words "social" and "market economy" was merely a "harmless pleonasm"[18] that made the 1948 reform look bland, unthreatening, politically less controversial. For all that, Ludwig von Mises (1966, 723) saw it as ill-disguised socialism — which is as it may be, and moves one to ask, once again, how long is a piece of string? However, what interests us now is that some adherents of the theory (supposing, *pace* Erhard, that it is one) deny that there *need* be any trade-off between efficiency and social justice or at least social appeasement. Redistribution engenders, as Rawls would have it, more willing social cooperation; it calms down strife, and establishes general consent (Starbatty 1993, 24). During the roughly three decades of postwar German economic success, many have in fact thought that the budding welfare state has actually contributed to efficiency rather than hampering it.

At all events, if redistribution produces more cooperation, consent and consensus, these things must be transformed into the ready money of better industrial relations, easier management, less absenteeism and malingering, a better work ethic, and so forth, in order to enhance

17. An authoritative study of modern economic development, that is, a model of the interplay between socioeconomic hypothesis and econometrics, advances the proposition that redistribution with some egalitarian bias has been an enabling condition of the continuing public acceptance of capitalism and market outcomes (Maddison 1991, 79–80). This is all the more incongruous as there is, in the nature of these things, no econometric test that could ever falsify the statement that "insufficient redistribution leads to the rejection of capitalism." At best, we can "verify" that a certain amount of redistribution was consistent with the "acceptance" of capitalism; the contrary remains unfalsifiable. We still do not know whether capitalism is not just as consistent with *less* or *no* redistribution. The idea of the trade-off remains simply unsupported.

18. In a personal communication to Hayek (Radnitzky 1993, 471).

efficiency. Indeed, they must enhance it sufficiently to offset the drag redistribution exerts on it by upsetting the particular distribution of factor incomes that would, given the pattern of ownership, be uniquely consistent with efficient factor allocation.

Since the sociopsychological assumption that workers work and managers manage better if enough redistribution is going on does not follow from anything in human nature that we know of, if other empirical evidence does not uphold it, nothing does. However, for those who have lived the industrial relations in pre-Thatcher Britain after decades of intensifying redistribution; absenteeism and disability fraud in Holland in the 1970s and 1980s; the breakdown of the "Swedish model" in the late 1980s; the devouring of public finances by the welfare state, the consequent menace of going under in a public debt trap in Belgium, Italy, Greece, Spain, Canada, and to a lesser extent the United States; for those who are witnessing these sad symptoms, the idea of buying efficiency with redistribution sounds like black humor.

Once democracy as the prime method of making social choice is thoroughly established, and the rule that decisions are voted and each vote counts for only as much as every other is followed, without regard to the quality, wealth, intensity of concern, and preference of particular voters, nor to the contribution each is making to the well-being of the others, politics becomes increasingly redistributive.[19] Moreover, the stability conditions of a democratically modified distribution are exacting, and may or may not be met: further redistribution may be provoked. This is an almost mechanical implication of the prevailing social choice rule system and has nothing to do with any grand bargain in which the rich few pay ransom to the poor multitude so as to be allowed to maintain capitalism. Nothing proves that there has ever been such an implicit bargain, nor that concluding one would be an equilib-

19. Democracy is a generalized and impure version of the elementary three-person pure distribution game. In that game, the distribution of the game sum among the three players is what any two of them agree on. This has the well-known result of producing, each time the game is played, a coalition of two players that redistributes the available sum in its favor, to the detriment of the third player. To maximize the gain of the winning coalition in a given round of the game, the loser must be the player who came out best off from the preceding round.

rium solution, representing the best strategy of each party compatible with the best strategy of the other.

III

Practical men, no less than ethical purists, might simply brush away the kind of polemics about redistribution sampled in the previous two sections. For pragmatists, the welfare state is a fact of modern life. It is unthinkable to "roll it back" by the means available in ordinary politics. Extraordinary means might, of course, put some kind of end to it, but would put God only knows what in its place. For moralists, the redistributive status quo cannot be undone without depriving its beneficiaries of their acquired entitlements. Even if it were the case that an economy free of redistributive distortions would be Pareto-superior, the case cannot be proved without actually performing the experiment. The holders of entitlements would not voluntarily give up their rights and permit the experiment without an assurance that they will not find themselves worse off—an assurance that, if given, may well not be credible, and if believed in, may well not be honored. The abolition of redistribution would almost certainly have to take place in what is arguably a rights-violating manner, contradicting the very condition of Pareto-superiority[20] which it would have been its purpose to attain.

20. On the usual definition, between two states of affairs x and y, x is Pareto-superior to y for a set of n persons if at least one in n prefers x to y and none prefers y to x. However, it is self-contradictory (irrational) for anyone in n *both* to prefer x *and* to insist on his right, if it is the case that x is devoid of this right, which must therefore be violated or voided to get to x. Rationally, if he prefers x, he waives his x-inconsistent right voluntarily. He is always free to do that. It is for this reason that the demand voiced by many commentators on A. K. Sen's "Impossibility of a Paretian Liberal" (Sen 1970), that is, that individuals should have a private sphere of rights protected *against* the claims of Pareto-optimality, is quite unintelligible (Sen, of course, merely states that these rights and Pareto-optimality may be inconsistent). If x, involving the abandonment of a right in the "private sphere," *is* Pareto-optimal, it is *because* the right-holder would rather waive (trade) the right than keep it. Against whom should it then be "protected"—unless it is against the rightholder himself?

Both the political and the ethical case for leaving well alone and muddle through, are strong. I for one consider them stronger than any of the pro-redistributionist pleas surveyed so far in this essay. One condition, however, would deprive both of much of their force if it were found that the status quo is not, in fact, sustainable over time. There are pointers that it is indeed unsustainable: that is, supposing that crime, teenage pregnancy, one-parent families, the failure of public education, endemic fiscal deficits, and the rest of the litany are in a substantial part imputable to the redistributive state. Plainly, however, no one can prove this conclusively to those who do not actively wish to be convinced. The imputation is an empirical matter, and the facts in question allow any number of interpretations. The object of this section is to take another pointer, chronic and apparently increasing long-term unemployment, and outline its causal relation to redistribution in a way that lays it as open as possible to purely formal, nonempirical criticism. The outline contains a largely deductive argument whose premises most trained economists would, I think, find fairly congenial.

The initial premise is that the demand for labor is a decreasing, its supply an increasing function of the wage rate or, in a concession to realism, the spectrum of wage rates. In another step toward realism, we may make the demand for labor also depend on the non-wage costs of employing it, and its supply on the non-wage benefits attached to employment. Let us now introduce redistribution.

How can the political authority, acting on the mandate of society, engineer redistribution in a simplified two-factor economy where capital is owned by the employers, labor by the employees, all income is factor income, there are negligible rents, and employment is full? Suppose that employers are made to pay a tax proportional to their income. In the short run, prior to any capital-labor adjustment, such a tax is, coincidentally, also proportional to the labor they employ. It functions as a tax on labor would function, and is added in full to non-wage costs. Let, however, the proceeds of the tax be fully paid over as a subsidy to employees in proportion to their income. This will add the same non-wage benefit to their wage as the non-wage cost the tax added to the employers' wage costs. The subsidy is thus a mirror image of the tax. Their joint effect is that the demand for labor shifts, in terms of the usual diagram, backwards to the left, its supply forward to the right. However, the two shifts, corresponding to the added non-wage cost and non-wage benefit respectively, perfectly offset each other. The cost of labor, the income from labor, employment, and total factor income all remain constant. The attempt at redistribution is void, nothing changes.

Let now the attempt at redistribution take another form, with the tax as before, but with the non-wage benefit given not as a money transfer, but as a gift of goods. The classic redistributive good is "security," embodied in a bundle of "social" insurance policies for the benefit of employees, with the premia paid directly by employers or by the government out of their taxes. The policies protect against such risks as ill health, unemployment, destitution in old age, and comparable adversities. How does an employee value this non-wage benefit?

To the extent that he has already been privately buying "security" against some of these risks, he can let his private policies run off. The employer-paid insurance is a perfect substitute, and the value to the insured at the margin is the premium he no longer need pay for private insurance. Depending on the relative efficiency of the two ways of providing insurance, and the actuarial loss expectation of the private versus the public scheme (which are likely to differ, especially if the public scheme does not discriminate by risk quality but offers uniform cover for a standard premium), the private premium may be either lower or higher than the cost of the public insurance, and so will be the value of the latter to the worker who has been a buyer of private insurance. We may, however, safely assume next that a substantial proportion of workers have not been buyers of private insurance, at least not against all their "social" risks. This, after all, is a principal reason for giving them public insurance cover in the form of an all-inclusive involuntary scheme they cannot opt out of. It is this proportion of employees whose subjective valuation of social security concerns us now.

It is tempting to say that the value of a good to the recipient who would not have chosen to have it if he had had to buy it, must be less than its money cost. This, of course, is the economic rationale of the long-standing statutory condemnation of "truck," the payment of wages in kind which in a perfect market for the wage good, would cost more to the employer than it was worth to the employee.[21] Opposed to this is the equally time-honored view that the preference-ordering of the improvident poor, and in a more self-confident version of paternalism, of everybody else, too, is a treacherous guide to the contribution various goods make to their welfare; consequently, merit goods are really worth more to them than they cost. Even without adopting the paternalistic position, one may well admit the possibility, if not the likelihood, that public provision of security is valued by some of the uninsured or underinsured at not less than its cost, although private insurance offering comparable security is not. Those uninsured workers who feel this way may indeed rather have social insurance than the money. Recognition of their own weakness of will—"compulsory insurance is worth it, for if I had the money instead, I would just fritter it away on beer and the races"—may be a possible reason, and we cannot exclude any number of others.

All we need for the present outline of a theory of unemployment to progress and prosper is that the condition "social security is worth as much or more than its public cost but less than what it would cost to buy it privately" should *not* hold for *everybody*. If it does not—a weak assumption I think we need not hesitate to make—there will be a marginal body of labor whose post-redistribution non-wage cost is higher than the non-wage benefit it confers upon them. Another way of saying this is that to some part of the employed workforce, the social security they are given is worth less than it costs to provide. Publicly providing social insurance, whatever else it did, will have achieved one effect: to make the marginal cost of labor higher than the marginal benefit from working.

The bare bones of the resulting static equilibrium stand out clearly. Just as it would in the earlier tax-and-transfer case, the demand curve for labor shifts to the left by an amount equal to the tax on labor. The supply curve of labor shifts to the right, *but by a lesser amount,* since at the margin the non-wage benefit in kind is less than the tax it costs the employers to buy it. In the apparent new equilibrium, the demand

21. In an imperfect market for the wage-good, on the other hand, employers may swindle their employees. It was this the anti-truck legislation was meant to prevent.

for labor and its supply are equated at a higher labor cost and at lower employment. As a result, part of the labor force is made redundant as enterprises "restructure."

This apparent new equilibrium, however, cannot prevail and is not one, because it is inconsistent with the insurance mechanism at work. The premium that was adequate to insure a fully employed active population against various risks including unemployment (the latter risk having in a full-employment economy a low actuarial loss expectation), is inadequate to provide the same insurance to a population that is partly unemployed. The reason can be formulated two ways: either we can say that the actuarial loss expectation rises to reflect the higher loss experience, or that the unemployed must be paid out on their policies. Whichever way the reason for it is put, the premium goes up and the extra cost must be met by somebody. The increase, which implies the same increase in the non-wage cost of labor, further depresses the demand for it: higher unemployment implies a yet higher insurance premium: a yet higher tax on labor; yet higher unemployment; and so on.

If the process is convergent, a finite equilibrium level of unemployment is eventually reached, and it is stable. If the process is "chaotic," we best not try to say what happens, but it is probably something even more unpleasant.

Guided by these fairly basic considerations, one would expect to find, in the less basic actual world, a certain number of salient features; their presence would lend a degree of confirmation to the theory.

First, unemployment corrected for cyclical variations would be rising, or leveling off at a historically high rate.

Second, in cross-national comparisons unemployment and its trend growth would be positively correlated with the level and growth of redistribution via social insurance of various kinds. The so-called "European model," as opposed to the American and East Asian ones, would show the highest incidence of unemployment. Among countries conforming to the "European model," the worst sufferers would on the whole tend to be the most "social" ones.[22]

---

22. Needless to say, countries with higher unemployment will spend more on unemployment pay. Therefore, lest we take effects for causes, we should be care-

Third, there would be in informed opinion an incipient recognition that the rise of non-wage costs, paying for non-wage benefits in *kind,* is the prime cause of unemployment. It would, however, be politically suicidal to act on this recognition and to start undoing the "social achievements" of the last two or three decades. Redistribution would continue, and continue to be treated by the typical commentator as a major virtue of modern democracy, well worth its putative costs. Classical liberals would continue to treat it uneasily as a fact of life, a peccadillo it is useless to fight against.

Fourth, cranks proposing intellectually discreditable remedies would get an increasingly sympathetic hearing. There would be a resurgence of Luddite beliefs: technology devours jobs, and not enough work is left to be done. There will also be a groundswell of neo-protectionism: foreign goods made by cheap labor devour jobs even more greedily than technology, competition from countries that protect neither the environment nor woman and child labor constitutes "social dumping."

Last, there would be a variety of tentative policy responses to "fight" unemployment. Encouragement of work-sharing, discouragement of layoffs by the imposition of penal severance costs, and an attempt to turn the burden of "social protection" from a tax on labor to a general tax, would be tried. These measures might shift the proximate incidence of the burden, but it is an open question what they could do to its ultimate incidence and its implications for allocative efficiency. As long as the good of "social" security is valued at the margin by its beneficiaries at less than the cost of producing it, somebody must absorb the loss. In technical language, the problem is that for a large part (in the lead welfare states, from a quarter to a third) of national product that goes to "social protection," the marginal rates of substitution and of transformation are forced apart by the policy of redistributing largesse in kind.

Most of these predictions of the theory are borne out by contemporary history. (I must not conceal from the rare reader who has not

---

ful in selecting a statistical proxy for the degree to which a country engages in "social protection." If we choose social insurance expenditure, we should probably exclude unemployment pay from it.

realized it unaided, that it was a great help, in sketching the theory, actually to see the contemporary syndrome the theory seeks to predict.) The long-term unemployed, and the angst-ridden young vainly looking for career outlets, are being smothered by the professed kindness and social conscience of the redistributive political system.

However, it is easier to shrug off, or deny altogether, some abstract loss of Pareto-optimality as the purported price of redistribution, than to accept its palpable manifestation, the emergence of chronic, large-scale unemployment. Two things seem to me totally unclear at the conclusion of these reflections: how democratic society could extricate itself from this self-made predicament, and how the situation could sustain itself for long.

8

Disjunction, Conjunction

A society can, for the purpose of understanding distribution problems, be seen as the aggregate of three groups of adult residents arranged in decreasing order by income per head or per household: the Top, the Middle, and the Bottom group. Let all members of these groups have two social options: to emigrate, or to submit to a social choice rule by which two groups together decide the distribution of aggregate income among all three. Any two groups can form a coalition and cause the redistribution, to themselves or to sub-groups designated by them, of some part of the pre-tax income of the third group. The relative sizes and initial pre-tax incomes of the groups is such that the potential gain from applying this distribution rule is greatest if Bottom and Middle combine to take income away from Top. In democracy with simple majority rule, Top and Bottom are ideally each 50 percent of the electorate, and Middle is a single person, the median voter; this maximizes the size of Top, hence also the potential gain to Middle and Bottom from redistributing Top's pre-tax income to themselves or to sub-groups they wish to favor. In real life, one may usefully relax this maximization condition, and think of Top as 40–45, Middle as about 10–20, and Bottom as about 40–45 percent of the electorate.

Under these conditions, rational use of the social choice rule results in a partial or total disjunction of benefits from costs in the politically determined domain of distribution. Benefits are unrequited cash

Reprinted with permission from *Can the Present Problems of Mature Welfare States Such as Sweden Be Solved?*, edited by Nils Karlson (Stockholm: City University Press, 1995), 20–27.

transfers and free or subsidized goods and services in kind. Resources to meet their costs come from two sources: taxes of all kinds (including "social" insurance contributions that, being mandatory, function like taxes) and net public borrowing. The former give rise to interpersonal, the latter to intertemporal redistribution. In the former, gainers and losers are both identifiable, and their gains and losses are simultaneous. In the latter, gains precede losses, the identity of the future losers is uncertain, but it is a fair conjecture that they are, broadly speaking, the young and the unborn members of all three groups, with future members of Top bearing a more than proportionate share.

If the full cost of a benefit is not borne by the beneficiary, excess demand is likely to be generated for the benefit. If the cost-benefit disjunction were total, excess demand for transfers and benefits in kind as a whole would be infinite. (If a particular good or service were subject to saturation, a non-saturated one would be demanded in excess of supply). Partial cost-benefit disjunction may be perceived as total. This will be the case if an individual ignores the effect of his own consumption of "free" benefits in kind and transfer receipts on his own taxes—an effect that is individually negligible though it may become significant at group level.

II. The "Mature" Welfare State

If the above mechanism, once installed and bolstered by doctrinal legitimization, requires time to operate, the demand for benefits will be met by some supply, not instantaneously, but by gradual increments. The welfare state will have relatively modest beginnings; it will then go on growing in terms of the size and diversity of the benefits provided; and a ratchet effect is liable to prevent any substantial reduction or withdrawal of a benefit once granted.

There is no obvious equilibrating tendency setting an upper limit that the growth of the welfare state may approach but not breach. Instead, it "matures" and its growth abates, and then it approaches one of two constraints.

One constraint is a complex set of dysfunctional effects that come into play as the share of incomes received in the form of unrequited transfers and "free" benefits in kind increases. These benefits are either independent of personal effort, or may indeed be inversely related to it; with other things equal, their increase reduces effort. It also reduces that part of personal saving that can be imputed to precautionary motives. Further, associated effects spring from welfare fraud, tax fraud, the erosion of the economic *raison d'être* of families, and a host of others that space does not permit to enumerate. When the growth of the welfare state presses against this constraint, heavy efficiency losses tend to arise.

The other constraint operates upon intertemporal redistribution through the well-known effect of the public debt trap. In as much as the public debt is not indexed nor denominated in foreign currency, escape from the debt trap is in principle possible through inflation. However, if holders of the debt understand this and anticipate inflation, this escape route will be rapidly closed. In addition, refinancing the public debt will probably require sharply higher real interest rates.

Allowing the economy to press against one of these constraints, let alone against both at the same time, entails serious material and moral losses. It is for this reason that the call arises for "reforming" the mature welfare state, instead of passively letting the above constraints do the work of limiting it, as it were, "naturally."

III. Collective or Individual Rationality

It is irrelevant, or nearly so, whether policy-makers or informed public opinion understand or not that society as a whole is in some sense worse off when the welfare state reaches the vicinity of these constraints. Even the more precise claim, that a reduction in the provision of welfare benefits would in fact increase potential well-being in the sense of meeting the Kaldor-Hicks compensation criterion, would not be decisive. For while reducing the benefits would presumably be "collectively rational," it would be individually irrational, as long as by imposing an excessive, collectively irrational level of welfare provision, a majority (e.g., the Bottom and the Middle) could still obtain some gain at the expense of the minority (e.g., the Top)—quite irrespective of whether the resource loss of the losers was larger than the resource gain of the gainers.

This is saying no more than the trivial truth that a player in a distribution game can do best by maximizing his own payoff even if his doing so causes the payoff of the other player(s) to decrease by more than his marginal gain (i.e., if individual maximization decreases the game sum). There is no known method of assuring that a "social" bargain is reached that would reconcile the conflict between collective interest and individual majority interest. It is even debatable whether such a solution is conceivable in the face of the dependence of the collectively efficient resource allocation on an income-distribution that favors a minority.

Nor is there much reasonable ground for believing that collective rationality can prevail at the constitutional level if it cannot prevail in ordinary fiscal legislation. If it is irrational for a winning coalition to forego potential gains, it is equally irrational for it to adopt a constitution that would oblige it to forego potential gains. If such a constitution is in fact accepted, it is not necessary; if it is necessary, it will not be accepted (or will be circumvented).

IV. A Fiscally Neutral Delayed-Action Reform

Recent history in both Western and Eastern Europe and the United States suggests that this logic does in fact operate most of the time, and political systems based on procedural social decision rules do not lend themselves to any radical rolling back of the welfare state. Voters do most of the time punish almost any curtailment of "free" benefits. In order to have even a minimal chance of success, a major reform attempt must for this reason meet two fundamental conditions. It must restore the conjunction of benefits and their costs at least at the margin; and it must incorporate this in an integrated, non-separable set of fiscal measures that is at least marginally favorable to a possible majority coalition, which may be the existing one or a new combination to replace it.

Is such a set of measures feasible? For feasibility, I shall assume, as minimum necessary conditions, that it must not directly clash with what seem to be political imperatives in mature welfare states (of which the Swedish political scene is probably one of the most characteristic examples); heavy progressive taxation of persons (combined with light corporate taxation to discourage the emigration of mobile factors, capital, and enterprise); egalitarian provision of welfare goods and services (no "first and second class" in health care, education, etc.); universal entitlements (no means testing) are features that, where they obtain, can only be undone at high political risk. However, should these political imperatives prove to be less compelling than expert opinion now believes, welfare reform would of course gain some degree of freedom. In broad outline, the following measures, taken together, take account of the several considerations discussed earlier in this paper, and might have some chance of attracting a majority coalition:

a. All cash transfers are to be broadly maintained.
b. Entitlements to welfare goods and services in kind are to be replaced by welfare credits (vouchers or credit cards). Some interchangeability between credits to particular goods or services may be admitted.
c. The total of vouchers or credit cards issued in the initial period is to be equal to, e.g., four-fifths or nine-tenths of the expenditure on these goods in the previous period, one-fifth or one-tenth being put in a reserve to meet exceptional needs (costly illness, incapacity to earn income, and other hard luck cases).
d. The total of welfare credits or vouchers is to be distributed to households regardless of pre-tax income, but having regard to the number of dependents and their age (infancy, school age, or retirement).
e. The major part of a household's vouchers is to be non-transferable and available only for the purchase of welfare goods and services; a minor part (perhaps one-third or one-quarter), however, is to be redeemable by the state at a moderate discount at face value in cash at the holder's option. This provision aims at two effects. One is that above some fixed level the consumption of welfare goods, i.e., the non-redemption of the voucher for cash, should have a positive marginal cost;

moreover, this cost is to be of the same order of magnitude as the good's cost of production. The other intended effect is that the probable shift of consumption from welfare goods to ordinary market goods and to private saving, permitted by the redemption of the vouchers for cash, should result in some public saving by virtue of the discount.

f. The total cost of these benefits is to be met, as before, from general state revenue. However, the mode of raising it is to be altered. A substantial part of the income tax, perhaps all of it over and above some low flat rate, is to be replaced by a number of earmarked welfare taxes levied on income at rates assuring the politically required degree of progressivity. Each welfare tax is notionally to be devoted to the (incremental) financing of a particular welfare good or service (education, health, pensions, etc.). At the margin, financing is to be met entirely by the tax in question, so that the rate of each tax becomes perceptibly responsive to any rise or fall in the cost of the welfare benefit in question. (The purpose of this provision is to reduce taxpayer indifference, and in some cases positive benevolence, towards increases of a particular benefit. There may be attendant advantages, including greater clarity and publicness about who pays what for whom.)

g. The set of measures from *a* to *f* is fiscally neutral in a first approximation, before allowing for the behavioral changes induced by the altered mode of benefit allocation and taxation. To encourage its adoption in preference to the status quo, it may seem advisable to make it more palatable either to the existing coalition of Bottom and Middle, or to a new one of Middle and Top. Changes favoring Bottom and Middle are *prima facie* more apt to obtain the support of Middle than their presumably more parsimonious opposites that would favor Top and Middle. This consideration would seem to speak for playing to the existing ruling coalition, and increasing the progressivity of taxation even beyond its existing degree. However, this would be undesirable for efficiency as well as other reasons, and seems a heavy price to pay for what is initially a fiscally more or less neutral reform. The alternative, shifting some of the welfare taxes from Top and Middle to Bottom, may or may not be feasible or decisive.

It is, however, quite possible that the electorally decisive element in these measures is the option to redeem some part of welfare entitlements for cash, albeit at a discount. While having the option cannot make anybody worse off, it is virtually certain to be preferred by many (by all whose preference for a freely chosen over a designated good exceeds the discount). The latter are likely to be randomly distributed over all income groups, loosening up the rigid income-determined division of interest groups, and *ceteris paribus* possibly tipping the electoral balance in favor of such a reform.

V. With the Grain

Clearly, as long as politics is unrestrained by deontological taboos about property and contract, men will always use it to disjoin benefits from their costs, get the former, and make others bear the latter. The reform sketched in Section 4 would, for evident reasons, fall far short of offsetting this primordial political drive. It would, however, establish at least a few cost-benefit conjunctions. They would be less efficient and less potent than the standard marginal equalities of cost and benefit prevailing in ordinary market exchanges. But though initially modest, they should have delayed and possibly important effects. For both the individual option to switch from welfare to market goods, and the closer and more visible links between welfare benefits and their costs, are likely to operate over electoral processes in future periods to curb excess demand for "welfare" by its consumers and willingness to meet it by its providers. With such mechanisms in place, the welfare state would acquire at least a modest built-in tendency to reform itself, so to speak, with the grain, rather than against the grain under the destructive pressure of its efficiency and debt constraints.

Part Three

Justice

9

Justice as Something Else

Why must nearly all the current normative theories of distribution represent justice as something else? Why are we led to see justice as fairness, as the greatest mutual advantage, as the minimax relative concession, as reciprocity, as the terms of a society-wide agreement that cannot reasonably be rejected, as reversibility, as impartiality? There is nothing in the lengthening series of aliases suggesting that the ingenuity moral philosophers deploy in reinventing justice as something else is about to run out of further variants.

Arguably, Kant has set the precedent. His categorical imperative identified justice as universalizability. However, his was not a principle capable of regulating all distributive conflicts, notably the conflicts that may arise from the distribution of initial endowments of talents, advantages, and possessions. A rule one wishes to apply to oneself is universalizable if it is a requirement of reason to wish it to apply to everyone else, and vice versa.

Universalizability, therefore, is incapable of generating rules of distribution that systematically favor the weak, the unsuccessful, and the poor. The strong, the successful, and the rich cannot plausibly be held to wish redistributive rules to apply to themselves that would predictably work to their disadvantage.

This Kantian defect, to call it that with tongue firmly in cheek, was radically remedied by John Rawls's "justice as fairness," where a sense of fairness impels all adult members of society to accept those prin-

Reprinted with permission from *Cato Journal* 16, no. 2 (fall 1996): 161–73. © Cato Institute.

ciples of justice that it would be rational to adopt in an "original position." In this original position, all initial endowments disappear behind a "veil of ignorance." If people had no endowments, or had equal ones, or were ignorant of what they had, it would be pararational[1] for them to agree that inequalities are to be evened out except if they work to the advantage of the least favored among them. This, Rawls's "difference principle," is the product of prudential reason once fairness has led all to ignore any initial advantages they may have.

Although Rawls (1971, 112, 343) defines fairness as submission by each to the same restrictions all others submit to, if each in fact shares in the common benefits secured by these restrictions—which amounts to "fairness as no free riding"—it is clear that the role he assigns to fairness is far wider.[2] Fairness in his theory requires the more favored to agree to the sort of distributive rule they would prefer if they were not more favored—a very different and more inclusive idea than "no free riding." If fairness were to mean something less than this, or if people did not feel bound to be fair in this radical sense, the sort of agreement that is supposedly rational in the original position (though not elsewhere) could not be reached. Fairness as initial equality is an axiom of justice as fairness.

Instead of simply treating it as an axiom, however, Rawls seeks to deduce it from the claim that initial endowments are morally arbitrary—a claim that might well not impress anyone who has not yet adopted moral rules and must first be induced, by the appeal to fairness, to enter into the "original position" by adopting some. Even if it were not dubious practice to invoke morals in order to generate morals, it is not at all clear why the fact that something is morally arbitrary should oblige us to take no account of it in deliberations about moral rules of distribution.

1. I call the agreement upon a maximin strategy equilibrium "pararational" (rather than rational), because while maximin is argued for by a reason ("make the worst possible outcome as good as you can, even if you must make the best possible outcome less good than it might have been"), the reason is obviously not the best possible one. The strategy that maximizes the mathematical expectation of utility is argued for by a reason that is by definition the best, hence better than maximin.

2. Compare Hart (1983, 119).

Among other "justices as . . . ," and next only to Rawls's, the most influential is probably Thomas Scanlon's (1982) justice as unrejectability. Brian Barry's (1995) "justice as impartiality" is a synthetic derivative of both, with a preponderance of Scanlon. The three together incorporate most of the currently dominant mainstream theory that, or so I shall argue, treats justice as a matter of social choice rather than, as in the traditional approach, a quality of individual acts.

Under Just Conditions, What We Accept Is Just

In Rawls, once he has led people into the original position (and some auxiliary assumptions are made), agreement on distributive principles is a matter of mutual advantage; it has instrumental value. In Scanlon's contractualist theory, in sharp contrast to Rawls, agreement need not yield mutual advantage in order to be reached. It may yield it accessorily, but people do not seek it to make themselves better off in the ordinary narrow sense.[3] They seek it because they are motivated by a common desire for agreement that is inherent in morality (Scanlon 1982, 128).

So far, there is nothing implausible or far-fetched in Scanlon's construction. Less extravagantly than Rawls, it does not require harsh and heroic renunciation of initial advantages. It is easier to take it that people wish to live in agreement with each other, on the basis of which they can mutually justify their conduct (ibid., 117) than that they commit themselves to a distributive rule that deprives the more favored among them of any advantage over the less favored.

However, this judgment about Scanlonian moderation compared to Rawlsian radicalism quickly turns out to require qualification. In

3. Whether the narrow sense makes sense is perhaps questionable. If people like to agree, they must prefer agreement to no agreement, with other things remaining equal. Can one nevertheless say that reaching agreement does not make them better off? One can, if preference is taken as a "subjective" and better off as an "objective" condition. If this distinction is upheld, it is a sensible statement that "he prefers to be worse off," or that "he is better off but ignores it"; if not, not. Austrian value theory and Paretian welfare economics are on one side of this divide, the utilitarianism of the Impartial Observer on the other.

Scanlon, for the agreement to produce unrejectable rules that will be morally wrong to transgress, the agreement must be both informed and unforced (ibid., 110–11). The information condition can, I believe, be safely accepted, but what about the condition of unforcedness?

Unforcedness, as Scanlon explains it, means not only that no party must be coerced to agree, but that none must be in a "weak bargaining position" enabling others "to insist on better terms" (ibid., 111). But better than what? Manifestly, there is a hidden norm both for bargaining strength (none must be in a stronger or weaker position than the norm) and for the terms eventually struck in the bargain (they must not be better for some, worse for others). But if such a norm is tacitly pre-set, the desired bargaining solution will be a disguised initial condition of the theory and not a theorem of it. Though Scanlon, to his credit, refrains from saying so, we may take it that people starting from initially equal endowments would find rules providing for continuing equality unrejectable — they are left with no ground for rejection. Hence, they would find inequality in breach of the agreement unjust. This is plausible, but how interesting is it?

Scanlon's argument is silent on whether reasonable unrejectable agreement could be found if initial conditions were unequal. However, given the norm for bargaining power and for the bargain itself, planted at the base of the theory, it seems that initial conditions that violate this norm could either not produce unrejectable terms, or if they did, unrejectability would cease to signify justice (i.e., cease to be a sufficient condition of it). In either case, the theory of justice as unrejectability would seem to hold if and only if initial conditions were just. If so, it is not justice that follows from unrejectability, but unrejectability from justice.

The Desire for Agreement, on What Terms?

Scanlon could well object that not all terms that were not in fact rejected were unrejectable in his sense. His unrejectability springs from the reasonableness of the terms, not from such contingencies as the pressing needs of one party and the ease and comfort of another. This defense fails to deal with the objectionable tactics of building equality into the foundations of the theory by the seemingly innocuous device of requiring equal bargaining power. In addition, such a defense also exposes another vulnerable flank of justice as unrejectability, and by extension of other "justices as," too.

All we know of the common desire for agreement is that all are "moved by it to the same degree" (ibid., 111). But what degree, how high? Given a very high degree, a variety of widely divergent terms may all be unrejectable. Nothing ensures a determinate solution. This might not matter much if the whole set of possible solutions were just by virtue of being unanimously agreed upon, or if there were independent means of identifying a unique just solution, or at least a just subset within the possible set. Would the test of "reasonableness" provide such a means? Or, what is a different proposition, is it that only reasonable terms are truly unrejectable? But what, then, is the test of reasonableness? How do we recognize it? One has the uncomfortable feeling of being led round and round in a circle.

I would submit that we are inadvertently moving back and forth between what are, in fact, two theories separated by the idea of reasonableness, which acts as a "cutout." On the near side, there is a theory in which the desire for agreement and initial equality jointly produce a bargaining solution, which is both unrejectable and normatively unique because it must correspond to the tacit norm built into the initial conditions (i.e., that the terms must not be "better for some and worse for others"). On the far side of the cutout, we find a much simpler theory. Among possible bargaining solutions, there is at least one set of terms that is reasonable. Since it is unreasonable to reject that which is reasonable, these terms will be unrejectable by reasonable persons, hence they will be just. There is no need for a desire for agreement, and it does not matter whether initial endowments were equal or not, for all will agree to their reasonable redistribution.

For reasonableness to exert the force this theory demands from it, it must signify a particular empirical content. It must function less like the word "warm" and more like the words "25 degrees centigrade"— that is, it must work with little intersubjective variance. Failing that, one man's reasonable terms may be another's cruel exploitation. There is little doubt, though, that "reasonable" works at best like "nice weather," which can mean anything from crisp and cold to sunny and hot.

Impartiality and Reasonable Rejection

The same or more, alas, is true of such words as acceptable, fair, unforced, equal footing, equal consideration, equitable sharing, and so forth. They are all unabashedly question-begging, in that they rely on a theory of justice (that tells us what is acceptable, fair, or equitable) and consequently cannot help in first constructing one. Yet it is such words that constitute the stuffing in Barry's *Justice as Impartiality,* the second volume of his projected three-volume *Treatise on Justice.* It is of course neither convenient nor necessary always to avoid terms that have no intersubjectively stable meaning at least within a language and a culture, let alone cross-culturally. But inherently vague words and concepts can only build an inherently mushy theory, ill suited to yield rules of justice whose chief function is said to be the avoidance of conflicts (Barry 1995, 12)—least of all if the conflicts are about who gets what, how, and at whose expense.

On the face of it, justice as impartiality is mainly about such concerns as freedom of worship, sexual practices, Salman Rushdie, crash helmets and seat belts, "multiculturalism" and race relations, and not or hardly about property and contract. Yet, the appearance of relative unconcern about what for most people is the central issue in justice is due to "economic" questions being held over for treatment in the forthcoming third volume of Barry's *Treatise.* Much of the treatment is foreshadowed in two essays (Barry 1991 and 1994), and will be taken into account in what follows.

Barry acknowledges a large debt to Scanlon, from whom he borrows unrejectability as the criterion of just arrangements, as well as seemingly innocuous defining features of the hypothetical "original position" that turn out, on inspection, to imply equal bargaining strengths and an independently postulated normative solution to the bargain ("not better for some and worse for others"). Following both Rawls and Scanlon, he equates distributive justice with the terms of a hypothetical contract to which all would give unforced assent if they found themselves in the "original position" as specified.

Unanimously accepted terms are liable to be trivial or confined to apple pie-and-motherhood issues. There are two ways of making sure that it is the "right" and nontrivial terms that are accepted. Trusting to belt and braces, Barry uses both. The belt, as we have seen, is to specify that the "original position" is one of equal endowments. From such a position the parties could plausibly be supposed to assent to distributive rules whose consequence is, in effect, equal endowments. If the initial position was accepted and just, rules that *perpetuate it* must presumably also be accepted and just. The rules are rules of impartial justice; they do not favor or penalize anyone relative to their initial position, and are not designed to promote anyone's values. They consecrate the status quo which, praise be, is one of equality that we must on independent grounds deem to be just anyway.

By way of braces, as if the belt were not strong enough, reasonableness is made to do the work all over again. Suppose that, instead of the idealized "original position," bargaining were to start from a position found in nature, entailing all kinds of unequal endowments. Alternative sets of rules are proposed to its denizens who must agree unanimously on one set. Suppose also that certain rules would permit some people to have more of what all want and others to have less. To prevent the adoption of such rules, reasonableness cannot be allowed to retain the vague and indefinite meaning it has in ordinary language and in most of Barry's *Justice as Impartiality*, but must be stiffened (as it is in Barry 1994, and presumably in his forthcoming *Principles of Justice*).

Under this stiffer meaning, that is not found in ordinary language, it is unreasonable for better-placed individuals to reject rules of distribution that do not allow them to be *so much better* placed than they were prior to the agreement. What counts is that this rule would still allow them to be somewhat better placed than others. The only people who *can* reasonably reject a given set of rules are those who are not placed better than anyone else—that is, than whom nobody is placed worse. Every set of rules that allows someone to be placed lower than someone else can reasonably be rejected by the lower-placed party as unjust. As long as anyone gets less than someone else, the rules under which this happens can be rejected; the only stable equilibrium set of just rules is one that *no one can veto*. This condition is fulfilled only when no one is worse off than anyone else. This is Barry's first (and only operative) principle of justice (Barry 1994, 67).

Justice as impartiality, then, whether obtained via the "original position" or via a special meaning given to reasonableness, entails equality of valuable endowments and the enforcement of that equality over time. Consequently, this notion of justice is incompatible with property and freedom of contract, institutions that, when combined, are a powerful generator of inequalities over time, and almost certainly a sufficient condition of them.

Justice as Social Choice

Justice as impartiality appears to be a feature, a trait, a distinguishing criterion of a complete state of affairs arranged by society: it is "a sign of an unjust arrangement that those who do badly under it could reasonably reject it" (Barry 1995, 7). Though they *could* reasonably have done so, they *did not* actually reject these arrangements, for if they had, these arrangements could not have come about. Since they did come about, it is up to society to rectify them and make them conform to the norm of reasonableness. Just "institutions should operate in such a way as to counteract the effects of good and bad fortune" (Barry 1991, 142). According to this formulation, impartiality must compensate for inequalities that are not imputable to one's deliberate and free choice. Which choice was deliberate and free is, of course, the whole question. It would seem that a choice by which we accept an arrangement we could have reasonably rejected, is not deliberate and free, but due to pressing need, hence tainted by bad fortune. The test for telling free choice from bad fortune is the reasonableness of what we accept. Impartiality, then, is defined by a substantive norm of reasonableness adopted and applied by society. The question-begging character of the claim that this is the substance of justice stands out clearly enough.

An obvious, and I think quite weighty, objection to Barry's view, as to other views of "justice as something else," is that it confuses the content of the rules of justice with the proper manner of applying them. It is one thing to say that the rules must be applied impartially, fairly, without fear or favor, treating like cases alike—which is of course consistent with the content of the rules being partial to the right, rather than impartial between right and wrong. It is another thing to require the rules to be such as to reduce unlike cases to like ones in an attempt to compensate for fortune, evening out the uneven, on the ground that leaving cases unlike and uneven would not be impartial.

Casting justice in this role is, in effect, to assimilate it to social choice and to merge the theory of justice into social choice theory. Justice becomes a matter of satisfying a selection criterion or choice rule (e.g., "choose the state of affairs no one can reasonably reject") by which a state of affairs is identified as "just," in the same way as other selection criteria, choice rules, or choice mechanisms identify a state of affairs as socially "chosen" or "preferred." Fairness, unanimity, non-rejection, veto right held by the "dictator" (e.g., the worst-placed individual or group) fit very well into the *modus operandi* of social choice theory.

It is almost as if Barry sensed and sought to carry through, yet also to evade, this conflation of justice with social choice. He energetically protests that his central concern, individual "conceptions of the good," is something quite different from the concern of social choice theory, individual preference orderings: one is a "system of beliefs," the other a "taste for strawberry ice cream" (Barry 1995, 167). But this is nonsense he must not be allowed to get away with. Conceptions of the good, if they are anything intelligible, are hierarchies of alternative states of affairs, ranked according to how good they are conceived to be. The rankings must be sensitive to every non-indifferent trait of a state, according to how well it is liked, approved, or coveted if it is a good trait, and disliked or disapproved if it is a bad one. Why exclude any trait, good or bad, as improper and irrelevant in judging a state of affairs? If the treatment meted out to Salman Rushdie can weigh in the ranking, why can't the availability of various flavors of ice-cream? Complete, comprehensive "conceptions of the good" must, almost by definition, take some account of both, except if the individual concerned is totally indifferent to Salman Rushdie or to ice-cream. So must complete preference orderings, subject to the same exceptions. The two are either indistinguishable,[4] or "conception of the good" is a woolly concept that corresponds to nothing in psychology and in practical reason.

It is fascinating to watch how current theories of distributive justice scuttle back and forth across the line that divides social choice theory into a Paretian or "soft" and a non-Paretian or "hard" version. (In the latter, Pareto-superiority is not necessary for "socially preferring" one state of affairs over another; imposing burdens on one individual in order to help another can be "better" than not doing so, while in Paretian theory the two alternatives cannot be ranked.) Rawls's insistence on unanimous consent and on the impropriety of political principles that expect "some citizens . . . to accept lower prospects of life for the sake of others" (Rawls 1971, 178) is Paretian "soft." Yet his difference principle is a "hard," non-Paretian social choice rule that makes some people better and others worse off than they would otherwise be.

Scanlon's rules and institutions, which no one can reasonably reject, can hardly be read otherwise than as Paretian: rejecting an arrangement all would prefer is self-contradictory; rejecting one that is indifferent is contrary to the desire for agreement, but I could no doubt reasonably reject (even if I did not actually reject) one that would burden me for the sake of strangers. Scanlon's theory then moves lock, stock, and barrel over to the "hard," non-Paretian side as it defines reasonable rejectability from an egalitarian original position. (In a just world, we would have equal endowments. I could not reasonably reject arrangements that equalized them. Therefore, it would be unjust to reject them even if I have more and must give some to you.)

Barry, too, is Paretian in his ambition to devise a social choice rule that will be neutral between "conceptions of the good," eschewing the attempt to aggregate them (which would involve the dubious exercise of adding together the positive and negative differences justice

4. Like many other political philosophers, Barry (1995, 135) is worried that some "conceptions of the good" place a premium on the suppression of the beliefs or modes of behavior of others. He believes that institutions giving effect to such conceptions are illiberal, and are contrary to justice as impartiality. He would therefore require institutions to "filter out" such illiberally other-regarding "conceptions of the good." The same requirement formulated in the language of preferences would have precisely the same effect.

as impartiality makes to individuals having different "conceptions of the good").[5] In almost the same breath, however, he defines justice as requiring that better-placed individuals give up some of their valued endowments, or the fruits thereof, in favor of the worse-placed—an overtly non-Paretian, "hard" choice.

This is hardly surprising. In "hard" social choice, almost anything can be advocated without risk of inconsistency; in "soft" social choice, hardly anything can. A theory that was Paretian throughout, and disclaimed any ability to say that as a matter of ascertainable fact, some forced interpersonal transfers made a state of affairs socially *preferred* or, by a hardly perceptible step from goodness to justice, more *just,* can only see distributive justice as a system of voluntary exercises and transfers of rights. Justice is upheld as far as it can be if voluntariness is safeguarded. It is then *just acts* that make for justice. The conformity of a state of affairs to a social selection criterion—fairness, nonrejectability, or impartiality as defined by the respective authors, or what a majority will vote for, or the dictatorship of the poor—is just that, conformity to the postulated criterion and nothing more. That the criterion is the embodiment of justice rests on no objective evidence, such as is provided by actual (as distinct from hypothetical) agreements to create or transfer rights.

5. Barry's test casts some doubts over his own conception of social choice theory. He makes the startling statement that "the Pareto principle is . . . the ordinal form of cardinal utility maximization" (Barry 1995, 135n). It is the non-admission of interpersonal comparisons that bars utility aggregation and would do so whether or not utilities were cardinally measured. Once the utilities of different individuals are taken to be incommensurate, they cannot be added up. It makes no difference how they are calibrated, ordinally or cardinally: in *either* case, only Paretian comparisons are possible, and aggregate utility maximalization is not. Cardinal apples cannot be added to cardinal oranges, any more than ordinal ones. To say that one is the ordinal, the other the cardinal "form" of utility maximization is, to put it moderately, apt to lead the trusting student into costly errors.

"Pre-Social" Rights and the Lockean Proviso

Acts that are not torts, breach no duty, and respect rights are just. Justice must then be explicated by an independent, noncircular account of torts, duties, and rights. The account must be noncircular in that, unlike fairness or impartiality, it must not rely on some concept of justice to derive justice.

Torts are recognized in immemorial and near-universal cross-cultural conventions that condemn and sanction murder, maiming, trespass, theft, and other offenses against person and property. They are not problematical for the present purpose.[6] Duties are conventionally recognized moral imperatives, and their breaches are conventionally condemned but typically not sanctioned. Unlike obligations, duties do not have the rights of another person as their logical corollary; but neglect of duty is generally taken to disqualify an act from being just. Duties, too, are largely unproblematical for the theory of justice. The ontology of rights and their corollary obligations, however, is more contentious. A plausible and noncircular theory of just distribution stands or falls with a plausible account of rights that does not presuppose some prior account of justice.

Barry (1995, 124) dismisses the idea of "pre-social" or natural rights as preposterous. Though his treatment is a little cavalier, his conclusion is incontrovertible in the somewhat trivial sense that an isolated, extrasocial individual cannot have any rights since the exercise of a right by a right-holder requires the fulfillment of the corresponding obligation by another person, the obligor. However, it is surely a *non-sequitur* to go from here to the proposition that for rights to exist, "society" must recognize them, hence they are the products of collective choice. This contention, however, is what Barry and his inspirators appear to believe when fashioning theories of justice within a framework of social choice theory.

6. Some torts, notably offenses against property, are rights violations, and the recognition of the right is implicit in the convention that makes its violation a tort. Other torts, however, notably offenses against the person, may be held to be wrong without necessarily supposing that there is a right they violate. It is, I think, not necessary to impute to the person a right to "self-ownership" in order to account for the full system of conventions against torts.

Revealingly, Barry (ibid., 205) speaks of property rights being "assigned" to persons without saying who "assigns" them. The underlying suggestion seems to be that society will assign property to persons to the extent that it finds it desirable to let them have "their own toothbrush" and, beyond strictly personal possessions, property representing some area of discretion. Barry makes clear, however, that this area must be neither large nor unequal as between persons.

Society, of course, does not create rights by way of voluntary agreements with itself, except metaphorically as in the social contract. (The creation of rights must be kept conceptually distinct from their enforcement. Whether society enforces rights, or more precisely what part of enforcement services it performs, is contingent on historical accidents and is an altogether different question.) The synoptic view of a set of rights as a product of social choice legitimized by some overall hypothetical agreement contrasts sharply with the more positivist and grassroots view in which each right is created by the assumption of a matching obligation, with value to be given for value received, in a formal or informal contract entered into by a pair of individuals. The contract is not hypothetical or metaphoric, but actual; it may or may not be reasonably unrejectable, but it has not been rejected; both parties would rather have it than not.

There are at least two (and perhaps more than two) ways of looking at such pairwise agreements. One is to find that the agreement, by virtue of being untainted by force, fraud, or unconscionability, is just, since those concerned jointly chose it, rather than something else. By extension, the distributive consequence of the totality of all such agreements, past and present, is a just distribution. The other view is that the agreement was just if and only if the values exchanged or promised under it have been justly come by. The employee acquired a right to a salary by assuming and performing an obligation to work as directed. That his right to be paid for his work is justly acquired does not seem to be in dispute. Any dispute is about the right to his labor acquired by the employer who, endowed with more property than the employee, has greater bargaining power.[7]

7. We may accept this supposition for argument's sake, though the very meaning of "bargaining power" is unclear, and if it were clear, we would almost certainly find that it is not correlated with property in any simple way.

Here is the final parting of the ways between justice as a socially chosen trait of a distribution and as a just distribution resulting from the totality of just acts. For the one, unequal bargaining strength is *eo ipso* unjust, and so is any formal right acquired by using it; such rights deserve no respect. For the other, no inequality—whether of bargaining power, property, or any other kind of endowment—is unjust as such, but only if it was brought about by unjust acts. Therefore, if the employer's greater wealth is the result of a chain of voluntary transactions, combined with his own abstinence from consuming capital, no injustice tarnishes it. Barring force and fraud, the only remaining source from which injustice might have sprung is inequality in first possession.

The essentially deontological theory of just acts corresponding to the exercise of rights and the performance of obligations, inspired by John Locke and most lucidly developed by Robert Nozick (1974), which justifies property by working backwards along a chain of voluntary transfers, loses confidence (and much of its consistency) when it arrives at first possession at the end of the chain. It subjects the justice of finding, enclosing, inventing, and thus appropriating valuable resources, to conditions. The chief condition is some form of the Lockean proviso that "enough and as good" must be left for others to appropriate. Nozick shows that in its stringent form the proviso can never be met. He then explicitly assumes that at least the weaker form, which can be met, must be incorporated as a condition in any adequate theory of justice.[8] One can, of course, assume anything, for any reason or none, but the assumption sits ill with the deduction of justice from rights, and of rights from agreements. Where rights must first be created, finding, enclosing, inventing, and appropriating that which was previously unowned is exercising one's liberties, for it cannot violate anyone's rights where *ex hypothesi* there are no such rights. In their absence, it is hard to see why the justice of appropriation of one resource by one person should be dependent on other persons having comparable scope for appropriating other, equally good resources, though of course it would be nice if they did have it. The supposition that they

8. "I assume that any adequate theory of justice in acquisition will contain a proviso similar to the weaker of the ones we have attributed to Locke" (Nozick 1974, 178).

must have it rests on the prior and tacit adoption of some egalitarian moral axiom.

Almost any form of the Lockean proviso can be levered up to a requirement that equates justice with conformity to some general feature of the social state of affairs. Equal initial endowments, or some other broad equality, is the privileged feature. Theories of justice can either do this, or they can define justice by reference to individual rights that are independently accounted for. They can hardly do both at the same time.

10

Justice

The concept of justice informs our sense of justice, rather than being formed by it. The concept escapes circularity, resting as it does on foundations that are independent of notions of justice.

I. Findings and Judgments

Answers to questions about what justice demands are commonly, and misleadingly, called judgments. Misleadingly, because the same word is used to denote two radically different types of statement, and much hinges on the difference.

One type deals with points of fact. They are true or false, for facts are ultimately ascertainable, and once ascertained, exclude *bona fide* disagreement. They are *intersubjectively* valid. Points of fact in a strict sense include "points of law," for what a text states, what the custom of a place is, or what conduct a social norm dictates, are also ascertainable. The world being what it is, texts may be poorly drafted, evidence may be blurred or missing, custom and convention may be falling into disuse. Findings in the face of such imperfect information may not be reached without a degree of help from judgments, which then appear as the product of personal intuition about what the facts would show if

From *The New Palgrave Dictionary of Economics and the Law,* edited by Peter Newman (London: Macmillan Reference Limited, 1998), 2: 400–409; reproduced with permission of Palgrave.

only they were fully accessible. For example, at one time interpersonal comparisons of utility were represented as "objective," more like findings to support advocacy of income redistribution. (Later, these efforts came to be seen as misdirected because the problem was no longer conceived as one of facts but of value judgments.) In their role as substitutes for information, judgments function as surrogate findings.

Judgments properly speaking are expressions of moral intuitions, sharply distinct from surrogate findings which seek to express empirical conjectures. Judgments reflecting moral intuitions answer questions of justice that are deemed not to be matters of fact. Such judgments may seem right or wrong to another, perhaps rival moral intuition, but they are neither true nor false. Nothing in the rules of logic or epistemology compels two *bona fide* persons to agree on the same judgment; there can be no question of intersubjective validity. A shared religion, shared value judgments, shared interests may bring different persons' moral intuitions closer to each other, and the contrary may occur when these influences affect different persons differently. Genuine judgments are intrinsically personal, enjoying a latitude that has no very obvious limits.

Latitude in judgment means discretionary justice. The task of a firm, well-defined concept of justice is to reduce discretion in which my say-so can oppose your say-so. It accomplishes this, in a seeming paradox, by constricting the scope of judgment in justice.

It will be argued in this essay that the world of justice is neatly divided into two adjacent realms, with no overlap between them. The two realms are ruled by two regulating maxims, "*suum cuique*" (to each, his own) and "to each, according to . . ." (i.e., one reference variable). In the realm of "*suum cuique*," the concept of justice leaves little space for judgments. Findings do nearly all the work. Where, on the other hand, "to each, according to . . ." is the master rule, there is an irreducible role left to judgment. This is perhaps no very bad thing as long as discretion is kept in its irreducible place.

If the thesis presently to be unfolded is anywhere near right, the concept of justice requires that where findings furnish complete answers, they should be left to do so. The persistent invasion of one realm of justice by the regulating maxim of the other brings incoherence, confusion, and discredit to justice.

DISORDERLY MINDS, DISCRETIONARY JUSTICE

Conceptual analysis often has recourse to two sources, the behavioral and the linguistic. They furnish evidence of how people understand a concept as witnessed by their reactions and by their use of the corresponding words in ordinary speech.

By the first source, then, a just state of affairs is one that people agree to. However, outside actual contracts, agreement may not be signified by any positive act. It may be tacit acceptance, which in turn may reveal nothing more definite than acquiescence born of indifference or impotence. An enormous latitude in states of affairs is compatible with tacit acceptance. Moreover, one and the same mind can manifest tacit acceptance of mutually incompatible states of affairs. Many theories of justice "finesse" the problem of tacit acceptance by postulating hypothetical agreements that would be reached under specified conditions, e.g., under ignorance of one's particular identity, endowments, and interests, under uncertainty, under a desire to agree to anything reasonable, under mutual insight into each other's intentions, and so on. However, what hypothetical persons would agree to in hypothetical circumstances, while perhaps an interesting subject of speculation, cannot reliably predict what actual people will agree to in actual circumstances, and reveals only one of many possible versions of what they understand by "just."

Is usage of words like "just" or "fair" in ordinary speech a better witness to the common understanding of the concept? People will unhesitatingly say "Due process of law should be observed (but) the wife-slayer should not get off by hiring high-priced lawyers"; "People are free to spend their own money as they choose (but) should not get better medical care by paying more for it"; or "The given word must be kept and contracts honored (but) great inequalities of income and wealth are unjust." The near-impossibility of reconciling the two members of these and similar pairs does not prevent them from being uttered in the same breath.

It is well known from social choice theory that it is not, in general, possible to obtain a coherent hierarchical ordering of states of affairs by aggregating, according to a plausible rule of aggregation, disparate individual orderings of such states. We may find X ranked above Y, Y above Z, but Z above X. If collective entities, such as a society, were supposed to have a collective mind, we should have to say that it was a disorderly one, unable or unwilling to sort out its own incoherences. When one and the same individual is found to hold incoherent preferences, opinions, judgments, unconsciously and without embarrassment disagreeing with himself, the disorderly mind is not a symptom of the impossibility of adding up orderly ones, but a fairly predictable feature of human imperfection.

Disorderly minds can harbor mutually incompatible judgments, and discretionary justice. This is not to suggest that people should wake up and tidy up their minds. It is to suggest that the concept of justice needs more coherent foundations than most people's understanding of what is just.

BEFORE JUSTICE: SOME FOUNDATIONS

Manifestly, justice is not a self-evident concept that reveals itself to the intuition of everyman. To what extent can one derive it from elements more basic, more self-evident than itself, and that are independent of, and prior to, any notion of justice? If it is a composite, what are its components; if an edifice, what are its foundations?

Five foundation stones seem to bear most of its weight, doing so unobtrusively, beneath the surface. They are *verifiability* and *falsifiability; feasibility; harm;* and *trust.* Only briefly identified here, their role in carrying the edifice will emerge in detail in subsequent sections.

"There is a hippopotamus in the room" is an affirmation we can both verify and falsify with the same ease. "There is a needle in the haystack" is a statement that the person affirming it can verify, but that we can only falsify with great difficulty and, in the limiting case of the infinitely great haystack, not at all. All data statements, i.e., statements with empirical content that, if confirmed, can pass for findings, are either verifiable, or falsifiable, or both. Which they are (and if they are both, which confirmatory operation is less onerous) appears, in an obvious but little noticed manner, to govern the placing of the burden of proof on one of a pair of contradictory answers to a question of justice. The allocation of the burden of proof, in turn, gives rise to such crucial principles as the presumptions of liberty, of innocence, of title, and of equal treatment.

Feasibility sets limits to the requirements of justice in the same truistic way as "ought implies can" does to the commands of morals. A person's feasible set of acts—what his environment and his possessions and claims on others permit him to choose—will generally contain some acts that sufficient reasons show to be inadmissible. These acts are unjust because they are inadmissible on independent grounds, and not inadmissible because they are unjust. No circularity is involved, as there would be if ruling an act admissible depended on prior knowledge of what justice required. All residual acts that have, for the time being, no sufficient reason speaking against them, are by implication, and for the time being, admissible. They are "liberties." Infringing them is unjust because they are liberties in the absence of reasons to the contrary, rather than being liberties because it would be unjust to infringe them. More concisely, liberty is the baseline; it is the restrictions upon it that need to be justified.

Sufficient reasons for ruling feasible acts inadmissible cannot be exhaustively classified, but some can be catalogued with some certainty. One class of such reasons has to do with harm, another with trust, both of which are foundation stones in their own right of the concept of justice.

Whoever cripples me, slanders me, or takes away what is mine and what I value harms me in a non-trivial way. This is not a trite proposition, and some may even consider it far from self-evident, if only because neither "non-trivial" nor "mine" are non-controversial. As to the former, it is perhaps fair to say that when a harm is really on the borderline, the question whether it just passes muster as non-trivial is itself relatively trivial. As to the latter, what is duly "mine" is clearly a central preoccupation of any analysis of justice. It cannot be resolved right at the outset, and must for a little while be held in abeyance. Notwithstanding any reservations on this score, harm is a robust enough idea to serve in the argument from feasibility to admissibility and hence to justice.

Trust enters into justice in a fundamental, constituent way through what one might call the belief-soliciting nature of statements. When making a statement, a speaker conveys words to a listener with the general objective of inducing in the latter a degree of belief—and the higher the better—that the statement is true or that he, the speaker, holds it to be true. The intrinsic purpose of saying *these* words must be to induce such a belief, for otherwise it would not matter whether it was these words or some others that were conveyed. The intrinsic purpose of a promise, a particularly important type of statement, is to induce a belief in the promisee that the promise will be fulfilled, or failing that, that the promisor intends to fulfil it. The promise is essentially a trust-soliciting statement. Breach of the promise betrays the trust that the promise was intended to induce. Contract is reciprocal promise. Whatever other reasons may be marshaled in support of the institution of contract, a self-evident one is that default betrays the trust the defaulting party has solicited. As such, it is an unjust act. It is perfectly possible to accept this conclusion, derived from the responsibility assumed by the promisor when he solicits the trust of the promisee, even if the proper remedy for the breach of promise is in dispute. An influential view in modern jurisprudence holds that when the breach of a contract causes no assessable damage, no remedy is applicable. In this view, when a contract is partly executed, remedy is restitution of the defaulter's gain or the damage caused by the default, while if the contract is unexecuted, remedy need only be brought for damage caused by the reliance of the plaintiff on its expected execution. This view appears to excuse the breach if it causes no damage to the promisee's interest. It reflects "rights-based" theories of justice that derive rights from interests and obligations from rights. Such theories commingle issues of justice with those of welfare, and are not conducive to a clear concept of justice.

II. Constituent Principles

Principles can be identified that rest on the foundations described in the preceding section and, perhaps together with other and compatible ones that are not specifically identified, constitute justice. Three such principles seem necessary, though we should not expect them to be sufficient, to constitute the essential concept: *responsibility, presumption,* and *convention.*

RESPONSIBILITY

The principle of responsibility results from the relation between a state of affairs and its putative cause—a relation that is normally a matter of empirical findings. A state of affairs in which we find disabled orphans, destitute old people, young people vainly looking for something useful and gainful to do, a region devastated by flood, an industry dying on its feet is readily described as an unjust world. Calling it unjust as distinct from sad or infuriating or crying out for some help, however, is implicitly to impute it to an unjust act committed by someone at some stage. Failing such imputation, one would in effect be saying that injustices can be self-generating—loose talk at best, nonsense at worst.

In the occasionally helpful language of game theory, Nature is a player whose moves have no discernible motive. Nature does not, as far as we can tell, seek to maximize anything. Nor does it deliberately help or hinder the human players who do. To say that an unjust state of affairs has come about without anyone committing an unjust act that could have caused it is saying that Nature has committed an unjust act. People sometimes do say this of Nature or of God in ordinary speech. They may even call Nature, God, history, chance, "the system," or some similarly elusive entity "responsible." But they do not mean the responsibility that is a ground for being called to account, and if they did, they would sound as strange as the primitive tribe that burns the effigy of the river demon for causing the flood, or the medieval villagers who punished the cattle guilty of straying into the standing crop. Such doings would be thought laughable by the very thinkers who hold that what justice demands first and above all is the undoing of the effects of chance, the accidents of heredity and history, and the acts of Nature on human lives.

It is not within our scope to speculate what the Herculean task of ceaselessly undoing what Nature keeps doing would require in terms of social and economic organization. On the other hand, it is pertinent to the concept of justice that the task of evening out the work of chance would entail arranging redress, not for injustices in the sense of acts that call for restitution and retribution, but for every human act that was either helped or hindered by chance. People would have to bear residual responsibility for the consequences of their own choices. Which consequence was imputable to choice and which to chance would have to be judged, offering almost infinite scope to judgmental justice and making it conceptually so vague as to be virtually indeterminate. This may not be the chief objection to it, but for the present purpose it seems telling enough.

It may be worth making it explicit that if an act of Nature, say a calamitous flood, is held to be an injustice to the flood victims, then the actor committing the injustice cannot be made responsible for repairing it. If the injustice is to be repaired just the same, the repair must be exacted from those who had the prudence or blind luck not to build their homes on the flood-plain; but making them repair the injustice they have not committed is an injustice, suggesting that a concept of justice that demands this is incoherent, a product of disorderly minds. If the non-victims are to be made to help the victims of the flood, some other ground than justice, e.g., some notion of an interpersonal sum of welfare, must be invoked to defend the injustice involved.

PRESUMPTION

A hypothesis and its negation form a pair such that it suffices to verify one member of the pair to falsify the other, or vice versa. A feasible act is either sufficiently harmless, unobjectionable, hence free, or it is not sufficiently harmless, objectionable, liable to sanction, unfree. A person is either innocent, or guilty. A holder either has title to an asset in his possession, or he has not. A case (raising a question of justice) is either relevantly like another case, or it is not. It is obviously redundant to prove one member in such pairs *and* disprove the other. The burden of proof need only be placed on one of the two, but it must be placed on one of them for a conclusion to be reached at all. Whichever side the burden of proof is placed, the opposite side is treated as the privileged hypothesis; a presumption is established in its favor. Unless the contrary hypothesis is successfully proved, the privileged hypothesis is presumed to be true and for the time being treated as such. Just as the presumption of innocence means that a man is treated as innocent until he is proved guilty, so the presumption of guilt means that he is treated as guilty until he is proved innocent. The two alternatives look symmetrical, though of course they are not. It is tempting to suppose that in our age and civilization we put the burden of proof where we do, because opting for the presumption of innocence, of freedom, of possession, of equal treatment of like cases, is intuitively just and ranges us on the side of the angels. Supposing this, however, is to suppose that we already know what is just and which side is that of the angels. There is, instead, an independent reason that makes these presumptions prevail, due to their being asymmetrical to their opposites in a way that makes them dominant quite regardless of ages, civilizations, and intuitions about justice.

Consider feasible acts. An actor proposes to perform an act. There could be an objector, an authorized representative of society, or just another party speaking for himself, who might affirm that the act would cause sufficient harm to a public or a private interest to justify its being stopped, prohibited, sanctioned. The presumption of liberty implies that the act will remain free and will not be stopped until the affirmation of its objectionable nature is not only made, but also verified. The opposite presumption would stop the actor doing the act in question until he could show it to be proof against possible objection. There is an indefinitely large number of potential objectors having a potentially infinite number of objections, some of which may be sufficiently strong. To falsify the hypothesis that the act is objectionable, and therefore not one of the actor's liberties, is a needle-in-the-haystack type of task, very difficult and costly if the set of potential objections is large, and logically impossible if the set is not finite (which, in a strict sense, it never is). Taking the haystack apart blade by blade to falsify the supposition of its harboring a needle would take long enough to mean an indefinite suspension of the act whose free performance depended on there being no needle. Taken literally, the presumption that every act may be harmful and hurt some interest would freeze everything into total immobility; this could only be attenuated by society granting advance clearance to a specific list of demonstrably innocuous acts, like visiting one's ailing aunt, whose safety and lack of threat to any conceivable aspiration, wish, interest, or value would not have to be established before they could be undertaken. However, opting for the presumption of liberty is hardly a matter of ethics, of a liberal temperament, or even of efficient social and economic organization. It is a matter of epistemology, of how knowledge works and how verification differs from falsification.

The way knowledge works directs, perhaps imperatively so, the burden of proof to be placed on interdictions, on the assumption of guilt, on the supposition that possession is illicit or title has some vice, and on the claim that some case is relevantly different from some precedent, some other case. The presumptions of liberty, of innocence, of title to possession, and of like treatment of like cases, do not stand on their particular merits, genuine as those may be, but are the automatic consequences of where the burden of proof falls—a matter about which sensible thought leaves little choice.

Equal treatment, with the burden of proving that two cases are relevantly unlike, has a pivotal place among the presumptions that enter into the concept of justice. If equal treatment is to be presumed, and if one person benefits from the presumption of liberty, of innocence, of good title or other favorable presumptions if there are any, then all other persons must also benefit from the same presumptions unless it can be shown that their case differs in a relevant respect from that of the first person. It is intuitively appealing that the principle of presumption is general because it is just that it should be so. However, as was argued above, its generality has an independent source in knowledge that can be recognized before any knowledge of justice. Circularity is avoided; we have a constituent principle of justice, rather than one that is derived from the requirements of a justice that already exists in our intuitive understanding.

CONVENTION

If there existed a truly pre-social state of affairs, or one where everyone was suddenly struck by amnesia, there would be no precedents to follow and no patterns of behavior to fall in with. Could questions of justice be resolved with any degree of predictability, or for that matter at all? Take two cases. In the first, two persons board a (pre-social) bus with only one empty seat. Which of them should sit and which stand? In the second, a man's honor is mortally offended. May he kill the offender, perhaps by giving him a chance in a duel? "Before justice," there is no predictable answer to either question; letting only their moral intuition speak, some people will give one answer, others another. Yet in a firm concept of justice, there must be guidelines that will narrow down the just resolution of such cases to a fairly predictable range. Once we all know what is just, the guidelines will be laid down in just laws. But if a concept of justice must precede just law, what will precede justice itself?

It is such considerations that suggest that there is a place for at least one more principle, in addition to the principles of responsibility and presumption, to enable the concept to be constituted from elements not dependent on prior ideas of justice. This principle is simply that where social conventions guide behavior, questions of justice should be resolved according to such guidance.

Conventions are most intriguing phenomena both as regards their origin and their enforcement. Lack of space forces us to take their emergence, their functionality, and their limited but nonetheless real self-enforcing features for granted here. For our purpose, they fall into two classes: conventions that foster civility, and those that discourage torts.

With two passengers aspiring to one vacant seat, they are both worst off when they fight each other over it. The next-worse solution is that they both remain standing, each fearing to look boorish if he sat down. If one sits and the other stands, at least one of them is better off and the other is no worse off. This is the Nash equilibrium solution, where neither can improve his own situation without the other accepting to worsen his. However, there are two equilibria, depending on who sits and who agrees to stand. This inequality of outcome is a source of conflict. Consequently, it is not self-evident that one or the other of the two equilibria will in fact be reached. Many if not most conventions of civility guide the parties in such conflicts round the issue and achieve an equilibrium. With the convention of first come, first served, both passengers know that he who boarded first is supposed to get the seat. We incorporate this into justice and have little hesitation saying that it is just that the first-comer should have first pick. For certain contingencies, a different and stronger convention may supersede the basic standard: for example, the aged and the infirm may get priority over the first-comer. Lest this story should give too Panglossian a view of social coexistence, it should be noted that conventions of civility tend to have a rather weak self-enforcing capability. The brutish driver, the lout spoiling the party, the queue-jumper face only mild sanctions, perhaps nothing more severe than contemptuous looks. It is also relevant to note that breaches of those conventions that are weakly sanctioned tend not to be called unjust acts in ordinary speech, and vice versa. Which way the causation runs should provide food for deep and probably fruitless thought.

Conventions against torts discourage serious harms to person and property and, more generally, non-trivial violations of the liberties of others except where this is done as a sanction employed to enforce the convention itself.

These conventions are largely self-explanatory. They are ancient, as old as society itself in the truistic sense that a society is formed by its members starting to adhere to such conventions in favor of each other. They are also cross-culturally stable, most societies treating much the same acts as torts. Doing one's bit to enforce the conventions, outlawing murderers, helping to catch the fugitive thief, watching the neighbors' property, putting peer pressure on defaulters, and lending a hand in getting contracts duly executed, used to be norms of behavior in conformity, as it were, to a convention to enforce the conventions. Though the enforcing function has to a great extent been taken over by state authorities, vestigial traces of it still subsist in many social groups.

The substance of the conventions against torts, including the mandatory character of the enforcement usually combining restitution and retribution, forms a stable and readily grasped part of the concept of justice.

III. The Two Realms of Justice

Standard usage talks of two kinds of justice, commutative and distributive. The first sees to the full commutation of deserts into rewards and punishments. The second ensures that rewards and punishments are distributed as they ought to be. Assuming that "deserts" means, broadly, all good grounds for rewarding and punishing, so that people in a just state of affairs get *all* they deserve, *and* deserve all they get, the supposed duality of justice is baffling. If commutative justice has been satisfied, it must have duly discharged the distributive function by the just allocation of rewards and punishments, benefits and burdens. Likewise, it is hard to see how distributive justice can be satisfied if it is not by the execution of commutative justice. The confusion has irked many logical minds, provoking them to deny that there could be any such thing as distributive justice. While this seems to be a mistaken view for reasons to be put forward in Section V, the commutative-distributive distinction is not very helpful, and obscures another kind of duality in the concept of justice. This concerns the two types of situation in which justice is a pertinent consideration.

The two kinds of situations are regulated by two complementary maxims. First enunciated by Cicero, the maxim "*suum cuique*" ("Render unto each his own") has survived as the common nucleus of two golden rules put forward by the third-century Imperial Roman legal thinker Ulpian in his *Digesta*.

The other maxim of "to each, according to" is the generalized schema of "to each, according to his needs, from each, according to his abilities," proposed by the revolutionary writer Louis Blanc in 1839 and made famous by Marx in the *Critique of the Gotha Programme*. Despite appearances, the two maxims are not rivals. They regulate two separate realms, and where one applies, the other does not.

Under "*suum cuique*," justice operates with an initial datum telling it what is a person's own. It is an ascertainable fact, or failing that, a presumption, that he has certain liberties, good title to his possessions and valid claims to what is owing to him under outstanding contracts. He has his own, and gets his own, as long as he and others do no more than exercise their liberties and fulfil their obligations, with their interactions being confined to voluntary exchanges and the rendering of unilateral benefits. "*Suum cuique*" is breached when a person's liberties are violated, his possessions are taken from him or trespassed upon, when his obligor defaults, or when he is forced to render involuntary benefits to others. Under "*to each, according to*" each person in some defined class must get some benefit, or carry some burden, according to some defined criterion. For Marx, the criterion for benefits was need, and for burdens ability, while he left open and undefined the class of persons who shall benefit or carry burdens. But the maxim in its general form leaves undefined both the class of persons and the reference criterion, to be decided on the merits of the case. All it lays down unambiguously is that all who benefit should do so according to the same reference criterion, as should all who are made to suffer or carry burdens. In "let all guilty persons be punished according to their crime," both the class of persons and the criterion according to which a punishment is to be meted out to them suggest themselves and appear to make the choice obvious enough. Yet even in this case, the choice remains a judgmental one, while in many other cases it is much less obvious and leaves great latitude to judgment.

Manifestly, both "*suum cuique*" and "to each, according to" cut right across the somewhat questionable distinction between commutative and distributive justice. Each has to do with just distributions and the rectification of unjust ones, where "distribution" must of course be understood in a general, all-inclusive sense.

The distinction between the two realms of justice ruled by the two maxims is a different, and very much sharper, one. Under "*suum cuique*," the exercise by everyone of their liberties and the fulfilment of their obligations distributes benefits and burdens. A just state of affairs prevails *unless* an unjust act violates it.

Under "to each, according to," certain benefits or burdens must be distributed to chosen persons according to a common criterion. The class of persons and the distributive criterion must be chosen justly. Unlike in the realm of "*suum cuique*," the distribution here is the product of a deliberate act. Failing that act, there is no distribution; failing it being just, the distribution cannot be just. An unjust state of affairs ensues *unless* a certain just act is performed.

IV. "Suum Cuique"

What is a person's own is fundamentally a question of what, within his set of feasible acts, he is at liberty to perform. By the same token, knowledge of what "*suum cuique*" implies can be reached by knowing what particular persons' liberties are. Most, if not all, of this knowledge derives from the foundations and constituting principles of justice which dictate the division of any feasible set into admissible and inadmissible acts.

ADMISSIBLE ACTS

Before Friday arrived, any act Robinson Crusoe was capable of performing he was at liberty to perform. There was no potential objector, raising questions of freedom, no one to tell him what to do, raising questions of obligation and duty, and no one his acts would inconvenience or harm, raising questions of civility, nuisance, and tort. Feasibility and admissibility coincide for the solitary person. This need not mean that all his feasible acts are morally irreproachable, that he cannot do any wrong that is not wrong on consequentialist grounds. What it does mean is that the solitary person may be restrained by ethics but need not restrain himself on grounds of justice; he cannot be unjust without being unjust to others. Nothing in the concept of justice suggests that doing oneself an injustice is anything but a figure of speech.

Admissible acts are either *liberties* we are free to perform unless sufficient cause is shown why we should not, or *obligations* we are not free not to perform if called upon to do so by the holder of the right that was created when the obligation was assumed, or *duties* that we have moral reasons to perform but are not obliged, and normally cannot be forced by others, to perform.

The simplest liberties are acts that are matters of indifference to others and create no externalities. My reading in my study is undoubtedly indifferent to everyone else. My walking in the wood could be a negative externality to some people who like to take solitary walks. My driving to work is almost certainly a negative externality to other road-users, as is their driving to me. However, society in its wisdom has not evolved conventions about not entering the wood when someone has gone for a walk there, nor about desisting from driving into dense traffic. In the absence of a broadly recognized convention, such acts, for all the negative externalities they generate, remain liberties. Smoking in public is an interesting borderline case; in some societies, a convention seems to be evolving against it, though the spontaneity of its emergence is questionable in view of the influence exerted by the public health authorities and by tort litigation. "Imposing a convention," an oxymoronic idea on a par with inventing a tradition or decreeing a custom, apart from other and probably more fatal flaws, confuses the issue of how we know what is just. For an "imposed convention," unlike ones that emerge unaided by what Edmund Burke called "artificial government," presupposes a concept of justice and is not an independent source of knowledge contributing to it.

A different and more serious problem is posed by imposed obligations. Making a promise or entering into a contract is to assume an obligation and to solicit the trust of the promisee that his right to the performance thus promised will in fact be honored. Not to fulfil the obligation is therefore *prima facie* unjust. However, certain schools of thought assert that rights can arise not only by promise or contract, but by the recognition that the right in question would serve a very important interest. Along these lines, a right to the satisfaction of basic needs, a right to work, a right to education are said to exist and may be decreed by government. For the rights to be exercised, others must be placed under the obligation to provide the wherewithal. Unless it can be successfully argued that the involuntary, coerced obligors are in fact responsible for the basic needs of others being unmet, employment opportunities or educational facilities lacking, it is an injustice to coerce them to provide redress and serve these putative rights, however important they are. If the coercion in question is to be justified, it must be on grounds other than justice, and more powerful than justice.

In addition to exercising one's liberties and fulfilling one's obligations, doing one's duty completes the typology of admissible acts. It suits the structure of our argument to treat it presently in its negative form, i.e., as the breach of one's duty.

INADMISSIBLE ACTS

Acts are inadmissible on general and on specific grounds. The general ground for inadmissibility is the prevention, frustration, or obstruction (without sufficient reason) of another's admissible act—what is sometimes called interference with his liberty. Questions of deliberate intent, negligence, or strict liability may enter here, affecting in particular the problem of redress and sanction. They cannot adequately be treated here. Deliberately raising the opportunity cost of an admissible act may or may not be inadmissible; this is part of the problem of coercion, and will be treated in that context. It is clear on the whole that to the extent that the reasons that make admissible acts admissible come to be integrated into the concept of justice, inadmissible acts that override these reasons are unjust.

The general ground for inadmissibility is that the act in question interferes with a liberty without sufficient reason. This means that, at least if sufficiency is so defined as to be empirically meaningful and verifiable, a reason may be furnished and may on occasion be found sufficient. Although the presumption of liberty prevails and therefore acts interfering with liberties are presumed to be inadmissible on general grounds, some such acts may nevertheless come to be admitted on examination of their merits. Inadmissibility on specific grounds forms part of the general case with, however, a particular reinforcing feature: the act in question is inadmissible *both* because it interferes with a liberty, *and* because it is in breach of a recognized rule, namely the social convention whose function is to protect that and other liberties. Thus, my stealing your money is inadmissible both because it deprives you of the chance to do certain things you would have otherwise been at liberty to do, and because it breaks the convention that forbids stealing. Roughly speaking, the first ground is consequential, the second deontological. Specific grounds for inadmissibility are, as it were, fully catalogued in the set of conventions in defence of civility and against torts. Anyone living in the society in question has ready access to the catalogue. If there can be sufficient reasons for interfering with a liberty, it seems immaterial whether they rest on general or on specific grounds. All one can say to reaffirm the difference between them, then, is that specific norms of conduct including specific interdictions, are not meant to be examined case by case on their merits.

Coercion calls for particular attention among inadmissible acts. Suppose racketeers offer protection against burglary to all shops in a street. Some agree to pay protection money. Those who do not become more attractive targets for the freelance burglars, and suffer increased losses. This raises for them the opportunity cost of not paying protection money, but contrary to how this predicament will be loosely described, does not "force" or "coerce" them to pay it. Coercion begins when the racketeers threaten the recalcitrant shopkeepers with burglary or worse unless they start paying. Short of threatening to commit a tort, the racketeers have not exercised coercion.

PROPERTY AS A LIBERTY

It seems self-evident enough that an act a person can perform and which is not inadmissible is one of "his" liberties. "*Suum cuique*" applies unambiguously. It is equally easy to grasp how and why a person's life and limbs, his good name, his personal belongings are "his" and what justice requires with respect to them. "Property" in a wider sense, going beyond personal chattels, and including the freedom of disposition over valuable assets, the freedom to exclude all others from access to them and to the income they produce, while perhaps no harder to grasp, is notoriously controversial, if only because many people feel less compunction about coveting, and wanting to redistribute to themselves or to others, the "impersonal" assets of some owner than about taking his personal belongings or the money in his wallet. What "to each, his own" dictates becomes apparently less obvious and unequivocal as the property becomes larger, more abstract, and more distant from the putative owner's daily life. Yet there is nothing intrinsic in property that would make it more or less legitimate according to its kind or size. The concept of justice speaks with equal clarity to its various manifestations, private or public, large or small, tangible or intangible, earned or inherited.

Owners acquire title to assets by two main means. One is by not consuming current income—what an earlier generation of economists approvingly called "abstinence"—the other by voluntary exchange or the acceptance of bequests and gifts. We must leave the third means, the finding of unowned resources, discoveries, inventions on one side for a moment.

Not consuming current income is *prima facie* not unjust, but is it perhaps unjust to have the income in the first place? Many would say that it is unjust if large enough to permit so much saving. However, since current income is the produce of voluntary exchanges including the exchange of one's personal exertions, and of income-producing assets, if these can be justified, then income need not separately be justified. Assets acquired from a previous owner in voluntary exchange, giving value for value received, is an exercise of their liberties by both and as such fully respect the command of "*suum cuique.*" What, however, of the previous owner? And what of the owner before him? There is an old and familiar argument that at the end of a long chain of voluntary exchanges, each of which is as legitimate and just as the one preceding it, we ultimately arrive, at the end of the chain, to an acquisition that was not an exchange with a previous owner. It is then argued, though this does not follow at all from the chain having an end, that unless the first acquisition at the far end of the chain was justified, the whole chain unravels and property loses its justification. It will be borne in mind through what follows that this reasoning rests on the presumption that possession, far from permitting suppositions about title, places the burden of proof of title on the possessor. In the chain argument, title is presumed to have a vice until the contrary is proven. This remains a requirement through the length of the chain.

Along these lines the Western, and especially the Anglo-American, doctrine of property is wedded to the Lockean tradition, in which first acquisition is by taking first possession of a resource, say land, and where this is justified only on condition that the well-known Lockean proviso, namely that "enough and as good" is left to others, is satisfied. Locke himself had no doubt that his proviso would in fact always be satisfied, both by virtue of the open frontier whose closing he did not foresee, and by virtue of enclosed land, as he put it, producing ten times or more of the produce of common waste. Perhaps comforted by his belief that what is valuable is not necessarily scarce, he did not seem to appreciate the logical quandaries his proviso creates.

In the first place, if resources are finite, any discovery, any finding and appropriation of a resource by the first individual reduces the probability of an equally valuable finding by each subsequent seeker. This can be seen either in terms of a declining marginal value of finds, or an increasing marginal finding cost of finds of equal value. With finite resources, the Lockean proviso cannot possibly be satisfied. The plain man, who finds that there is not "enough and as good left" for him as some others possess, need not be able to appreciate the fine logical point to be convinced.

In the second place, however, one must ask the more fundamental question: why ever should one accept the Lockean proviso as a condition of the justice of property? Speaking in terms of land, if an individual must safeguard the interests of others before taking first possession of a tract of land, this *means* that the others had some interest in that tract, i.e., that is was not unowned, but had already been appropriated by them in some way. In equity, he must compensate the others; yet the others cannot object to his appropriating the tract if, in equity, they are compensated. The situation is manifestly one of a joint tenancy. The first individual is one of the joint tenants, and the tract he takes out of the joint tenancy must be small enough to leave the remaining joint tenants as well off on their remaining land as they were before. It is only this situation that makes the Lockean proviso just.

However, imputing some kind of prior ownership to a joint tenancy just shunts the conundrum a little way off, to be faced again. For how does the joint tenancy justify *its* appropriation of the land? Only two ways can be tried. One is by showing that it has satisfied the Lockean proviso and taken the land out of an antecedent, and more encompassing, joint tenancy by leaving to the latter "enough and as good" as it took. This, in turn, begs the question of how that more encompassing joint tenancy came to own the land, and leaves the Lockean proviso dangling from the end of an infinite regress. The other way to try is to assert that while the individual, taking first possession, owes a liability to a joint tenancy, the joint tenancy owes no liability to anyone because the land it had taken possession of was unowned, unclaimed, unencumbered by anybody's prior interest. Accepting this purely hypothetical assertion is to give the benefit of presumption of title to the joint tenancy while refusing it to the individual who had taken first possession. The joint tenancy is *presumed* to have good title, while the individual is expected to *prove* his good title by showing that he has satisfied the Lockean proviso. If this is its last line of defence, the doctrine of property had better not be based on the Lockean proviso.

Intellectual property merits a minor digression at this juncture. If one creative act, e.g., an invention, does not reduce the probability of an equally valuable one by someone else in the future, the Lockean proviso with respect to intellectual property is meaningless, for how can you fail to leave "enough and as good" of infinity?

For property of all kinds to find its place in the scheme of justice, it needs a doctrine that is neither impossible to observe when resources are finite, nor nonsensical when they are infinite, nor unjust in distributing the burden of proof.

"Finders, keepers" is a starting point that, perhaps alone among starting points, is a question of ascertainable facts and does not beg questions of justice in order to draw conclusions about justice. To find something valuable is an admissible act as long as no one can show a valid prior claim to the find; it benefits from the presumption of liberty. It also benefits from chance, over which justice neither can nor must pretend to rule, and it is protected against arbitrary challenges by the convention of "first come, first served." Where valid prior claims exist, acquisition is justified by the voluntariness of exchange. Incremental acquisition of property *means* saving from income and is justified as an admissible act, a liberty, if the income itself is justified and if income is understood at large, to include windfalls. Bequests raise problems when they are mandatory, but if both the leaving and the accepting of them are free, they can be assimilated to voluntary exchanges, as can gifts for the same reason. If finding and appropriating what is unowned is a liberty, abstaining from consumption is a liberty, and voluntary exchange is a liberty, then property is a liberty. Under "*suum cuique*" a person's property is *his* if and because the acts that led to his possessing it were *his* liberties.

If this is established, the problem of property without possession is easy to fit into the concept of justice. Property is a liberty, or more precisely a set of liberties that the owner can choose to exercise. He is also at liberty to surrender such liberties, by voluntarily exchanging them for value received. He may, for example, let the use of his house to another in exchange for rent. By entering into such contracts, others acquire certain property rights and assume certain obligations, and so does he. His former liberties become pairs of obligations-and-rights, which are the reciprocals of the rights-and-obligations of his contract parties. Speaking of "property rights," instead of simply of property, draws attention to the presence of as yet unexecuted or partly executory contracts of this kind, signifying undischarged obligations.

DUTY AND ITS BREACH

An obligation is a relation between two persons, the obligor and the obligee or right-holder, on the one hand, and an (onerous) act on the other that the obligor must perform at the right-holder's option. The relation is a consequence of a special kind of reciprocal promise, the contract whose existence and terms are normally verifiable. Breach of contract is inadmissible and an injustice. The conventions against torts provide for remedies against breaches of contract at least within the bounds of unconscionability. What, however, is a duty and how does it arise? One of our less errant and more uniform moral intuitions leads us to say that parents owe certain duties to their dependent children, employers to their employees, officers to their men, judges to the accused, kings to their subjects, and that these duties are matters of justice in a different way from obligations. Duty appears to be a complex consequence of a relation between a person in authority and others depending from it, with the authority exercised in the distribution of certain benefits or burdens, rewards or punishments among the dependents in a just manner. What inserts duties into the concept of justice is that only some distributions pass for just.

There is good reason, in the presumption of like cases requiring like treatment, why we hold that it is unjust for a parent to overfeed one child, and starve another, for the teacher to give teacher's pet better marks than his course work deserves, or for the officer to assign the dangerous or unpleasant mission always to the same men. The parent, the teacher, the officer are in breach of their duty, yet the victims of the unjust use of their authority, unlike parties to a contract who have, so to speak, bought rights to the performance of certain obligations, have little recourse beyond grumbling, sullen resistance, and the hope of one day getting their own back.

At best, the dependent recipients of a distribution by authority have a legitimate expectation that the authority will be exercised in a just manner. But if it is not, since they are not being deprived of anything that was theirs to begin with, "*suum cuique*" does not take care of their case.

In an attempt to repair this gap, it is sometimes said that relations of authority and dependence, command and obedience must really be understood as tacit contracts between the parties concerned, one agreeing to respect authority in exchange for the other exercising it in a non-arbitrary manner, though what the latter condition is meant to entail may call for further definition. A classic version of this attractive metaphor is the social contract between ruler and ruled. Evidently, if such relations were as good as explicit contracts, the requirements of justice could be derived from them; all distribution would fall into the realm of "*suum cuique*" and ensuring its justice would be reduced to contract-enforcement. With voluntary cooperation and command-obedience brought under the same rule, the concept of justice would be a simpler one than it proves to be when it is stripped of such pleasing fictions.

Where "*suum cuique*" stops, ceasing to offer reliable or indeed any guidance, "to each, according to" takes over to fill the void, though its manner of doing so is neither above *bona fide* contestation nor always predictable.

V. "To Each, According To . . ."

When the parent has pocket money to give his children, the teacher papers to mark, the officer duties to assign, and the judge sentences to hand down and the government taxes to levy, the salient common feature is that without certain persons in authority performing certain acts within their competence, the children would get no pocket money, the papers would not get marked, the fatherland would not be defended, criminals would not be sentenced, and the tax burden would not be allocated. Under the rule of "*suum cuique*," at the end of a day of liberties exercised and obligations discharged, everybody has got his own and nothing is left to distribute. Under "to each, according to" things fail to get distributed unless someone sees to their distribution. He can see to this in infinitely many different ways, for the rule he must follow, namely "to each member of some class of persons, distribute the benefit or the burden according to something they have in common," is so general as to be virtually useless as a constraint. Can one be any more definite about which distributions will be more just than others?

IS THERE A PRESUMPTION OF EQUALITY?

The same questions of justice must have the same answers; it is self-evident that like cases must be treated alike. However, every case is like every other case (for otherwise they would not all be *cases*), yet every case is also unlike every other (for otherwise they would not be *other* cases but one and the same case). Likeness in some respect is coupled with unlikeness in some other respect. Which respect is relevant?

The general proposition that the case of one person differs from the case of another in some respect that is relevant to what share each should get in some distribution is a needle-in-the-haystack hypothesis, unfalsifiable if the number of respects that could be relevant in a distribution is undenumerable. Therefore the burden of proof cannot be borne by the negation and must be placed on the assertion of a relevant difference between cases. This appears to establish the presumption of equality, interpreted to mean that until some difference between the cases of two persons is proved relevant, they should get the same share. Such a presumption, in turn, may partly explain why the idea of equality carries a connotation of justice, albeit in a somewhat vague and diffuse way.

However, there is some misfit between this presumption and justice. "To each (child), the same (pocket money)," "to each (student), the same (marks)," "to each (athlete), the same (laurels)," "to each (criminal), the same (sentence)," "to each (patient), the same (medical attention)," "to each (poor family), the same (allowance)," "from each (taxpayer), the same (tax)" makes for an implausible and incongruous series of recommendations that radical egalitarians might be the first to protest against.

EQUIPROPORTIONALITY

Clearly, if the presumption of equality means "to each, the same," its general application would yield bizarre results. We would all want athletes to get laurels according to their prowess, and at least some of us would want good students to get better marks than bad ones. We would usually think it just that sentences should be the heavier the graver the crime, and wish that serious illness should get more medical attention than a head cold. What appears to have gone wrong with "to each, the same" is that it is a special case of "to each, according to" where the relevant reference criterion, that triggers off the distribution of a reward or a penalty, is not a quality, condition, or circumstance of each person's case, but the person himself. It is the athlete and not his prowess, it is the patient and not his illness, the family and not its need, the criminal and not his crime. In this special case, the chosen reference criterion is the person, and since the reference criterion is a constant as between the cases to be treated, the result is also a constant: "to each, the same."

Were the reference criterion a variable, such as prowess, scholastic achievement, illness, need, crime, exertion at work, capacity to pay taxes, or any other among the variety that may be thought suitable as the "according to" of a distribution rule, the result would of course also be a variable. For the general form of the rule, to which the presumption of equality guides us, is that in each distribution there shall be an equal proportion between the reference variable and the distributive share it triggers off. The generalized form of the rule produces equiproportionality ("Aristotlean equality"), of which absolute equality is a special case that will obtain when the reference variable is held invariant between persons.

Nothing in "to each according to" determines how the blanks shall be filled, who shall be included in the distribution, and what reference variable shall be taken as relevant. The rule leaves the filling of the blanks ultimately to moral intuition.

To find that intuition enters dominantly into deciding what is just, is to see the flashing of warning lights. Self-evident propositions, findings of ascertainable facts, the logic of the burden of proof, agreements, and conventions go to shape a concept of justice that is largely unequivocal in resolving questions arising from "*suum cuique.*" Given the facts of the case, there is a vast area of determinacy about who owns what and what others owe to him. Just acts lead to just states of affairs without seeking to do so. Manifestly, however, this ceases to be true when distributions, instead of emerging as the by-products of the sum of just acts serving other purposes, must be consciously chosen by a distributor. The choice is left indeterminate in two of its variables, leaving it to moral intuitions, value judgments, and perhaps also to partisanship, ideological fashion, or sheer opportunism to decide what shall be deemed the just distribution.

When a distributor distributes something, all the concept of justice tells him is that he must treat like cases alike, different cases differently, i.e., follow the presumption of equality. However, for each set of possible recipients of a distribution of a benefit, positive or negative, there are indefinitely many ways of following the presumption of equality. Should everybody do military service, or only the young, or only able-bodied young males? Should family allowances be means-tested? Should all students get scholarships, and should they all get the same?—and if not, should grants vary according to parental income, some measure of honest plodding, or innate ability and the prospect of glory to the school? Formally, equality is satisfied by each and every one of these alternatives, and by none more than any other. And how else can one satisfy equality, if following the rule satisfies it only formally and doing it formally fails to warm the heart?

The latitude left to decisions about who shall share in a distribution, and according to what his share should be fixed, leads to a predictable consequence. The value judgments, and related uses of moral and emotional discretion that enter into the rival answers different people finally give to these questions, are mistaken for parts of the concept of justice itself.

ALL IS THERE TO BE DISTRIBUTED

The vast bulk of the world's goods, tangible and intangible, is produced and distributed as a matter of course as and when liberties are exercised and mutually agreed obligations are discharged. In this, the realm of "*suum cuique,*" no distributive decisions as such need, or indeed can, be taken. The question of the justice of distributive acts can properly speaking only arise in the realm of "to each, according to," where judgment and discretion are dominant and where theories of justice may play a role in educating, and perhaps explaining if that is indeed possible, our moral intuitions that inspire them.

Contemporary theories of justice, however, tend to maximize their scope by obliterating "*suum cuique.*" The space thus vacated becomes one where everything worth having or escaping, and that is transferable among persons, is necessarily the subject of a deliberate distributive decision that is either just or unjust. Where "*suum cuique*" is tacitly or overtly laid aside and distributions are not *prejudged* by it, they can and must be *judged*. All things function like cakes waiting to be sliced and shared out by respecting the presumption of equality. One theory may favor one reference variable as the basis of distribution, the other another, but all have in common the starting point of the cake that is just there. Nobody had to provide the wherewithal for it, nobody had to bake it, no prior claims attach to it, and its distribution would be unjust or fail to take place altogether unless it was effected according to a just act.

The move to take an unowned cake, baked without anybody having been responsible for baking it, as the natural starting point may be overt or veiled. An example of the overt move is to propose to deduce justice from the solution of the problem of an agreed sharing out of manna from heaven. Covert moves are less blunt. Perhaps the best-known one is to take it that fair-minded people will accept, as a matter of fairness, principles of justice they would agree on if they ignored all the advantages with which nature or luck had endowed them. Given such a veil of ignorance, it is not known who contributed how much to producing the cake, and it is equally unknown who must contribute how much to reproduce it once it is eaten. Finally, "*suum cuique*" was set aside by some theories by claiming that the past and present exercise of liberties and rights does not establish title to property. For one thing, it is contended that it is society, by a collective effort, that provides for individuals the legal framework they need for exercising liberties and rights. No one could own property if society did not protect it from predators, and no one could earn income if society did not enforce contracts. Any distribution is really willed by society, and it is incumbent upon society to bring about a just distribution by a just act. For another, *pace* the marginal productivity theory of income distribution and Euler's theorem, it is argued that what people get in current income is no indication of what they really contribute to the social product, nor is the pattern of wealth ownership evidence of past contributions to the stock of wealth. Everybody's share is owed to everybody else's contributions in effort, saving, invention, and the transmission of experience from Day One to the present. The stock of material and moral wealth is one vast positive externality, as is the current product. It is said to be meaningless to pretend that anybody has contributed any particular quantity of it and as a result owns any part of it: there is no "*suum cuique.*" Instead, there is a social obligation to distribute goods and bads according to proper criteria conforming to the presumption of equality what would otherwise be distributed randomly and unjustly.

It is in these various ways that all that is valuable and transferable is assimilated to the basic fiction of the cake that nobody baked and that needs cutting into just slices. "To each, according to" is extended over all aspects of life where justice can have any relevance. Being judgmental and indeterminate in specific content, it is invested with criteria that would indeed have plausibility in a fictitious situation, or to which fictitious persons might indeed agree in such situations. The interest and significance of the theories that set aside "*suum cuique*" and make "to each, according to" the universal rule is the greater, the less importance is attached to real facts and notably to real, as distinct from hypothetical, agreements. However, the importance we do attach to such things is not altogether a matter we decide at our pleasure. Its short anchors in logic and epistemology, conventions and agreements allow justice but little leeway.

11

On Treating Like Cases Alike

Idealism, intelligence, and importance are a rare combination. *Politics by Principle, Not Interest,* the book on "non-discriminatory democracy" by James Buchanan and Roger Congleton, achieves the feat of combining them, though the occasional strain shows that the three are not natural bedfellows. The book is enormously ambitious: it sets out to prove that by enshrining the principle of treating like cases alike ("the generality principle") in the constitution, the body politic could be purged of much sordidness and conflict. There would be no winning and losing coalitions, for coalitions could no longer take wealth from one another. Yet with "politics as taking" barred, the deadweight costs of redistribution and rent seeking would be saved, and all sides would be not only more fairly treated but also better off materially. Imposing the generality principle on politics would be a Pareto-improving move. *Politics by Principle* pleads for the move to be made.

The book is remarkable in at least two respects. The first is its courage in exposing the sacred cow of what it calls "majoritarian" democracy (is any "real-existing" democracy not majoritarian?) in all its immorality and inefficiency. Admirable, too, is the painstaking application of the analytical schema to such fields as externalities, public services, fiscal policy, interpersonal and intergenerational redistribution, and social insurance, implying that if the generality principle works, it

Reprinted with permission of the publisher from *The Independent Review: A Journal of Political Economy* 4, no. 1 (summer 1999): 107–18. © 1999 The Independent Institute.

does so right across all fields usually regarded as the proper domain of collective choices.

Three theses are put forward. The first, best called Contract, argues the possible legitimacy of coercion by collective choice and establishes a link to the contractarian tradition that now constitutes the mainstream of political thought. The second, Cycle, argues that because collective choices dealing with distributions of benefits and burdens are unstable and every distribution is dominated by another, winners cannot win permanently and would in fact be better off under a constitution that, by imposing generality, abolished the rotation in which winners become losers and vice versa. The third and main thesis is Generality, a formal rather than a substantive principle that, if applied, puts distributional conflict out of bounds by equal treatment, the treating alike of like cases.

Here is a massive job for the Devil's Advocate. The present essay traces the line of attack he could be expected to follow. The author of the essay wishes to add, for the record, that he would not be displeased if, on some judgment day, the plea of the Devil's Advocate were found to have failed and that of Buchanan and Congleton to have prevailed.

Contract

Pivotal to the argument is the lesson to be drawn from David Hume's parable about draining a swampy meadow by what is called "collective action" in modern jargon. In his *Treatise of Human Nature*, Hume tells us that some neighbors agree to dig a drainage ditch, to the benefit of their adjacent farms. "Agreement" here means more than the shared opinion that it would be nice to have a drainage ditch. It is a reciprocal promise by the neighbors to dig it. It is, in effect, a contract. Hume goes on to say that such promises are the means by which men achieve shared ends, from the digging of ditches and the building of bridges, harbors, ramparts, canals, and armies to the formation of governments. He is quite explicit in giving contract causal priority over the state, which most other theorists say is needed before a contract becomes a binding commitment. The contract here binds the parties because it is self-enforcing. In modern parlance, we would say that the parties see this interaction as a single link (a "node") in a chain of interactions stretching indefinitely into the future, with a probabilistic and ever-receding endpoint. The parties ("players") choose to perform according to their contract, as well as future ones to be entered into, because in comparing the relative merits ("payoffs") of performing as promised or defaulting, they consider the present value of two streams of expected payoffs along the whole chain. Performing prolongs the chain; defaulting (taking the "free rider" strategy) damages the chain or breaks it off altogether, so that the defaulter gets few or no chances to default again. Hume, in fact, implicitly employs the Folk Theorem of modern game theory, which shows the cooperative strategy in repeated prisoners' dilemmas under certain conditions to be a Nash equilibrium.

Buchanan and Congleton, taking the drainage ditch as an isolated collective enterprise, present the usual, and perfectly correct, solution that for each farmer, not digging is always a better strategy than digging, whatever the other farmers do; hence there will be no ditch, nor any other collective action. The farmers cannot credibly bind themselves by contract, and for their own good they need to be coerced by a contract enforcer, the state.

By this reasoning, contractarian philosophy explains the individual's willing subjection to a collective choice mechanism, backed by a monopolistic coercive agency, as a "social contract" that could be agreed to by all rational persons. The necessity for coercion breeds consent that, in turn, lends legitimacy to the state.

Buchanan and Congleton's restatement of the doctrine is more explicit and precise than most. It presents a clearer target for the Devil's Advocate than do more fudged and elusive versions. It has, or so he would argue, three easily identified chinks in its logical armor.

The first has long been recognized by critics of all forms of contractarianism, but to the best knowledge of the Devil's Advocate, no effective defense of it has ever been offered. If man can no more bind himself by contract than he can jump over his own shadow, how can he jump over his own shadow and bind himself in a social contract? He cannot be both incapable of collective action *and* capable of it when creating the coercive agency needed to enforce his commitment. One can, without resorting to a bootstrap theory, accept the idea of an exogenous coercive agent, a conqueror whose regime is better than anything the conquered people could organize for themselves. Consenting to such an accomplished fact, however, can hardly be represented as entering into a contract, complete with a contract's ethical implications of an act of free will.

Because prior to the construction of the collective choice mechanism the purported agreement must be unanimous (for, remember, there is as yet no rule for reaching non-unanimous decisions), no party to the social contract must be asked to accept a worse position, taking good periods with bad, than he would occupy without the contract. Here is the second chink in the doctrine's armor. Buchanan and Congleton stress that contractarianism "rules out payoffs that are sensed to be negative by any participant . . . over the whole set of anticipated political choices, the base point being defined by positions achieved when the majority rule, collective action game is not played at all" (p. 18). However, life without any collective action is difficult to imagine except on desert islands. If it is conceivable at all, it entails unmitigated misery. Because the authors believe categorically that collective action presupposes a coercive authority, and because almost anything is a better payoff than that available at the "base point," it follows that almost any terms, no matter how harsh or lopsided, must be accepted by the rational player. In terms of the economist's familiar device, the situation is like a very, very long Edgeworth box with a very, very long contract curve running inside it, with all points on it from one end to the other being bargaining solutions, better for both (or all) players than no contract. The actual solution may be outrageously good for one player and outrageously bad for the other; we do not know how the bargain will turn out, except of course that it will be Pareto optimal. But if the alternatives are rigged in such a way that the terms of mutually acceptable bargains can vary from one gross extreme to the other, from princely privilege to abject submission, the condition of universally positive payoffs and unanimity is trivial.

The third weak spot reveals itself in the attempt to remedy the second. Contractarianism uses a veil of some kind to obtain certain behavioral results. In the original Buchanan and Tullock version, the social contract was concluded behind a veil of uncertainty; the lack of visibility concerned the future. People did not seek social-contract terms favoring one situation over another, because finding themselves in one kind of situation seemed no more probable than finding themselves in another. John Rawls, of course, operated with a very different device, the veil of ignorance, behind which people were unaware of their personal endowments and indeed of any differences that distinguished them from one another. Behind the veil of ignorance, contracting parties became, in the strictest sense, each other's clones. Somewhat drastically, Buchanan and Congleton resort to a double veil they call "the veil of uncertainty and/or ignorance," presumably obliterating knowledge of the future, or one's self-knowledge, or both, to suit all occasions. They argue, plausibly enough, that the veil or veils will powerfully narrow the bargaining problem, because parties unaware of their own interests cannot have conflicts over terms and should find it easy to agree on what seems fair and impartial to both.

It is no doubt as easy to reach unanimous agreement on innocuous terms (and perhaps on any terms whatever) under these conditions as it is to agree with oneself. The result is still trivial, no less so than the one reached without the help of veils. But it is a little disappointing to find perhaps the foremost champion of methodological individualism of our time producing this result by resorting to a device that effectively obliterates individuals and opens the back door for some holistic entity to take the place they can no longer usefully occupy.

Cycle

Politics by Principle recalls the well-known, and somewhat overworked, proposition of formal social-choice theory that if "society's choice" is taken as the largest number of individual preferences attracted by one alternative state of affairs, certain preference configurations will produce an incoherent result under which, given pairwise choices by at least three persons (or groups) among at least three alternatives, any "socially chosen" alternative will be dominated by another. Consequently, the actual choice must go round and round the available alternatives in a cycle. It is widely accepted that such cyclicality, in which any distribution of income or wealth is overturned by another that is "socially preferred" to it, should obtain in a society where majority coalitions are freely formed and able to expropriate the minority. For Buchanan and Congleton, the rotating nature of distributions, with today's gainers becoming tomorrow's losers, is the saving grace of majoritarian democracy, ensuring that no group in society will be a permanent loser from redistribution.

The Devil's Advocate will contend that this conclusion would undergo radical revision if due distinction were drawn between a pure and a non-pure distribution "game" and also between distributional and electoral rotation. He will consider these distinctions in turn.

Consider a pure three-person Neumann and Morgenstern distribution game, where a coalition of two players can decide how a fixed stock of goods, say, one hundred golden eggs, shall be divided between them and a third player. With players A, B, and C entitled to form one two-person coalition and take one distributive decision per period, and with an exogenously given bargaining solution to tell us how the members of the coalition will share the golden eggs between them and how many they will leave for the third player, the following table shows how the solution will rotate over a full cycle of three periods. In each period, the payoffs in italics indicate which two players will form a coalition in the next period.

		Player		
		A	B	C
	1	50	*40*	*10*
Period	2	*10*	50	*40*
	3	*40*	*10*	50

Whatever the bargaining solution (provided it does not vary from period to period), over any full cycle the three players come out even, with an average share of thirty-three golden eggs. The present values of the three streams of payoffs differ a little because of the timing of high and low payoffs, but this difference is a minor matter if the discount rate is not exorbitant. Any coalition can lift its average payoff over the three periods by sticking together. For example, once A and B have secured their ninety golden eggs in the first period, if B sticks with A, both will keep having the permanently higher payoff of ninety between them, whereas C will be permanently exploited.

Myopia and bargaining difficulties may, for all we know, weaken the dominance of the stable over the cyclical solution. Consider, however, the incomparably stronger likelihood of the stable, noncyclical pattern of exploitation as we move from a pure to a non-pure three-person distribution game. There is now both production and consumption in each period. When, in period 1, player A has the most golden eggs, the redistributive payoff available to the coalition of B and C dominates that which any coalition that includes A can gain; hence the coalition BC will form to exploit A in period 2. B and C consume what they take from A. Player A, however, is a goose laying golden eggs. She produces, within the period, the same number of eggs that B and C take from her. Under this condition, at the end of period 2 the distribution is the same as at the end of period 1, and forming the coalition BC is still more profitable than forming any coalition that would include A—and this remains true at the end of every subsequent period. The "socially preferred" solution is perfectly stable.

Empirical evidence clearly demonstrates that in modern democracies redistribution is, broadly speaking, always from the richer half of the electorate toward the middle (which harbors within it the median voter) and the poorer half, with no rotation, which is what we should expect from looking at the distribution game with production and consumption, as well as on grounds of common sense. The richer half is not made poor and the poorer half is not made rich, by turns, as the Cycle thesis would predict.

However, Buchanan and Congleton invoke a different set of historical evidence to the effect that democracies tend to display an irregular but inevitable electoral rotation; sooner or later the team of political entrepreneurs in power is voted out and another team is voted in. Here, the authors seem to equate an electoral with a distributional outcome, instead of distinguishing between the two. One team of politicians will normally demarcate itself from the other by adopting different slogans, professing different values, and proposing different policies whose impact on the pattern of redistribution is small or opaque, hence difficult to perceive. It is, however, almost inconceivable that the first team should offer redistribution from rich to poor and the second team from poor to rich, which is what would be needed if electoral rotation were to amount to distributional cycling. The second team's offer would be strongly dominated by that of the first in terms of transfers and "targeted" public goods and services. We can assume that the larger sums in the first team's offer would swamp any effect that might be exerted by the intangible elements of the two teams' offers. To have a chance of winning the bid for the votes of one-half of the electorate *plus* a margin to make sure of the median voter, both teams have to formulate rich-to-poor redistributive offers. One would expect to capture the poorer half's allegiance, the other that of the richer half, with the latter voting for the lesser of two evils. Schematically, this is how democracies must function, and do in fact function.

However, although neither the rotating solution of pure distribution games nor electoral rotation is relevant to real-life redistribution under majoritarian democracy and there is no cycle, still it is always the same half of society that it is exploited by the other half. Stopping this exploitation by inserting an appropriate rule in the constitution would not simply put an end to futile and costly back-and-forth sloshing of wealth, as Buchanan and Congleton appear to believe. If generality were such a rule and had the effect in question, it would permanently hurt the exploiters and permanently help the exploited. It could hardly be Pareto-superior. If it were, we should have to wonder why society has never groped toward adopting it.

Generality

Politics by Principle proposes that constitutions should prohibit the makers of collective choices—whether democratic majorities, dictatorship, or anything in between—from resorting to other than general rules in determining distributions of benefits or burdens.

Such reform may or may not be feasible. Assuming for argument's sake that it is, principle would replace interest, and the reformed constitution would be going against the grain, forbidding the very things the decisive force—for example, the majority coalition—most wishes to do. What entitles us tacitly to suppose that such a constitution could be durably enforced? Following the public choice tradition of treating constitutional rules as being on a different plane and being determined by different interests from the "in period" choices such rules permit, Buchanan and Congleton do not treat this problem. Even if such difficulties were not prohibitive, but could be overcome by paying whatever enforcement costs were required, it is legitimate to ask whether such costs would not offset the savings that the greater political efficiency of general rules promises to bring.

However, this objection is but a quibble compared with the major and fundamental one that concerns the very concept of generality. Indeed, the Devil's Advocate submits that it is logically impossible to formulate constitutional clauses whose strict respect would constrain the lawmaker from passing any rule on the sole ground that the rule would violate the generality principle. Generality cannot be sufficiently defined to allow us to tell rules that are general from rules that are not.

Statute laws, judicial precedents, conventions, bylaws, customs, taboos, decrees, regulations, and administrative directives are all *rules* of varying degrees of stringency and precision. Every rule resembles every other in at least one respect: each rule is an invariant relation between a class of defined circumstances (here denominated "cases") and a set of consequences (sanctions for the breach of behavior norms; distributions of benefits and burdens) that must result if the rule in question is applied to the case within the class in question. The same cases must bring forth the same consequences if the rule is in fact applied.

Buchanan and Congleton plead, in the name of fairness and what they call "political efficiency," for rules in all domains, and notably in the political domain, to conform to the generality principle. If rules applied in politics were general, some of the worst features of majoritarian democracy would be purged or at least greatly mitigated. Distributions would be stabilized; they would become better in the normative sense of being less dependent on the will of the politically stronger battalions. The socially wasteful expenditure on promoting distributional interests would cease. The outcome would be Pareto superior; no coalition under majoritarian democracy could expect to do better, taking good years with bad.

What meaning is being imputed to such a promising principle?

When the authors speak of "treating like cases alike" or "equal treatment under the law," they seem to be saying, uncontroversially, that a rule must be applied to all the cases to which it is applicable, that there must be no positive or negative deviations in treatment between such cases according to arbitrary whim, fear, or favor unprovided for in the rule itself. In short, they state that a rule is a rule—an analytic statement that conveys no additional information about generality, for in this sense every rule is a perfectly general rule and conforms to the principle postulated.

More controversially, they use "generality" in a different sense when they say that general rules do not discriminate among persons. Two objections arise. One is a shade pedantic but not wholly superfluous, for it adds some clarity to what might easily degenerate into confused rhetoric about equal "rights"—though, to their great credit, Buchanan and Congleton never resort to such vocabulary. The objection is that rules do not directly target persons, much less discriminate among them, but are directed at cases in which persons may play various roles. Breaches of contract, for example, are cases in a class to which a rule applies and provides for certain consequences. In such cases, particular roles are played by plaintiffs and defendants. The rule discriminates between them. For example, it places the burden of proof on one party rather than on both of them. Likewise, a rule about lawmaking may attribute certain powers to representatives, others to senators. There is discrimination between them, but the rule about lawmaking is a general one for all that—if the term *generality* is indeed more than a tautology.

The more serious objection provoked by the authors' recurrent characterization of generality as non-discrimination is that this requirement contradicts the very logic of rules. Their function is to separate the cases that require a particular uniform treatment from the rest of the universe of cases that do not require the same treatment. Non-discrimination is inconsistent with treating like cases alike and different ones differently, except in the logical limit where from some infinitely distant celestial perspective, every case is like every other.

The more nearly we approach this logical limit, the more curious is the resulting "generality," understood as non-discrimination. Suppose a rule requires that the destitute be given food and shelter by some of those who have these things. Generality is doubly violated, both in the entitlement to alms and in the selective nature of the obligation to give. To satisfy generality, either nobody must give nor get or all must give and get. There are a few sound reasons for the first alternative, though most people would think the balance of arguments is tilted against it. But there are no good reasons speaking for the second version, whose very generality raises the suspicion that satisfying the generality principle, even if it is interpreted as more than a tautology, may not in itself make for better rules.

By way of demonstration, consider alternative rules for distributing punishments. One rule might lay down one punishment for all felons ("off with their heads") and another for minor offenders (a suspended jail sentence). This is obviously not a general rule, discriminating as it does between felonies and misdemeanors—though it is vastly more general than any real-life criminal code with its fine gradations of offenses and punishments. A large step toward greater generality would abolish the discrimination between types of crimes. It would require that all criminals have their heads chopped off or all get a light suspended sentence, but not that some should be beheaded and others not. Buchanan and Congleton, incidentally, make the case that general rules are politically efficient in that they reduce the cost of administering the system as well as the wasteful expense people incur to avoid the negative or to benefit from the positive discrimination available under non-general rules. This cost-reducing effect is clearly visible as we move, in the hypothesized case, from a more to a less discriminating rule of distributing punishments. In the true logical limit of the generality principle, however, where every case is like every other and is treated as such, it is the final discrimination, that between criminals and noncriminals, that falls to the ground; everybody's head is chopped off or everybody gets off scot-free.

Although the "treat like cases alike" meaning of generality is no more than a tautology for "apply the rule," the "non-discrimination" meaning clearly does not bear pushing anywhere near its logical limit —a telling sign that it has some defect that comes to light when the meaning comes to be stretched a little. In fact, Buchanan and Congleton are far too intelligent not to sense this problem. They are fairly diffident about providing a working definition that would tell us, in every case, what rule would pass for general.

In one basic case, though, they are perfectly confident about what rule would be the truly general one. This case is the two-person (or two-coalition), two-strategy game of benefit- or burden-sharing, as exemplified by Hume's farmers digging a drainage ditch. A two-by-two matrix describes four alternative allocations of the workload. Along what the authors call the diagonal, both farmers dig for two days or neither digs. Along the off-diagonal, either one digs for three days and the other for one, or the other way round. Which of the two off-diagonal, asymmetrical alternatives is the actual solution depends on which "farmer" is enabled by the political choice mechanism to coerce the other. A rule applied to this type of case is general if it outlaws the off-diagonal solution, so that only the symmetrical, equal-sharing solutions remain available. Both farmers work the same length of time. Obviously, the Pareto-optimal solution among all the symmetrical ones is that they should both work as long as it takes to complete the ditch; but this is not the point. The point is that generality has been found to reside in symmetry.

From here, a promising avenue seems to lead toward a more developed form of generality. The simple version of the rule would say that the farmers, when placed in the circumstances described, should dig the same number of days, preserving one kind of equality, albeit a rather rudimentary one.

However, there is no compelling reason why equality of days worked should be regarded as the best, let alone the sole valid criterion of symmetry. If one farmer is frail, old, or arthritic, or if one has a higher opportunity cost because when he digs he cannot attend to the calving or lambing, or if his end of the ditch has a nasty, sticky, clayey patch, then a rule laying down equality of labor time might well be held to produce asymmetrical shares of pain or cost. Likewise, it might also be argued that symmetry calls for labor time to vary inversely with productivity or directly with the benefit each farmer will derive from the drained meadow. Symmetry in the relevant variable must prevail, but why is labor time the relevant variable rather than pain, productivity, opportunity cost, benefit, or something else?

The "equal treatment" schema of a distributive rule is "to/from each, according to. . . ." The blank space is filled in by some function $f(x)$, where x is the reference variable common to a class of cases, deemed relevant for holding that those cases ought to be treated alike, and differently from other cases. The treatment is coded in $f(x)$. If x is a constant, the rule becomes "to/from each that is x, the same" (that is, absolute rather than proportionate equality).

What this formula fails to decide is whether the relevant variable is x, y, w, z, or none of them. Which, if any, meets the generality principle? Don't they all do so despite being mutually inconsistent?

One of the most famous dialogues in *Through the Looking-Glass* could well have been written about symmetry, non-discrimination, and the generality principle: "When *I* use a word," Humpty Dumpty said in rather a scornful tone, "it means just what I choose it to mean—neither more nor less." Alice is doubtful about this declaration: "The question is," said Alice, "whether you *can* make words mean different things." But because it is a matter of opinions, feelings, and "values," not of "facts," which variable is the relevant one that makes one case like another and unlike a third one, and because different people may legitimately hold different views, generality can mean neither more nor less than what each chooses it to mean. Alice is wrong, and Humpty is right.

Before like cases can be treated alike, it must be decided which case is like which other case. Any one case is described by an indefinitely large number of variables, many of which would be dismissed as unimportant by most reasonable people, leaving a number that are important for at least some people. Every case is like every other, because all are "cases." A rule incorporating a reference variable is applicable to all cases that are relevantly described by that variable. These are, then, the "like cases" that the rule treats alike. Many things can be said about the chosen variable: that it is not as relevant as some other, that it is insufficiently inclusive (hence discriminating) or too inclusive (hence indiscriminate, perhaps absurdly so). Ultimately, however, all such observations are intrinsically subjective and can be reduced to my say-so against your say-so. My general rule is your special one; my non-discriminating rule is your indiscriminate one. How does a constitutional court tell my generality from yours?

The inconclusive search for generality is inseparable from arbitrariness and discretion. Between the two extremes "every case is like every other" and "no case is like any other," certain cases are like certain others if one variable is chosen as relevant for rule-making, and other cases are like yet others if relevance is judged differently. The champions of each rule will claim that theirs is the truly general one, but such claims are irrefutable and function as value judgments.

What would be the general rules of public finance? Buchanan and Congleton consider that to ensure generality, the relevant variable for the rule governing transfers of all kinds should in fact be a constant, namely, "human being"; whether pauper or millionaire, each should get the same poll grant. However, to ensure generality on the revenue side, the relevant variable should be "income," and the rule should be that all incomes are taxed at the same flat rate (making some people pay more tax than others). Rival "political entrepreneurs" might well appeal to some constitutional court against this rule, arguing that a rule that does not discriminate between incomes but taxes them all at the same rate does manifestly discriminate among income recipients, by treating bachelors and the rich more favorably than heads of large families and the poor, or by failing to compensate for positive and negative externalities associated with the earning and spending of certain incomes, and so forth. Who can decide whether generality requires, permits, or excludes taking account of such matters? And if on the expenditure side a poll grant satisfies generality, why does an income tax (whether flat or progressive) and not a poll tax satisfy it on the revenue side?

The answer seems to be that Buchanan and Congleton seek rules that combine a measure of simplicity and inclusiveness with a curb on redistributive infighting without being hopelessly impractical (as combining the poll tax with the poll grant would be). Once they have selected rules likely to fill this bill, they call them "general," or more general than alternative ones. But this approach involves arguing from desirable effects to generality, rather than from generality to its desirable effects. Their rules are good rules, perhaps the best one can think of if one shares their political predilections. The Devil's Advocate does. Yet he would not be doing his job if he did not insist that although the tautological sense of generality ("a rule is a rule") is unhelpful, no meaningful sense of generality is as yet in sight, to be proposed as a formal constitutional constraint on admissible rules. Disappointingly, legislating for generality seems to be about as effective, and as constraining, as legislating for the common good.

Suppose, however, that the defense of generality were to admit that ultimately it is a value judgment to say that one rule applicable to one class of cases is general, another applicable to another is not, or is less so; but then to point out that everybody's value judgment rejects as a basis for classifying the cases certain notorious "reference variables," such as the race, sex, color, or religion of the persons playing certain roles in a class of cases. Would this approach not serve to ward off the charge of subjectivity and special pleading, and provide an unassailable, firm foundation for generality to rest on? Such a universally rejected set of variables can tell the constitutional court that rules differentiating between cases according to these variables are not general, if indeed generality is no more and no less than "general approval," that is, unanimity in value judgments. However, the rejected set cannot help determine which of the countless remaining, actual or potential, rules differentiating between cases according to the countless remaining unrejected variables is general and which is not. Moreover, whatever the foundation of the taboo variables, it is not a firm but a shifting one, contingent on cultural change. Currently taboo variables are liable to be eroded or swept away by the next wave of political correctness, whose reigning value judgments might well seem outrageous, and outrageously un-general, to our own generation.

Conclusion

Here, the Devil's Advocate rests his case. Buchanan and Congleton have had their day in court. Additional submissions may come, from them or from sympathizers or adversaries, believers or agnostics, before the jury can retire. An interim summing up, however, may be in order at this stage.

Idealism or intellectual convictions persuade Buchanan and Congleton that constitutions determine politics, rather than the other way round. If so, it may be possible to purify politics by constitutional reform, making both the winners and the losers of the old, sordid game of political tug-of-war better off. Enshrining the right clause, hitherto missing, in the constitution would force people willy-nilly to give up the politics of interest. Generality is said to be the clause that would achieve this result. Only rules that satisfy generality in governing distributions of benefits and burdens, rewards and punishments should be constitutionally admissible.

In treating like cases alike, all rules satisfy the generality condition; it is, in this sense, a tautology. Is there another, meaningful sense that would permit rules that are general to be distinguished from those that are not? Does generality require us to treat every case like every other? Or does it permit us to treat each case on its merits as unlike every other? If the answer to both questions is "no," where between these extremes does generality lie? Inclusiveness and non-discrimination, besides their logical and semantic defects, raise the difficulty that equal treatment of cases according to one variable will normally entail their unequal treatment according to other variables—offering free public education to all children treats families with children better than the childless, and so on through endless examples. What is deemed to satisfy, and what to violate, the generality principle does not appear to rest on any intersubjective criterion but ultimately on somebody's value judgment. The question to be decided, then, is whether a proposition whose meaning is contingent and discretionary—like the value judgment that lies behind it, with no stronger claim to validity and truth than its rivals—can function as a major constitutional constraint on the domain of collective choice.

12

Slicing the Cake
Nobody Baked

Explanatory theories of distribution can get along, after a fashion, without recourse to the notion of rights. Normative theories of distributive justice, on the other hand, presuppose matching theories of distributive rights. Outlining a set of principles of distributive justice without accounting for the rights, or their absence, that such justice would presuppose strikes me as incomplete. It amounts to laying down rules for sharing out manna, a windfall, a cake that nobody baked, a pool of goods that have no prior owners. Consequently, the problem of conflict between *prior and posterior claimants* to goods need not be dealt with: all claimants reach out from the same baseline for what they think they ought to have.

This very incompleteness speaks loudly about the nature of the principles in question. Revealingly, Barry proposes principles, provides some (I think precarious) underpinnings for them, and draws out quite awesome policy implications, without any reference to property, except at the end of his argument, as an afterthought.

Presuming Equality

Of Barry's six proposed principles, the key one is the "presumption of equality." It is the hardest to underpin and the most in need

Originally published as "Comment on Brian Barry, 'Justice, Freedom, and Basic Income': Slicing the Cake Nobody Baked"; reprinted with permission from *The Ethical Foundations of the Market Economy,* edited by Horst Siebert (Tübingen: J. C. B. Mohr, 1994), 90–98.

of underpinning. It is also the only one that tells society what shall happen in cases where the distribution of resources and opportunities is in dispute, since it gives rise to a "reasonably" clear collective decision rule. (On the power of the word "reasonably," more must be said presently.) The other five principles are either subsumed by it in the sense that application of the decision rule implicit in the first principle would, all by itself, produce the results the other principles are intended to bring about, or are so vague and so open to interpretation as to be vacuous.

Barry interprets his "presumption of equality" to mean that only the departures from equality must be justified. Once this is granted, it remains to choose the criterion, substantive or procedural, that makes the justification adequate, conclusive. How to tell that an inequality is "really" justified? There is no recognized adjudicator, only interested parties to the dispute. However, if even those who are least favored by it find an unequal distribution acceptable, it is justified. This criterion directly gives rise to a social choice rule for bringing about distributive justice.

By the rule, any distribution can be vetoed by those, but presumably only by those (a class? a group? a single individual?) who get the least under it. Consequently, the only distribution *immune to veto* is an equal distribution, under which nobody gets less than anybody else, hence nobody is entitled to a veto.

Barry qualifies this somewhat forbidding result by adding an adverb to a double negative ("cannot *reasonably* [emphasis added] be rejected"); but it is surely unworldly, in philosophy as in practical politics, to rely on the low-powered word "reasonably" to guarantee a *reasonable* result.

The "anti-aggregation principle" merely specifies, using a triple negative, that a change in distribution need not be accepted by those who lose by it if and only if it is those who get the least who lose. But by the first principle, they can veto it anyway and need no extra authority to do so. This is so because, prior to the change, the distribution was equal subject to a Paretian proviso, for otherwise it would have been vetoed. As the result of the change, the losers would automatically become less well off than anybody else, and the first principle would allow them to veto the changed distribution. Hence the "anti-aggregation" principle is redundant. The same is true, for analogous reasons, of the "compensation" principle. The victims of misfortune can veto a distribution that leaves them worse off than the nonvictims. Prior to the misfortune, all are equally well off. After the misfortune, the victims can insist on being compensated in whichever way will restore their condition to equality with the nonvictims, simply by virtue of the principle of equality. No principle of compensation is needed. The "vital interests" principle, if it means anything, is also redundant because it is already taken care of by the first or equality principle: a situation where some people can satisfy their nonvital interests while others cannot even meet their vital ones could be vetoed by the latter without benefit of a new principle to that effect.

The remaining two principles add little of substance. The "principle of personal responsibility" leaves it indeterminate what must, and what need not, be recognized as a consequence of one's own choice.[1] Failing its restatement in far sterner language, it is no guide to distributive justice. At best, it is inconclusive. At worst, it becomes the "it is not my fault" principle. Finally, the "principle of mutual advantage" or strong Pareto improvement merely lays down that if the least-favored prefer an (albeit unequal) distribution, they do not *have* to veto it. However, this is not worth stating, and nor is it a "principle." By the first principle, inequalities are subject to veto rather than to interdiction. Hence, it is clearly optional, and equally clearly not mandatory, to suppress an inequality that is to everybody's advantage, making even the worst-off better off than they would be under a more equal distribution.

Barry alternates between three stratagems for underpinning his key, nonredundant principle of "the presumption of equality." Without prejudice to logical priority, I take "hypothetical agreement" to be the first, "equality as the basic normative idea" to be the second, and "equal treatment of equal subjects" to be the third stratagem.

---

1. In an earlier essay on "Chance, Choice and Justice," Barry (1991) suggests that the question of personal responsibility, reducible as it is to the question of free will, is an open invitation to endless and inconclusive argument.

Hypothetical Agreement

Barry employs a variant of the contractarian device: principles of justice are those that people in a "negotiating situation" would unanimously accept. All such variants are beset by a common dilemma.

Either the "negotiating situation" is defined in such a way that people are required to ignore the particular features (notably talents, skills, endowments) that distinguish them from other people, and would in prudence cause them to prefer principles different from those preferred by others who are characterized by other features. This is logically equivalent to all participating "featureless" individuals being reducible, for the relevant purpose, to one and the same individual. He, of course, unanimously agrees with himself about principles of justice, as about everything else. But the hypothesis of agreement is then trivial and carries no weight with real people.

Or, as Barry at one point claims for his version, the people in the precontract negotiating situation are real people, in which case they are aware of their capacities and circumstances, strengths and weaknesses. Consequently, they can by and large assess the likelihood that one set of "principles of justice" will serve their prudential interest better than another. (Indeed, the same is true more generally of one non-Paretian social choice rule rather than another.) A procedural rule giving veto power over distribution to the worst-off would prima facie damage the interests of the rich, the able, the industrious, and the thrifty. The converse would be true if dictatorial power were ceded to the best-off instead. Stipulating that "nobody's interests count [for] less than those of anybody else" (whatever that may mean) clearly does not help: if anything, by awarding equal weight and influence to everyone, it makes it more difficult to reach this kind of agreed solution. Among real people it is unworldly to look for a bargaining equilibrium that could pretend to the Kantian universalizability that Barry, taking Scanlon's formulation of it as the standard, claims for his "hypothetical agreement."

Equality as the Basic Norm

We are asked to accept that "the equal claim to consideration of all human beings" is "at the root of justice." This is not hard to do, since accepting it as it stands does not commit us to anything. To create a specific commitment, "equal consideration" must be amplified. It cannot, for instance, mean that we must accord Donald Trump the same veneration, approval, and respect as Mother Teresa, nor that we should extend the same protection to the liberties of a multiple rapist as to those of his potential victims, for strong arguments can be found against doing so. Barry's notion, however, must be held to be beyond argument, for or against; he tells us that it cannot be derived from anything more basic than itself.

Barry's idea must, in other words, function as a final, noninstrumental value neither requiring nor admitting justification. At the same time, it must commit us to an identifiable course of action so that, in the present context, all of us can tell whether the norm it lays down is or is not actually being met. Reading Barry, his only idea that both functions like this and involves this kind of commitment seems to be equality of well-being. Alternatives and complements, such as equality of the range of each person's available options, are too indefinite.

Declaring this idea to be a final value makes it invulnerable to arguments except those appealing to other, rival, "noncompossible" final values. Thus, it becomes a matter of (if we may put it so) "moral tastes." It ceases to be a matter of agreement, unless it be the agreement to differ, to *non est disputandum*. This is a feasible stratagem, and a very safe one. But it fails in underpinning principles of distributive justice; for stating that equality is an ultimate value is one thing, to establish that it is just is another. The two are neither coextensive nor even commensurate.

"Equal Treatment"

The third stratagem one can detect in Barry's argument avoids the dead-end appeal to a final value that it is as rational to embrace as to reject. It relies instead on the generally compelling nature of cer-

tain moral precepts. It attempts to derive the proposition that equal
well-being is a requirement of justice from the maxim of equal treatment that commands moral beings to treat like cases alike. This is the
command of impartiality in justice which no just man can, on pain of
self-contradiction, reject.

Impartiality in commutative justice is trivial. It goes without saying
in the sense that it is simply a corollary of the meaning of law. Equality
before the law is a pleonasm. It insists that "a law is a law"; that it treats
equal cases equally, without condoning arbitrary exceptions, is one of
its defining features. In distributive justice, however, while impartiality
is still a constitutive requirement, not every distribution must be impartial, for not every question of distribution is a question of justice
requiring impartial treatment.

It is a question of distribution, but not of distributive justice, that
a passer-by gives his small change to the first beggar, leaving nothing for the second; that a woman bestows her favors on one man and
not on another; that a patron of the arts accords his patronage only
to some artists, and the housewife her business only to some shops,
rather than spreading it "impartially." Cutting closer to the bone, "finders, keepers" denies any place to impartiality between finders and non-
finders in recognizing title to what is found. Bequests are left only to
the legatees, to the total neglect of impartiality.

Why do these apparent violations of "equal treatment" fail to strike
us as morally repugnant? One reason is no doubt our belief that being
the owner of something confers at least some discretion over its disposal. Denial of this would empty ownership of all meaning, and
though some would be ready to take this step, it is far from clear that
taking it is, and ought to be accepted as, a compelling moral imperative.

In Barry's scheme, ownership apparently never justifies a distribution. Hence for him ownership could not preempt the requirement of
equal treatment. Provisionally, let us take him at his word and argue on
his own terms. A second reason is still left then for explaining why apparent violations of impartiality are not always perceived as apparent
injustices.

It has often been pointed out (notably by Leoni 1961, 64–66; Berlin 1978, 82–83; Raz 1986, 218 ff.), that equal treatment applies to all

cases or all subjects who are members of the same class. It does not apply to nonmembers. Subjects can, of course, be classified in indefinitely many ways. Two subjects are entitled to the same treatment if classified one way, to different treatment if classified another way. In "finders, keepers" each finder gets title to what he found, and no nonfinder gets title to what the finders found. Likewise, the class "workers" is, under "equal treatment," treated unequally from the class of "nonworkers," the former justly being and the latter justly not being paid wages. Needless to say, it is all too easy to classify in bad faith: it is equal treatment to concede all power to members of the Politburo and no power to nonmembers, and it is likewise equal treatment to concede a veto over the distribution of goods to the class of the least favored and refuse it to the more favored.

Since equal treatment leaves the justice of a treatment indeterminate, it cannot possibly underpin a particular set of "principles of justice" better than any other set. Finding distributive justice at the end of an argument for equal treatment depends on finding the just division of cases and subjects into classes, and only *then* on treating the members of each class equally.

The Irrelevance of Distinctions

Salvaging egalitarian principles from the debacle of the equal treatment stratagem involves maximizing the size (minimizing the number) of classes into which we order people for purposes of treatment in distribution. Owner or nonowner, worker or nonworker, clever or dull, sucker or free rider must, for the egalitarian result to come out, all become irrelevant distinctions.[2] There are to be only the "adult resi-

---

2. Seeing society either as one large homogeneous class (or two: the "least favored" and the rest), or as a heterogenous association of many interacting, interlocking, and overlapping groupings, are the marks of two opposing political philosophies. The distinguished previous holder of Barry's chair ascribes the former view to the "anti-individual," who is "intolerant not only of superiority but of difference . . . seek[ing] his release in a state from which the last vestiges of civil association have been removed, a *solidarité commune* . . . from which no one was to be exempt" (Oakeshott 1962, 278).

dents" of the country or indeed, when Barry generalizes the argument, which he finds can be done with "surprising ease," of the whole world. All must be guaranteed a locally adequate basic income, "adequacy" being presumably judged by the least favored. (They must also all have the same freedom. It is not evident why Barry feels he must separately stipulate this, for in his treatment well-being and freedom seem to merge into one inchoate whole. It is as if for him being free were, to put it unkindly, what our uncles and aunts used to call having "independent means.")

One need not pursue this argument much further. That equal treatment of such a megaclass as "all adult residents" or "all human beings" should imply a distribution assuring equal well-being to each (subject only to local variations and to a proviso for Pareto-superior, agreed-to deviations) runs counter to many moral intuitions. It is also a repudiation of the most important conventions that have, at least so far, enabled civil society to function. That the quasi-infinity of obvious differences between them should all be irrelevant in judging what each human being should be getting is a demand that has cropped up sporadically throughout history on the fringes of political discourse. It has never gained the status of a moral axiom generally agreed to be compelling. It seems safe to say that, luckily for mankind, it never will.

Pereat Mundus

Maybe justice should never be judged instrumentally; maybe *fiat justitia, pereat mundus* is the right position to take. Barry would probably do well to take it, so as further to immunize his principles of justice against temptingly easy consequentialist criticism. He does not take it, and he does not believe that his just principles would cause the world to perish. On the contrary, he supposes their policy implications to be highly beneficent.

Why he is confident of this is not obvious, for, as he cautiously puts it, "we can only imagine in outline what a society would be like in which this reform had worked its way through." Other, perhaps more pedestrian, imaginations would readily conjure up much less reassuring consequences from his proposals. Mine certainly would. But it is not within the proper scope of this paper to match utopian against dystopian imaginations. Once the logic of the principles is taken care of, the policy implications can probably take care of themselves without their having to be tested by rival flights of imagination.

Other principles than Barry's have for long implicitly guided the Humean conventions at the base of civilized societies and productive economies. They have not served too badly, and except on the fringes of society, they have not passed for unjust. *Suum cuique:* that each is entitled to what is his by virtue of finding it, making it, or acquiring it by agreement with those similarly entitled; that value received for value given in valid contracts is justly acquired; that freedom of contract must not be denied, and exchanges must not be imposed—these and related conventional beliefs have at least as good a claim to the rank of moral axioms as Barry's presumption of equality. They are consecrated by long practice.[3] They belong among the building blocks of any theory of distributive justice. They are conspicuously missing from the egalitarian one. Their absence, if not their outright repudiation, is the most striking feature of Barry's attempted construction.

He takes a peculiar position with regard to contract, property, and more generally rights arising from voluntary exchanges. He accepts them as first principles. He notes that they (conjointly with certain others) entail a ban on redistribution. He sees no objection to them, provided they are subordinated to some other "basis on which to establish an economic system." This other basis is redistributive, and for that purpose overrides the first principles alluded to. But first principles cannot be overridden and subordinated as the occasion demands. They can either be accepted, or are repudiated.

The repudiation is of course entailed in Barry's notion of justice. Nobody owns the cake to be distributed, nobody has baked it, nobody provided the wherewithal for baking it. If anyone did, they were jolly

---

3. It seems true that the practice is declining. Barry is no doubt right in pointing out that some existing trends in our society suggest "a bleak future." His detailed diagnosis is, of course, controversial. At least two of the prevalent symptoms of social dysfunction, chronic unemployment and dependency, that Barry treats as arguments for radical reform, seem to me, on the contrary, to be the effects of our progressive abandonment of the old conventions that, in the present text, are loosely associated with *suum cuique.*

foolish and imprudent, for they get no thanks for it under the new "principles of justice." In fact, the world as we know it cannot stand under them. It need not necessarily perish, but it must be totally transformed, to borrow Barry's phrase, in ways "we can only imagine in outline."

Property, Usufruct, Income as Public Goods

In this new world, there is no place for property. Barry does not choose to recognize this, and allots a rather squeezed place for it under the proviso that such property as is in private hands has a relatively equal distribution. In strict logic, this proviso cannot be met over time without continuous and unrequited redistribution of property, requiring the administrator of distributive justice ceaselessly to violate with his left hand the remaining property rights that his right hand is meant to uphold. This inconsistency can only be removed by going all the way to full-blooded socialism, a move Barry, for freely avowed reasons, shies away from.

Worse, however, is to come. Putting his principles into practice supposes that "the link between earning and income has to be weakened" by a high marginal rate of tax and, as regards "basic income," cut altogether. Benefits must be tendentially dissociated from contributions; they must become increasingly *non-contingent.*[4] Both the usufruct of property, and nonproperty income, are to be, to use a technical term, "nonexcludable," for egalitarian justice would not allow their benefit to be reserved for contributors, i.e., owners and workers, only.

Nonexcludability is generally taken to be the critical feature that makes public goods "public," and necessitates coercion in calling forth contributions to their cost. In ordinary parlance, the state must tax incomes to pay for public goods. What, however, if the incomes themselves are made to converge towards the status of public goods? Do we

---

4. Barry suggests not only that income *ought not* to be dependent on work but—puzzlingly—that it *is* not. His analysis is said to yield the point that "incomes derived from work are less and less reliable and adequate as a means of supporting the population." What other, let alone more reliable and adequate, means are there?

then coerce some to make them produce incomes for all? After reject-ing "productivism," how do we get enough production to allow man-kind to enjoy the income it is "entitled" to without working for it? Can a society, or the whole world, "be helped out from accumulated savings, contributions from other people"?

The questions are not rhetorical. They are implied in Barry's theory of distributive justice, and mutatis mutandis in all egalitarian schemes. They require some answer. None is forthcoming that I can see.

Part Four

Socialism

13

Ownership, Agency, Socialism

The failure of the socialist command economy directs attention to purported alternative mechanisms of resource allocation that would be self-enforcing, simulate certain capitalist processes and outcomes, yet would preserve some socialist values. Tracing the effect of alternative types of ownership, severalty and commonalty, upon systemic behavior, the present paper argues that the principal-agent problem obstructs any self-enforcing efficient solution unless severalty becomes the dominant form of holding property. The latter, however, is inconsistent with other essential socialist goals.

The economies of the greater part of the Eurasian land mass have lost steerage way, and seem to have great difficulty in getting up steam again and setting a course. At the same time socialism as a doctrine of government has exhausted its intellectual credit and, to survive in some version, must seek new theoretical foundations—an endeavor that has not been crowned with much success so far. These two quandaries are of course closely related. Both have their origin in a fudged image of economic and social institutions as they really work, leading to a boundless overestimate of their mutual compatibility and the results they can be asked to deliver. The present paper is aimed at the center of the fudge, the dependence of a particular mechanism of resource allocation on a particular type of property right. It seeks to help clarify the question: are markets intrinsically capitalistic?—or, to put it the other way round, is "market socialism" a contradiction in terms?

Reprinted with permission from *Government: Servant or Master?*, edited by Gerald Radnitzky and Hardy Bouillon (Amsterdam; Atlanta: Rodopi, 1993), 125–37.

1. Enforcement

Socialism in its undiluted, genuine version implies a command economy. There is nothing pejorative in this term: it is factually descriptive. It means that all significant production and distribution decisions are taken by "social choice" and backed by the sovereign power vested in it.[1] They are broken down by central planning into detailed instructions concerning factor inputs, product outputs, incomes, and prices. The instructions are meant to be coherent and capable of being executed by agents of "society" from managers down to workers. Coherence *ex ante,* if it is achieved, does not secure coherence *ex post,* because the system is necessarily rigid yet exposed to random shocks, shortfalls, and stoppages. *Any* variable not subject to a specific instruction or target backed by adequate sanctions, has a natural propensity to follow the line of least resistance and take on the "wrong" value; inputs, prices, wages, and investment expenditures will be too high for given outputs, outputs will be too low for given inputs, labor productivity too low for a given equipment, quality too low for a given price, and so on. This tendency necessitates an ever finer breakdown of targets and constraints, and runs counter to attempts at simplifying and decentralizing the system by one ingenious reform after another. The agents of the political authority owe it obedience, but the more exacting are their orders and the greater is their complexity, the stronger will be the likelihood of laxism in execution and dissimulation of failures. For these and other reasons, the nature of the genu-

1. I use "social choice" in the ethically neutral legal-positivist sense, to mean any decision reached in conformity with the "constitution," rules, and procedures, whose observance entails that the decision will be enforced by the power of the state. "Social choice" corresponds to a broad class of decisions, including not only laws passed by elected legislatures and decrees issued under such enabling laws, but also the commands of a dictator or of a totalitarian party exercising effective sovereignty. "Social choice" does not imply that it has been arrived at by following any particular decision rule. "Democracy is a form of government, and in all governments acts of state are determined by an exertion of will. But in what sense can a multitude exercise volition?" (Maine 1885, 104). The only answer that *does not sanctify social choice* by imparting ethical value to it is a legal-positivist one.

inely socialist economic mechanism demands severe enforcement in order to perform anywhere near as intended—yet severe enforcement is costly. However, the innocent belief that the corresponding "Stalinist" features of socialist systems are merely residual effects of the personal proclivities of the individual of the same name, seems nevertheless ineradicable from much public discourse.

The typical by-products of the genuinely socialist economic steering mechanism are twofold. First, despite the humanitarian strands of the creed, the need for severe enforcement brings into being an authoritarian political system that must make heavy exertions to legitimate itself and leaves little room for democratic trappings. Political relaxation is quickly translated into a worsening economic performance that may degenerate into uncontrolled rout. Second, even under fairly rigorous authoritarian rule, the mechanism lends itself poorly to its intended purpose. The "social choices" it is supposed to put into effect prove in general to be partly or wholly unenforceable.

2. *Efficiency*

Unenforceability of its "socially chosen" instructions and targets, and the high moral and material cost of attempted enforcement, are primary weaknesses of genuine socialism. Its secondary weakness— secondary only in the sense that the empirical evidence for it is indirect and not wholly conclusive—is that even if its instructions were wholly coherent and fully enforceable, they would still be inefficient, wasteful by failing to hit upon the factor combinations, techniques, product mixes, and foreign trade patterns that would jointly place the economy on the "socially preferred" (i.e., politically chosen) point on the production possibility function. Even if the steelworks gets built and functions exactly as planned, it would have been more economic to build tourist hotels instead, and import the steel. The reason is presumably that prices in genuine socialism serve essentially recording purposes, but do not generally clear markets, do not reflect relative scarcities, and are not "truthful" signals calling for any particular resource allocation, let alone the "optimal" one. Prices are *not formed* in a progress of *discovering* opportunities for profitable exchanges, and once formed *do not convey* the sort of information that, if acted upon by buyers and sellers, would bring about the best available outcome.

3. Self-Enforcement

Having made a diagnosis along these lines, socialists who for one reason or another put a high value on economic efficiency or political democracy, and of course those who think the two are Siamese twins and come and go together, are intellectually ripe for abandoning direction by command; they typically suggest recourse to the market as the remedy. (Whether buying efficiency and democracy at this price would really be in socialism's best interests, is a moot point that we will leave on one side.) Reliance on the disciplines of the market makes input-output instructions redundant; at the most, limited intervention should suffice to make production and distribution respond to "needs" as well as to demand, when the two are deemed to diverge too blatantly. If there are few or no instructions to obey, there is little or no need for their enforcement. The market is a mechanism with a built-in allocation of rewards and punishments that generally make it preferable for all participants to *act as they should if it was to fulfil its purpose.* Briefly, it is self-enforcing.

Where there is no enforcement in the above sense, there can be democratic decision-rules; where there is a quasi-automatic feedback mechanism for sorting out waste and seeking out the most economical solutions, there can be a reasonable approximation to efficiency. For all this, there must be no capitalism. These three conditions form the hopeful crux of "market socialism."

4. Equality at the "Starting Gate"

There must be no capitalism because, in the first place, socialism seeks its own renewal and would rather not make away with itself. In the second place, it derives such legitimacy as is left to it, from a conspicuous commitment to equality and what it is pleased to call "distributive justice." It is part of its creed that capitalism is actively destroying these pre- and post-capitalist values. Therefore the cohabitation of inconsistent systems must not be tried; capitalism must be abolished, not mitigated. The social democratic or "American liberal" compromise, whereby capitalism is allowed to produce wealth, whose spontaneous distribution is then forcibly rearranged by the institutions of the welfare state, is not ambitious enough for the emerging "market socialist" program. For under the welfare state compromise, capitalism keeps creating unacceptable inequality and injustice which "social choice" must keep correcting and redressing. The desired end-result must be *continuously enforced,* and as one unjust head is chopped off, two grow in its stead. Under market socialism, on the contrary, the basic institutions themselves must be such that no unjust end-results are created in the first place, the very system being *self-enforcing* with regard to both of its intended outcomes, economic efficiency and social justice.

While the former is to be achieved by "reliance on the market," the latter is to come about as the spontaneous product of "equality at the starting gate." Private property of productive assets, even if equally distributed in some imaginary initial position, tends over time to cluster unevenly as a combined result of random chances and systematic processes, with winners winning even more and losers eventually losing all. Hence people's capitalism is an illusion; at best, it is transitory. Productive property under market socialism must therefore be "socially owned," both to preserve "starting-gate equality" from the accumulation of private property, and for numerous other reasons that seem to me secondary to the program's main objective.

5. *Severalty*

"Social ownership" is market socialism's secret weapon, in that its exact nature is kept behind a veil of verbiage, leaving it to the imagination of each to discern through its opacity particular charms, a particular potency. Trying to identify it by working back from other market socialist theses (employee ownership is not socialism but workers' capitalism; decentralized ownership creates conflicts of interest among particular sets of owners, and between each such set and society or the superset), one would have to conclude that "social ownership" is merely a coy euphemism for state property. However, most market socialists vigorously deny this without saying plainly what is meant by it. They variously allude to distinctions between private and public, individual and collective, exclusive and inclusive, selfish and unselfish, conflictual and cooperative, as elements of the definition of "social ownership." Manifestly, however, these allusions only help to make the notion woollier still. Since "social ownership" must mean *something* if it is to be discussed at all, some minimal definition of it should be agreed. Here, we will proceed by first identifying its polar opposite, severalty.

When property is held in severalty, each individual member in an owner-set has rights to a *quantified* part of the whole by virtue of original occupation (*"finding"*), *contract* or *bequest.* In the absence of specific contractual provision or custom resting on good reason to the contrary, each individual owner can exercise the rights pertaining to his part of the property at his discretion. In the limiting case, the owner-set is simply one natural person, the sole owner, whose discretion to exercise his rights is complete. In the general case, the owner set can of course have any real positive number of individual members, from one to many. A good reason for *limited discretion* in the exercise of property rights by members of a multi-person set of owners is that the property is indivisible or would lose value in division. It is not feasible to cut a ship in two so that its two owners may each sail away with half the hull. Less obviously, it is not always feasible or at least not convenient to let one part-holder of an usufruct to exercise it one way, the other another way. Thus corporations distribute the same dividend to each share of a given class of stock even if one shareholder prefers high dividends, the other a high ploughback. However, under severalty the limited discretion in the exercise of property rights, due to *physical indivisibility* or high cost of division, is to a substantial extent overcome by potential *value-divisibility.* The owner of half a ship cannot cut off his half nor use it in ways the owner of the other half objects to, but he can claim half the income it yields and half the residual value when it is sold. He can, in turn, alienate a part or the whole of these claims,[2] a

2. The latter right presupposes freedom of contract and bequest—freedoms which the present writer would consider as being entailed by ownership. Many

right that renders income and capital both divisible and *convertible* into one another. Likewise, the shareholder who disagrees with a corporation's profit reinvestment policy can supplement his low dividend by selling each year such fraction of his shareholding as will keep his investment constant while that of the corporation as a whole increases; in fact, subject only to tax considerations, he can decide his saving or dissaving at his discretion in complete independence from his fellow owners in the corporation.

The principle of severalty, greatly aided by value-divisibility, does not eliminate every possible externality arising from multi-person ownership of undivided chunks of property, but in its purely economic effects comes close enough to sole ownership; in the limit, it *is* sole ownership. It is quintessentially capitalist in that each benefits from his ownership in proportion to his *equity* in the property, rather than in proportion to the *work* he contributed, or his *deserts,* his *needs,* his *age,* or some other criterion. It is the form of property right where, despite indivisibilities and potential externalities, costs and yields are internalized to the greatest practicable extent.

6. Commonalty

Commonalty is almost the obverse of severalty. Under commonalty, a property has a single owner who, however, is always an abstract holistic entity whose individual members, unlike members of partnerships, joint stock companies, or other owners in severalty, have no definite shares in the property by virtue of contract or bequest. Such rights as they have individually are derived from their "belonging" by virtue of *residence, place of work, admission,* or *citizenship*—a quality that may be acquired at little or no cost by simple entry and lost by exit, and that is

---

others, however, view ownership as a loose bundle having "variable geometry," that may contain some property rights but not necessarily all, e.g., the right to rent out residential property to any tenant at any rent he will pay is not considered by everyone nor by every jurisdiction as an integral part of the ownership "bundle." In this view, ownership consists in *distinct* rights which are detachable from each other. The question is a vast one and cannot be gone into here.

in many cases as loosely defined as the benefits to which it entitles the member.

There is little doubt that commonalty is a very old form of property right, probably older than severalty in general though not older than the special limiting case of severalty, i.e., single individual (or family) ownership. Historically, commonalty declined *pari passu* with the economic role played by the tribe and the clan. An instance of commonalty that has survived is the village owning the "common." While all have certain access rights, no individual villager owns a definite fraction of it, or of any right pertaining to it. There may be a presumption that everybody has the same right to it as everybody else, but this is not translated into quantitative limitations of use or equity; what it really means is that the members' property rights are quantitatively *indeterminate*. Any villager can free-ride on his fellow villagers by overgrazing. Costs and yields are to a large extent externalities. Hence, contrary to severalty, economically optimal solutions (e.g., as to the number of cattle to be grazed) are not self-enforcing (in technical language, "co-ordination games" involve conflicts), and the avoidance of waste may need specific enforcement if it can be done at all. Physical indivisibility and its attendant inconvenience and cost cannot be evaded by recourse to value-divisibility. Hence an individual seeking, for instance, a change of use or a change in the time-profile of the income stream, can only obtain it if the owner entity as a whole has the corresponding right *and* decides to exercise it—a requirement that, failing unanimity, raises all the problems of collective choice, notably the choice of a choice rule, cyclical preferences, the status of minority rights, dictatorship, and so forth.

As the villager is to the common, so is the club member to the golf course, the syndicalist to the worker-owned "self-managed" enterprise, and the citizen to state property. The latter is in practice the overwhelmingly most important form of commonalty. We do not know which of these property forms socialists really have in mind when they call for "social ownership." They do not seem to have thought out their own position on the question. The mainstream view used to be, and perhaps in a latent fashion still is, that the state must own all productive property over a certain size. Other proposals would allow workers' collectives and non-profit institutions to own restricted rights in them, the rights of alienation and change of use being reserved for the state. All "market socialists" would, however, exclude any right that gave individuals a precisely quantified negotiable equity in a property, permitting the "exploitation" of labor and "unearned income." Their rejection of capitalist property rights implies, however, that which-ever abstract entity is the rightful "social owner," it holds its property in commonalty, with consequences for the resulting economic system that may not be immediately obvious.

7. Simulation

How would market socialism "rely on the market" under common-alty? How, for that matter, does it know that there *would* be a market to rely on, and that if some kind of market did emerge, it would be efficient in some sense and hence *worth relying on?*

Since exchange needs at least two contract parties and a market a plurality of them, there can of course be no market in producers' goods if they are all owned by the same "social owner," the state. A market is difficult to conceive of even if there are many "social owners" of use rights, but these rights are not value-divisible and negotiable. The state may put shadow prices on capital goods and may set interest rates in order to calculate the "costs" of consumer goods, but these would not be market prices and rates in the proper sense, and would not benefit from the presumption of truthfulness about relative scarcity. However, if there is no true market in producers' goods, there cannot be one in the consumer goods they serve to produce, nor of course (for these and other reasons) true factor markets. The more intelligent kind of market socialists have been aware of this at least since the start of the "socialist calculation debate,"[3] and have proposed a series of alterna-tive solutions involving some method of simulation of the process by which prices, corresponding to efficient resource allocation, are deter-mined in a competitive market.

3. The basic literature is in Hayek (1935), Lange (1936), Lange (1937), Berg-son (1948), and Bergson (1967). For a survey, see the "Introduction" by Vaughn (1949).

The oldest is the computing solution, first envisaged and rejected by Pareto (Pareto, 1909, 233–34) because it would require solving an astronomical number of simultaneous equations incorporating an astronomical quantity of information, much of it difficult to extract. Three generations after Pareto, this objection looks less decisive, for data storage, retrieval, and processing are well on the way to tackling problems of astronomical complexity. The true obstacle to the mathematical solution is not the technical one of gathering and manipulating too much information, which an imminent science-fiction civilization might presumably overcome. It is the more fundamental fact, rightly stressed by Hayek and Kirzner, that some market participants do not act on pre-existing information, but discover it, so to speak, for the first time; it is their search for innovative, "economic" solutions to problems posed by competition that generates the knowledge in the first place about prices, costs, techniques, etc., and it is this information that is needed for efficient resource allocation.

Many half-way solutions between command and market socialism have been proposed, and some have been tested by the many abortive "market-oriented" reforms of the late planned economies, especially in Hungary, Poland, and the Soviet Union. Common to each were the ambitions to decentralize, to direct the economy by setting broad parameters rather than giving detailed instructions, to allow a measure of price flexibility and accounting and managerial autonomy in state enterprises. Probably the strongest single reason for their failure was that they tried artificially to transplant and insert into the "socially owned" economy a number of features that characterize market economies and that grow out of decentralized capitalist property rights. In the absence of the reward-and-penalty structures that arise out of ownership in severalty, they are like plants with their roots up in thin air. A "socially owned" enterprise is autonomous and independent in the sense that a weightlessly levitating object is autonomous and independent. There is no reason why it should "economize" and tend to move in any particular direction, let alone as it ought to in order for competitive markets to come into being and perform their optimizing function.

To overcome levitation and indeterminacy in enterprise behavior, theoretical models of market socialism postulate various types of conduct to be mimicked. In one version, the enterprise is instructed to adjust output and price until, by trial and error, it just clears its market. However, the enterprise can clear its own market with a suboptimal output at a price above marginal cost, and may well prefer to do so. In a tighter version, it may be instructed to expand output until price equals short- or long-period marginal cost, i.e., to simulate some ideal type of profit-maximization. Once again, it has no evident interest to do so, may prefer to maximize peace and quiet, or conversely size and influence, or perhaps the managers' popularity among the employees. The instruction to maximize profit would in any event have to be enforced—the simulated market mechanism would not be self-enforcing—but enforcement might well prove to be impossible because the enterprise could, within reason, simulate to have whatever level of marginal cost suited its own purposes. It might choose to innovate and "economize" in a wide sense, but more probably it would not, and there is nothing much anyone from the outside could do to make it.

If ownerless enterprises, held "in commonalty," cannot with any certitude be *made* to simulate some acceptably profit-maximizing behavior, they have to be given incentives to make it worth their while. The corresponding version of market socialism might be called "motivated simulation." It is of course not the enterprise as a legal person, but the natural persons influencing its conduct who need to be motivated. They can be promised bonuses depending on their own performance, or that of their department, line, or function according to orthodox business school teachings, with the top man's or men's bonus directly tied to some measure of total profit. Provided it is a linear function of the latter, the bonus of the ultimate decision-taker is then the tail that should wag the dog, i.e., make the enterprise adopt the profit-maximizing output and price.

8. When Agents Have No Principals

Can the "socially owned" enterprise's top manager be made to *act* like a capitalist without first *becoming* a capitalist? The problem is the notoriously intractable one of *agency*. The last-resort impossibility of simulating an efficient market under socialism resides in the peculiar nature of the principal-agent conflict when property is held in commonalty. In general, the agent responsible for the management of property reports to another agent, responsible to its owner or to yet another agent who, in turn, is responsible to the owner; no matter how indirect the responsibility and how long the chain of agency, it must end somewhere.

Under capitalism, the end of the chain is held by a natural person aiming to maximize the value of his equity, or an aggregate of such persons. Profits and losses are their profits and losses: they are *principals.* How the principal obtains that the agent should put his interests first, or (less naively) how a mutually acceptable solution is found to the obvious, albeit partial, conflict of interest between them, is a long story that continues to be told, mostly on the financial pages of newspapers. In the modern large corporation with a multitude of owners, many of whom hold their stakes through institutional intermediaries, the solution, such as it is, is provided by the latent possibility of the takeover bid that threatens the tenure of the managing agents who, whatever their excuses, fail to maximize the owners' equity as valued in the market. The solution is a self-enforcing market sanction, blunted as it may be by legislation that can be turned to entrench the sitting management. It may not be a perfect solution—no agency problem can have one[4]—but at least it has a logical structure.

Under "social ownership," however, property is ultimately held by an abstract entity which cannot but be *represented* by an agent, an agent's agent, or an agent of the agent's agent. There *is no principal* at the end of the chain, for whom the discounted value of all future income from his equity in the property would be a sensible, rational maximand. At best, an individual "owner" in commonalty, if the term "owner" can be employed at all, would seek to maximize the value of the rights *he* held or that benefited him personally. The villager, subject to how he expected his fellow villagers to act or react, would put as many cows on the common pasture and cut as much timber from the common wood as he

4. A perfect solution of an agency problem is one whose result is the same as the result that would be obtained if the principal acted directly rather than through an agent, but this trivializes the premiss that there *is* an agent.

could. The member of a worker collective would lobby for the greatest possible capital-intensity (machines per worker) in his enterprise, and for having as few fellow-workers as possible provided his cousins and nephews were co-opted into the happy few. The ordinary citizen, holder in commonalty of all state property, would probably be just indifferent to the fact and not bother about who maximizes what.

When there are no principals, the question of solving agency problems through overt or latent bargains between principals and agents cannot even arise. Property may still be managed, but it will be managed as if it belonged to nobody.

9. When Simulated Capitalism Becomes Real

Now a principal-less agent will have no constraint, except perhaps public opinion, to stop him from maximizing the variable, or bundle of variables, that *he* prefers. He might put various values on various combinations of the income, non-pecuniary agreement, and safety of his managerial tenure. Having said this, we have said next to nothing, for almost any managerial behavior can be alleged to be consistent with such vague unquantified objectives. In other words, the principal-less agent is largely unpredictable. There are nevertheless a few things we can safely say he will *not* do if he is rational, i.e., fits means to ends. He will *not* maximize profit if only part of his income from his post is a bonus geared directly to profit while the rest depends on other variables that are not co-variant with profit. He will *not* maximize profit if his evaluation of risk is different from what it would be if it was his own equity that profited or lost from unpredictable outcomes. (Not risking his own money may, of course, as easily lead to undue aggressiveness as to timid passivity.) Finally, he will *not* maximize profit if his own tenure is finite for any reason: because he is mortal, must retire, cannot bequeath or sell his job, or may lose it upon a turn of the political wheel. With finite non-negotiable tenure, his rational maximand is not the market value of his equity, but only the discounted value of profit over some limited, perhaps brief, period—a very different objective dictating a different policy for investment in facilities, research, quality, reputation, and goodwill.

Once the conditions are stated under which the heads of "socially owned" enterprises, if they are rationally pursuing what is best for them, will *not* manage their business in such a way that outputs and prices should fairly closely simulate those that capitalist enterprises would adopt in a competitive market, a simple conclusion becomes blindingly obvious. Before there is any hope for "market socialism" to perform as expected, these conditions must be removed though their removal, while necessary, may not be sufficient. Removal of the anti-efficiency conditions, however, would effectively transform the agent-manager into a principal, a capitalist with a negotiable and heritable part-ownership in the enterprise. Of all the market-socialist versions of simulation—by giant computer, by instruction to clear the market, to equate marginal cost to price, and by "motivated simulation"—this is the only one that is not logically condemned to fail, basically because this is the only one that does not simulate capitalism, but admits it and resigns itself to its domination.

Though this conclusion will not seem original to the common-sense reader who "knew" all along that socialism "cannot work," it is perhaps a comfort to his worldly wisdom to find that one can also be guided to the same result by the disciplines of deductive reasoning.

Under this version, where socialist simulation flips over into real capitalism, the head of each enterprise and perhaps his close subordinates, would be owning a perhaps minor stake in its equity in severalty, the "social owner"—the state, the municipality, the "work collective"—the remaining stake in commonalty. The capitalist tail would well and truly be wagging the socialist dog. In important respects, the effect would be much the same as if the managers had taken over the economy in a gigantic avalanche of leveraged buy-outs, leaving the "social owner" with an ill-defined interest that is, rather like "junk" bonds, neither really a prior charge nor really equity; it is neither the wellspring of incentives nor a basis for influence. The individual "social owners," if they can be said to exist as such, would in such a situation be very much at the mercy of the owner-managers, for even if they could muster the collective will to do so, they could neither remove nor buy out the latter without defeating the object of the exercise. "Social ownership" could not regain the upper hand without actually liquidating market socialism and going back to the genuine command version of socialism. Once more, this is perhaps unsurprising once it is argued and stated, but seems worth stating all the same.

10. When the Starting Gate Is at the Finishing Post

Can anything at all be saved from the socialist program, or must the establishment of a self-enforcing and efficient market mechanism crowd out the socialist norms of equality and "distributive justice" — unless they are squeezed back in by the system-alien compromises of a hybrid "social democracy"?

Market socialists would hardly admit to this stark alternative. The belief that in fashioning society one can have it both ways, is fundamental to their intellectual constitution. If some system of social organization does not achieve all they hold dear, there *must* be another that does, and all they need is to design it by informed thought. A secondary reason for their confidence is that to my knowledge no market socialist is on record as realizing that property in commonalty is inconsistent with the efficiency they think their system must have in order to be accepted. They have never come to terms with the thesis that, as was shown in Sections 6–9, "social ownership" must be superseded by capitalist ownership for their program to succeed. Should they, however, come round to this recognition, they might still not give up hope and renounce certain normative demands. They might fall back on the prima facie plausible case that the ethical features they want society to have, ought to and can be secured by a form of equality of opportunity. If that is achieved, any type of property rights, even capitalist ones, and even the market processes such rights generate, can be consistent with social justice. "Equality at the starting gate" would, according to this fallback position, mean that even unequal results at the finishing post would be ethically acceptable; for acceptance of the outcome of just initial conditions and of due process is, after all, the essence of the American liberal idea of "procedural justice."

Equality at the starting gate needs careful definition before it has any meaning worth serious discussion. Here, let us merely note that since the "race" (the market economy) is a continuous process without a beginning where all start to run and an end where all stop, any arbitrarily chosen "finishing post" where we assess results to date, doubles as the "starting gate" for the rest of the race that is still ahead. Unless the runners have all passed the finishing post marking the end of any given lap in a dead heat, they have ceased to be (if they ever were) in a position of "starting-gate equality" *for the next lap.* The market solution implies that some of the "runners" gain advantages as they run, and *get to keep them,* for if they did not, they would not race but only simulate. One can have a real race, or "fix" the result, but not both. This is by no means a compelling argument for having real races which *upset* equality, rather than phoney ones whose results are "fixed" in advance to *uphold* equality. It is merely a statement of the mutually exclusive alternatives that each kind of race implies.

Refusing to choose between "market" and "equality," proclaiming that one need only ask to have the best of both worlds, is self-delusion or self-contradiction; it is nonetheless the position market socialism is now adopting. On the long retreat from the original doctrine, past one humiliating accommodation after another, it can no doubt accommodate itself to that, too.

14

Market Socialism:
"This Square Circle"

Never kick a doctrine when it is down; the present is hardly the time to rub in the humiliations of socialism, in disarray as a political and economic theory and failed as a practice of government. This is not a rubbing-in essay. On the other hand, now is very much the season for attempts to reformulate, or as we have learnt to say, to "restructure" socialism, openly defaulting on its heaviest liabilities, and taking it out of bankruptcy under some less tarnished identity. If only to protect the public, these attempts should be submitted to fairly beady-eyed scrutiny. The present, beady-eyed essay looks at the favorite candidate for such a new, post-bankruptcy identity.

In *Market Socialism*,[1] a team of Fabian social science teachers presents a collection of papers avowedly designed to rebuild an intellectually tenable position for the Left. The authors proceed partly by jettisoning some of the doctrinal baggage socialism has found too heavy to carry, partly by cross-breeding "socialism" with "market" to demonstrate that the union is both possible and desirable, and would have as its progeny a richer mix of efficiency and justice than any type of organization that has yet been tried.

Reprinted with permission from *Market Socialism: A Scrutiny "This Square Circle,"* Occasional Paper 84 (London: Institute for Economic Affairs, 1990).

1. Julian Le Grand and Saul Estrin (eds.), *Market Socialism*, Oxford: The Clarendon Press, 1989. Subsequent references to authors' papers in this collection are cited in brackets in my text, with page references where appropriate.

I

There is a minor and a major move in this exit from bankruptcy's Chapter 11.[2] The minor move, which may serve as a hedge against the major move not succeeding, consists in denying that the realization of socialism entails recourse to *any* particular set of means (Estrin and Le Grand, 2). This must mean, conversely, that the employment of a particular set of means need not signify that it is socialism or anything like it that is being built; the means does not identify the end pursued. Hence if nationalization, planning, regulation, price or rent control, queuing, sharply progressive taxation, or a certain type of public education prove to be counterproductive in practice and untenable in theory, it should be easy for socialists to repudiate them without in any way abjuring socialism, for the former are merely contingent features of a possible socialist system; some other socialist system could do without them; and their presence neither qualifies a state of affairs or the thrust of policy as socialist, nor discredits socialism if they are condemned. This a more refined echo of the perennial and unbeatable defense which makes all tangible evidence irrelevant by declaring about Soviet Russian experience that it did not discredit socialism because it was not socialist, but Stalinist and bureaucratic.

The authors of *Market Socialism,* quite astutely, generalize this defense: *no* objectionable feature of an existing system that calls itself socialist counts as evidence one way or the other. No empirically observable detail of its policies can serve as an argument that socialism is not a worthwhile goal. Thanks to this defense, socialism becomes a highly mobile and elusive target. Its definition is purged of falsifiable propositions. Such alternatives as "the means of production are/are not privately owned," "workers hire/are hired by capital," or "access to food and shelter is/is not regulated by purchasing power" no longer necessarily distinguish a capitalist from a socialist society. It is only clear what socialism is *not*—no existing arrangement is—while what it *is* will be revealed only by the future, and then only if we have the good taste and judgement to embrace market socialism.

2. Chapter 11 is a U.S. form of corporate re-organization which falls short of liquidation.

ARE MARKETS COMPATIBLE WITH SOCIALIST ETHICS?

The question whether reliance on markets is compatible with the ethics of socialist man "cannot be fully resolved until we have a working model" of market socialism (Miller, 48)—a test which does not threaten by its imminence. The internal contradictions of the Yugoslav system of worker ownership are no arguments against it, since "as our understanding of co-operatives increases, we are [*sic*] able to devise alternative arrangements which preserve both enterprise-level democracy and economy-wide efficiency" (Estrin, 184)—though the profane reader wonders why, in that case, forty years of experience did not enable the hapless Yugoslavs to have either democracy or efficiency, let alone both at the same time.

Dissociation of socialism from empirically falsifiable descriptive statements (e.g., "in socialism, workers hire managers," or "unearned income is taxed more heavily than earned," etc.) and indeed from all empirical precedents (e.g., "Sweden" or "Yugoslavia"), should protect it from positivist attacks, and ease the major move, the projection of a new identity. Its new name attractively couples the currently fashionable ("market") with the nostalgically retro ("socialism"). For this union really to work, however, it is necessary to dissolve another, that is, to "decouple capitalism and markets" (Estrin and Le Grand, 2), for the two are wrongly yet strongly linked in the public mind.

There are, in fact, two links, one philosophical, the other historical. The philosophical link was first asserted by Mises[3] in 1920, for whom the information embodied in prices, necessary for efficiency in resource allocation, could be generated only by a competitive market. His argument was completed by Hayek[4] who added the essential element of a discovery process, developing and spreading otherwise unavailable, latent information, that is part of price formation by a multitude of economic agents.

The socialist counter-argument, that no logical links existed be-

3. Ludwig von Mises, "Die Wirtschaftsrechnung im sozialistischen Gemeinwesen," *Archiv fuer Sozialwissenschaften*, 1920, trans. as "Economic Calculation in the Socialist Commonwealth," in F. A. Hayek (ed.), *Collectivist Economic Planning*, London: Routledge, 1935.

4. F. A. Hayek in Hayek (ed.), *ibid.*

tween capitalism and efficient pricing, set out in the 1930s by Lerner and Lange,[5] centered around the theoretical possibility of finding market-clearing prices by simulating the responses capitalist producers would make to perceptible shortages and surpluses of exchangeable goods. This controversy, which went down in the history of economics as the "Calculation Debate," in my view cannot be usefully pursued on a purely formal logical level.

On the substantive level, the key question to be settled is the reason adduced for expecting participants in a market to behave in a manner that will make the market an efficient instrument of resource allocation. In the context of the "socialist market," this calls above all for settling the principal-agent problem. While it is present in both a real and a simulated market, there is good reason to hold that it works one way where property rights are private (i.e., attach to *individuals*), another way where they are collective (i.e., attach to *holistic entities* like the workforce, the commune, the state). The difference is fundamental, and suggests that managers of collectively owned, non-capitalist enterprises neither would nor could successfully simulate capitalist responses and reproduce the market processes and the resource transfers they induce. This argument is strongly supported both by the micro-economic theory of property rights and agency, and by the depressingly monotonous failure of repeated "market-oriented" reforms in socialist economies—reforms that have always fought shy of reassigning ultimate, properly sub-divided, and clearly defined property rights to *persons*.

Even if these arguments were not conclusive and the issue were open, the onus would still be on socialists to show that, contrary to the record and to the state of the Calculation Debate, anything a capitalist market can do, the socialist one could do as well. No trace of meeting this obviously central requirement appears in *Market Socialism,* except for a bland and platitudinous reference to the calculation problem (Miller, 30–31) as a reason for recourse to markets, rather than as

5. A. P. Lerner, "Economic Theory and Socialist Economy," *Review of Economic Studies,* 1934–35; Oskar Lange, "On the Economic Theory of Socialism, I–II," *Review of Economic Studies,* October 1936 and February 1937.

a reason for questioning *whether* socialist markets, too, *can* "calculate." Why markets under socialism should be expected to achieve efficient allocation, or indeed to exist at all except as fakes—which is the sole really contentious issue in the Calculation Debate—is passed over in complete silence and incomprehension. Instead, we are airily told not to fret, because for reasons that are not revealed, "in a socialist market economy . . . the makers of cheese will adjust their supply week by week to match the demand" (Miller, 38), and that is all there is to it. But it is not at all clear *why* they would adjust week by week, or ever, especially as doing so is neither always simple, nor convenient, nor costless. Simply to suppose that they would is begging a fairly basic question the authors may or may not have grasped, but have certainly not answered.

THE MARKET: A TOOL OF CAPITALISM OR SOCIALISM

The historical link between capitalism and market, in turn, is not (*pace* Marx) a matter of historical necessity—the capitalist "mode" entailing "production for exchange," other "modes" entailing "production for needs." It is merely a matter of historical coincidence that the abstract institution of the market, which is of course more than just the heir to the medieval fair, happened to evolve at the same time as, and in the frame of, the capitalist "relations of production," though no doubt it could have evolved in other "frames" as well. Apologists for capitalism usurp the market, appropriating it as if the market—an efficient institution—depended for its functioning on capitalism—a repugnant and alienating system. However, the suggestion that market and capitalism go together is but "a sleight of hand" (Miller, 25). Traditional socialists fall for this trick, and think they dislike and mistrust markets when in fact it is capitalism they reject. This is a confusion (Miller, 29), a failure to see that the market can be trained to serve socialist goals just as it now serves capitalist ones. Indeed, though the authors do not say so, they tacitly treat the market as a neutral tool in the hands of its political master who can use it in fashioning the kind of society he wants. Gone, then, is the characterization of capitalism as a design for the pursuit of profit, socialism as one for the satisfaction of "needs"—as is the clear distinction between obedience to impersonal market forces under capitalism, to conscious social choice under socialism. We can, in sum, have the best of both at one and the same time.

For market socialism is nothing if not pragmatic. Markets appear to be good for some purposes in some areas, planning is good for other purposes in other areas, and there is no apprehension that the two may not mix admirably well. Worker co-operatives "may not be optimal for all industries at all times" (Miller, 36), but then they surely must be for some industries at certain times. "[I]t is not clear that one would want to rule out capitalist acts between consenting adults altogether" (Estrin and Le Grand, 15; Winter, 154). "[G]overnment could seek to make the market responsive to social goals such as greater social justice, equality and full employment" (Plant, 52). "[C]entral planning of an entire economy is unfeasible" (Estrin and Le Grand, 11), but one must choose the right balance between market and planning, and indicative planning is valuable, notably as a "guide to medium-term economic development in the medium term [*sic*]" (ibid.). Above all, market socialists can safely count on the market for delivering material welfare, yet need not condone the unjust, "morally arbitrary" way it distributes it. Only social democracy, untroubled by principles and systemic clashes, is as confident of having its cake and eating it as market socialism.

IS MARKET SOCIALISM MERELY SOCIAL DEMOCRACY DRESSED UP?

Does this self-assured eclecticism in fact mean that market socialism is nothing else but re-packaged social democracy, with at its base an economy capitalist enough to work, and capable of holding up a strongly interventionist and redistributive super-structure, pushing union power, regulation, egalitarianism, and welfarism, but only to the point beyond which adverse economic and social trade-offs become unaffordable, and never quite going over the brink? The answer appears to be "no," for reasons that are not wholly clear and turn out to be surprising when they are elucidated. The main point seems to be that, unlike social democracy, market socialism will do more than merely *redress* capitalist outcomes; it will *do away with* the institutions chiefly responsible for these outcomes—and first of all with the main culprit, the limited liability company (Winter, 140). The latter is noxious because it facilitates private concentrations of power outside government control (a tendency which, if true, would surely be a contribution to the preservation of individual freedom by virtue of the counterweights it provided against the omnipotence of the state), but also because it separates ownership and control, and therefore—whatever the modern theory of the firm may say—it cannot be "relied upon to produce efficient results"; on the other hand,

> [b]oth the inefficiencies and the abuse of economic power can be reduced, if not eliminated, by placing both ownership and control in the hands of the entire work-force. (Winter, 142)

It is hard to take this sort of statement seriously but one must try. Market socialists ought to be especially aware of what markets are suited to do. The separation of management control from ownership, while admittedly a possible source of inefficiency, is broadly taken care of by the market for corporate control or, in plainer English, by the threat of the take-over bid. The more open and free is that particular market, the less the likelihood of inefficiency due to the principal-agent problem. The owner-manager, who has total security of managerial tenure, is potentially more inefficient than the professionally run corporation, since he is much freer not to "maximize," and can indulge his fancies—as the history of so many family-owned firms and of capricious robber barons demonstrates. Unfortunately for the market socialist thesis, however, worker co-operatives are *a priori* worse than either, their weird and hybrid incentive structure pushing them to choose "socially" wrong, inefficient factor proportions and a suboptimal scale. The authors of *Market Socialism* appear to be aware of this (Abell, 98; Estrin, 175–76, 183), yet they let stand the bizarre juxtaposition of capitalist inefficiency/co-operative efficiency. For the structural deformities of the latter, they propose truly lame remedies that might or might not work if they were tried but, perhaps fortunately for the market socialist argument, have not been, and the fact that they have not been is surely significant.

WHAT IS MARKET SOCIALISM?

If one is to believe the disclaimer that market socialism is not so-cial democracy (Estrin and Le Grand, 13), nor the putting into prac-tice of any particular set of reputedly socialist policies (Estrin and Le Grand, 2), what exactly is it? The answers, such as they are, have to be found by exegesis, for the authors do not tempt Nemesis by setting them out in the shape of a clearly visible target. We do know, how-ever, that it is a system where, contrary to socialism proper, decisions to allocate resources are taken in response to price signals emitted by market mechanisms. But why are these signals heeded? Innocently, the book takes it for granted that, quite simply, they are, "[s]ince market producers are generally motivated by profit" (Estrin and Le Grand, 3). However, it is clear on reflection (and the hurt surprise of socialist countries that tried to abandon the command economy without also re-defining and de-centralizing property rights and found themselves with an economy that heeded no signals of any sort, shows it conclu-sively), that this is by no means "generally" the case. It will be the case only if property rights are private in the sense that whoever is entitled to allocate certain resources is also entitled fully to profit from good allocations and is made to suffer from bad ones—either directly if he is the owner, or through some control mechanism if he is a manager. In the latter case tricky problems may start to arise, which, however, are as nothing to the problem to be faced when the manager is not the agent of the owner, but the simulated agent of a holistic pseudo-owner.

So far, however, market socialism looks not too unlike a kind of capi-talism in discreet incognito. Yet as one looks closer, troubles of identity emerge. Consumer goods are permitted to be privately owned by firms (which, in turn, may or may not be privately owned) and by individu-als but only within the limits imposed on the wealth and income of the latter by the requirements of equality. Subject to these limits, they can be bought and sold; at least one necessary condition of a market for consumer goods is thus fulfilled. Ownership of producer goods, and of their assemblies, however, is subject to more stringent restraints, which react back on consumer goods and negate other necessary conditions of a market for the latter.

"Provided that the capitalist acquired the productive assets legitimately, and here *I would rule out inheritance*" (Winter, 154, my italics), puts narrow bounds on the permissible size of asset holdings, for since the market must not permanently reward one participant more than another, and incomes after tax are to be broadly equal, the capitalist, barred from *inheriting,* cannot *accumulate* from his profits either. The size of a privately owned firm, moreover, is to be decided at the discretion of its employees:

> An attractive solution [*sic*] to the problem of how large a company should be before it ceases to be privately owned is to allow the workforce to make the choice. (Winter, 157)

What is more devastating, and indeed startling in the context of a proposal to rely on markets, is that "private ownership is tolerated so long as the owners do not wish to sell their assets" (Winter, 162). The ban on negotiability, reinforced by the ban on joint-stock limited liability, would put paid, in the name of market socialism, to any chance of having a market for producer goods, and assets as claims on producer goods or on income streams. The question then arises as to how a market for consumer goods alone can function efficiently or at all, if there can be, for practical purposes, no market in the resources that it takes to make consumer goods.

"A BRICK WALL OF SELF-CONTRADICTION"

It really seems that market socialism has, at this point if not before, run into a brick wall of total self-contradiction. Does it have some clever way around it, by inventing a species of property rights which permits exchanges on *all* markets, and permits market disequilibria to result in profits for those who best read market signals and thus do most to eliminate the disequilibria? Can it, in other words, devise a hitherto untried type of ownership that would be private in its effect on people's motivations, yet non-private in that it would not reproduce capitalist domination, capitalist inequality, capitalist "moral arbitrariness"? Miller declares, as if this were obvious once you thought of it, that "[i]t is quite possible to be for markets and against capitalism" (Miller, 25). Yet the possibility is remote, and certainly not evident. It depends on the discovery of this new institution of "both-private-

and-not-private" ownership—an attempt whose success has yet to be demonstrated.

As we shall see, if the theoretical attempt can be made, let alone made successfully, it calls for mental contortions of greater improbability than market socialists seem to realize. They appear to think— and if they do not, they unwittingly convey—that property rights which have both these attributes at the same time, are inherent and can be discovered in what they choose to call "social ownership." Once again, the meaning of the term is hidden in verbiage, and is rendered positively enigmatic by assertions that it does not mean what the lay reader would think it meant. It is *not* state ownership: if it were, nationalization would be an identifying characteristic of the building of market socialism, and we have been explicitly told that it is not. The authors of *Market Socialism* profess to think little of it as a policy. Is, then, "social ownership" ownership by the workers? Again the answer is "no." Communal ownership is potentially market-socialist if it concerns a mere island "in a hostile capitalist environment" (Estrin, 185) but becomes "workers' capitalism, not socialism" (ibid.) if it is the prevalent form of ownership, since each commune would be motivated to act selfishly with respect to society as a whole. The plot thickens; the puzzle gets ever more insoluble. Market socialist property rights "preclude any direct ownership or control by workers. . . . Ownership of co-operatives . . . must therefore be *social*" (ibid., my italics). Under social ownership, "the capital stock is owned collectively by society, and is merely administered by particular groups of workers" (Estrin, 173).

Who, however, *is* society? Is it not the entity represented by the supreme proxyholder, the state? How can ownership be vested in "society" without the ownership rights being exercised by the state? If the owner is not any of its subsets (a municipality, a co-operative, a commune of kindred spirits, or whatever), but really society "as a whole," social ownership is *ipso facto* state ownership, social owner decisions are government decisions (however unsatisfactory a proxy the government may be for society, there is no other above it), and no linguistic fig-leaves will alter these identities by one iota. The state, then, owns the capital stock, and "democratically run" groups of workers "administer" but do not "control" it. The reader who thought that elsewhere in this "reconstruction of the intellectual base of the Left" he saw market socialism held up as a superior *alternative* to nationalization, must be rubbing his eyes.

"SOCIAL OWNERSHIP" EQUALS STATE OWNERSHIP

"Social ownership," if it means anything at all beyond chatter, is clearly state ownership, for only the latter satisfies the apparent requirements of neutralizing the owner's selfishness *vis-à-vis* society; it is only society as such that has no "particular will" in conflict with the "general will." Yet it is not certain that market socialists realize that it is state ownership they are calling for. Only sundry *obiter dicta* suggest that in a vague way they do. One of them describes the passage to market socialism thus:

> . . . the state would transform all publicly and privately held equity into debenture stock, upon which the (self managed) firms would have to pay the going interest rate. At the same time, the authorities would create a number of new holding companies, to each of which would be entrusted certain assets in the national portfolio. Since the state has the task of creating the holding companies, *it might choose to retain ownership* itself. . . . (Estrin, 192, my italics)

But does market socialism leave it any other choice? It must not hand back the equity in the "national portfolio" to the citizenry at large, for that would in no time recreate capitalist institutions and capitalist outcomes; then market socialism would have to be introduced all over again. Nor must it hand it over to firms, letting them be not only "self-managed" but also "self-owned," for this would be taking a wrong turning, leading to workers' capitalism. The state, in sum, not only "might choose" to be the universal owner, but *must* do so unless market socialism is to degenerate into mere social democracy. A good deal of perhaps unconscious camouflage, in the shape of state holding companies acting as competing venture capitalists, and so forth, is going on in the book to avoid having to face state ownership openly. The words "social ownership" are the recurrent motif in this camouflage. It is no more a genuinely new type of ownership, holding out the stimuli of private rights without their propensity to reproduce capitalism, than market socialism is a genuine doctrine.

If taking capital into state ownership is mandatory—for any alternative would negate essential market socialist postulates—market socialism is no longer a moving target. We find that, perhaps unbeknown to its inventors, it has been nailed down, committed to at least one "particular means," nationalization, if it really seeks to realize its avowed ends. Can market socialists live with this? Perhaps understandably in view of the dilemma, they choose not to say.

An ironic consequence of their implicit commitment is that, even if other self-imposed constraints did not confine the "market" of market socialism to consumer goods alone, "social ownership" of productive assets would. Genuine market exchanges presuppose among other things a plurality of principals owning goods to be exchanged, and having dissimilar preferences or expectations. When the state is the sole owner of the assets to be exchanged, it can at best organize exchanges between its right hand and its left hand, getting up a "simulated market" generating simulated asset prices, a simulated "going" interest rate, simulated gains and losses of simulated efficiency, and, at the end of the road, simulated shops pretending to sell simulated goods.

"THE STATE-OWNED MARKET"?

Undaunted, market socialists will have both state ownership and market, and introduce a near-perfect oxymoron, the state-owned market:

> Under a scheme of this sort, the internal structure of productive enterprises would remain largely unchanged [thanks for small mercies!] although of course their system of control would alter. However, an entirely new *state-owned capital market* would have to be created. (Estrin, 192, my italics)

What these words can possibly mean, and how such a market could be "created," are details that remain unrevealed due perhaps to modesty, perhaps to the author's belief that a "state-owned capital market" is self-explanatory in the same way as "state-owned steelworks" or (in what is probably the crowning example of self-explanation) Engels's "state-owned brothels."

Other contributors commit themselves even less in the matter of how real markets in non-capitalist property rights are to arise. In characteristically pragmatic spirit, it is suggested that all manner of arrangements could be envisaged, ranging from various types of co-operatives to "labor-capital partnerships" (Abell, 95, 98), excluding only the joint-stock company. Labor-capital partnerships differ both from capitalist enterprises and from pure co-operatives; in fact, they appear to embody the vices and virtues of both in a diluted form. They look like the corporatist fudge, much tried by British governments of both parties since the Second World War, that may be the least unacceptable short-run *modus vivendi* for producer interests, but regularly ends up in the worst of both worlds for producers and consumers alike.

Fudged or clear-cut, non-private ownership is a core requirement of market socialism, and genuine markets must somehow prove to be compatible with it. It is the pivotal place of this condition that really differentiates market socialism from the bankrupt doctrine of orthodox and, as I would insist, genuine socialism, as well as from the *ad hoc* compromises of social democracy. Market socialism, in order to rid itself of the crushing liabilities of genuine socialism while still making good its claim to being more than just the boring old welfare state, must invent something desperately original by way of what property rights should entail and in whom they should be vested. It is dismaying to find, then, that the particular author whose lot it was to go beyond airy anti-private generalities and to spell out these matters, is not familiar with the meaning of ownership and has not mastered the distinction between creditor and owner, debt and equity, interest and profit. In the same breath he (probably rightly) condemns workers' capitalism and communal ownership, prescribes the vesting of productive capital in "society as a whole," yet assigns to the labor force of each enterprise "one element of the entrepreneurial function: the right to the residual surpluses (profit from trading after all inputs have been paid for)" (Estrin, 186), the right in question being none other than equity ownership.

Manifestly, then, it is not "productive capital" as such, but only some kind of gigantic prior charge on it, that is to be "socially owned" by the state. The equity of each enterprise is to belong to workers' collectives (always provided that they do not buy or sell it or parts in it—a condition that is sure to give rise to lively and efficient asset markets). Back we go, then, to "each of these groups of workers acting selfishly with respect to the broader society" (Estrin, 185), which was the reason for prescribing state, instead of group, ownership in the first place. At this point, one abandons vain exegesis; the more one looks to see how the circle could be squared, the rounder it stays.

II

Market socialists are on intellectually less unfamiliar ground when, instead of dealing with such contrivances as equity, debt, market, and profit, they turn to the final values—equality, freedom, distributive justice, the satisfaction of needs—that they expect the market as an instrument, allied to some ingenious if not wholly comprehensible reform of property rights, to procure. Arguing for these values and about ways to reach them has always been congenial to socialist thought (though more to its Proudhonian than its Marxist strain), in contrast to the value-neutral tendencies of liberalism. In addition, Plant and Abell, the authors whose contributions particularly address these issues, happen to reason better and less glibly than the others, and deserve more serious attention.

For genuine socialists, the notion of freedom conveys above all mankind winning mastery over matter, liberating itself from the tyranny of things, the blind caprice of "reified relations." It is a notion that alludes to scientific progress and political revolution, and whose subject is a collective, holistic one. Its bearing on individual choice is at best derivative and contingent; at worst, it dismisses choice as a selfish indulgence. Market socialists, by contrast, associate freedom primarily with individual choice in the classical liberal manner, and are pleased to note that the market is the economic institution *par excellence* that responds to preferences, just as democracy is the political institution *par excellence* that does so, though each weighs the preferences of different individuals in a particular manner. The democratic weighting—one man, one vote—is always egalitarian, the market weighting may be grossly inegalitarian if one man can back his preference with more money than another. It is for socialist policies to see to it that grossly unequal weights disappear. Various means can be employed to this end. Whatever they are, they are prefaced by a blanket dismissal of the costs and pains of applying them, and of the feedbacks leading back to the market economy:

> Nor is there any reason why a market socialist economy should not operate effectively in the presence of an active enforcement of such policies. (Estrin and Le Grand, 22)

Perhaps there isn't, but how do they know?—and how do *we?* Gratuitous assertions such as this one, only just acceptable in a party policy statement but not in an argument addressed to intellectuals, are not helpful for the declared aim of rebuilding "the lost intellectual base" of the Left and "its philosophical and economic foundations" (Preface, v).

HOW MUCH "ACTIVE ENFORCEMENT"?

A good deal of "active enforcement" would be required to establish "market democracy," and more than we should at first think to secure freedom of choice, for the latter is not simply what it says. It is more than the non-imposition of any particular alternative out of a given set of them—what has unfortunately come to be called "negative freedom." It is also their availability, according to Miller, as "real" rather than merely "formal" options. On inspection, a formal option is one that is not one, while a choice is said to need resources before it can be acted upon. It would be better English not to call them "options" when they are unreal, nor "choices" when they cannot be acted upon, but the inept language about unreal options and impossible choices helps to slip in the similarly muddled notion of "positive freedom." As Miller clumsily puts it,

> freedom can be diminished not merely by legal prohibitions but also by economic policies that deprive people of the material means *to act on their choices.* (Miller, 32, my italics)

More lucidly, and without talking of *choices* when he means *desires,* to shape one's life means "to have abilities, resources and opportunities—that is to say, some command over resources," and cannot be separated from "the capacity for agency and its associated resources" (Plant, 65). In the terminology of economics, negative freedom is the unobstructed faculty to take any option that falls *within* the individual's given budget of time, money, and knowledge, while positive freedom has to do with widening the budget constraint. Having more positive freedom is a code word for having more wealth, more leisure, more knowledge—in sum, a richer life. But then why not *say* so?—why have recourse to the special code? For are not wealth, knowledge, or leisure less emotion-laden words, and have they not a more settled and precise meaning, than freedom? Or is that precisely why market socialists, and others, draw them under the umbrella term of "freedom" instead? They plead that "it would be perverse" to regard "a wealthy genius and a poor illiterate, both living under the rule of the same liberal law, as equally free" (Abell, 84). Users of the "negative" freedom concept would have no inhibitions so to regard them; they could increase the information content of the comparison by adding that while both were "equally" free, one was richer and cleverer than the other. This would tell us substantially more than the cryptic socialist statement that one had more "positive" freedom than the other.

One suspects, however, that the call to give "equal freedom" to all gets a wider and more favorable hearing than the seemingly far stronger demand to equalize everybody's wealth, leisure, and knowledge. Hence packaging the latter demand under the bland name of "positive freedom" masks the sting of a very demanding egalitarian norm. Indeed, when postulating that equality is a value in its own right, it is explicitly the equality of "positive and negative freedoms" that is being stipulated (Abell, 80), for defined as they are, their equality will *ipso facto* give socialists all the equality of wealth, income, education, and status that they are likely to want.

They want a good deal, but it is never finally clear just how much, for despite a few defiant assurances that we can safely afford social justice, since the market will go on delivering much the same riches regardless of how "society" decides to distribute them, several contributors to the volume have some gut awareness that redistribution of the rewards market participants hand to each other must have some effect on the performance of the market economy; the goose will hardly remain forever indifferent to what happens to her golden eggs. Plant warns, pertinently, that "[i]f people know in advance that there will be equality of result however they act in the market, this will be a recipe for inefficiency" (p. 72)—to put it no higher. Since they could not be fooled for long, and *would* know in advance if there *were* to be equality of result, presumably there *must not be* equality of result—or so one would surmise, although as we shall see presently, one would be wrong.

STARTING-GATES AND END-STATES

Unease about the goose may have a small part in shaping the sort of equality market socialists are calling for, philosophical differences with genuine socialists a greater one. In the trendy words that have come to pollute the stagnant pool of political philosophy, they do not wish distribution to be governed solely or even mainly by "patterned" or "end-state" principles, but want distributive justice to emerge from just "process"—their great remaining difference with liberals being that, for market socialists, just process yields acceptable end-state outcomes only if it begins at a specially designed "starting-gate" of equal opportunity. Provided, however, that in socialism *starting-gates themselves are "patterned"* as they should be, the outcomes of market processes will call for relatively little further state intervention to make the right, egalitarian end-state principle prevail—for it will then to a large extent prevail, as it were, of its own accord, assisted by the invisible hand.

This, then, is the great promise of equality of opportunity, the species of equality that offends least and is easiest to get past a somnolent moral consensus; for while there is no single end-state principle of equality that would not offend some strong moral intuition, some material interest, or both, equality of opportunity is at first sight soothing and almost wholly unexceptionable. Its appeal to our sense of justice (or, more insidiously, to our sense of "fairness") is as broad as it is weak, while any vague threat it may represent to our vested interests looks tolerably easy to live with.

Proponents of the idea convey this impression (and, I dare say, convince themselves of it, too) by employing a particular paradigmatic imagery. Participation in the market economy is a trip, or a race. It has an "entry point" or "starting-gate," and a finishing line where prizes await the runners who win them in order of arrival. The winners get larger prizes than the others, but this inequality is a legitimate outcome of the process of matching the runners on a level track, provided the winners had no "unfair" advantage, nor the losers a handicap, "at the starting-gate." Calling advantages that have helped winners to win *"unfair,"* and that we only recognize as such because their possessors have won, is of course vacuous in itself unless it gets content from a prior delineation between fair and unfair advantages. All market socialists would put greater wealth, a better education, a more extensive and highly placed network of friends and protectors on the wrong side of the dividing line. Many would hesitate about more brains, rare gifts, better looks, greater sex appeal. Most of them would not (though those who took the "moral arbitrariness" of natural endowments seriously would clearly have to) classify greater industry, hard work, relentless application as unfair advantages, because they are owed to character, innate guts, and strength of will that are, in turn, unearned. Great perplexity would surround the fairness or otherwise of sheer luck, which is the residual cause of differential performance after all other, specially identified advantages have been accounted for.

Evidently, if all differential performance on a level track is attributable to some advantage, whether innate or acquired, and if *all* advantages at the starting-gate are unfair, the only fair outcome of the race is all-round dead-heat—that is, "equality of outcome." Dead-heat is engineered by stripping the contestants at the starting-gate of their *alienable* advantages, such as wealth, or redistributing them until all possess them in equal measure, while compensating for *inalienable* advantages by a system of head starts and handicaps (positive and negative discriminations). However, racing history suggests that perfect handicapping is probably impossible, for residual advantages always manage to subsist. Nor would market socialists really want it, most being content to allow desert in some sense to earn differential rewards (Miller, 44), and believing that they can tell rewards due to some kind of desert from rewards due to unfair advantages.

EQUAL OPPORTUNITY: "FAIR" AND "UNFAIR" ADVANTAGES

In sum, under equal opportunity people retain some "fair" advantages at the starting-gate to make the race interesting, but the rest of their advantages, inherited or acquired, are unfair and must be evened out one way or another. Lest we should think that, once that is done, the rest is really up to the individual contestants, it turns out that the end-state resulting at the finishing line, albeit a product of pure procedural justice, will still require adjustment guided by "a theory of distributive justice, equality and community" (Plant, 76), which cannot "be achieved without a powerful state" (ibid., 77). Nevertheless, "starting-gate redistribution" will have done much that would otherwise fall to "end-state redistribution" to achieve, and this will bring to life a remarkable hybrid, "market-oriented" in that it permits random outcomes, and socialist in that it does not.

The prize formulation of this clever synthesis is once again contributed by Miller:

> the system might have some of the features of a genuine lottery in which punters win on some rounds and lose on others, the net effect being relatively insignificant . . . the socialist objection is . . . to the kind of luck which, once enjoyed, puts its beneficiary into a position of permanent advantage. (Miller, 45)

Now winning on the lottery *is* a permanent advantage, unless there is a specific, built-in provision to *undo* it, ensuring by some means that the winner loses it again without undue delay. For instance, a combination of poor odds and an obligation to go on playing as long as he is ahead, would suffice to make him rapidly lose again the advantages he has won. Failing such a combination of adverse odds and obligation to play on, he could either take the money home, or profitably use it to buy more tickets for the next round of the lottery, since a sufficient proportion of tickets would be winning ones. At the odds offered by the "lottery" of a market economy—that is, where the return on the average investment is better than zero—an initial advantage has a better than even chance of becoming cumulative, as each round is more likely to add to than subtract from the player's winnings.

But market socialism works by a different logic. It insists that the market shall be a "*genuine* lottery," not a game of "*cumulative* advantage" (Miller, 45, my italics).

THE CONFUSION OF LOTTERIES

The confusion about lotteries is not a pardonable slip of language or logic, for it leads to a gross confusion of the whole issue of equal opportunity in a market economy. A lottery is genuine if the distribution of all (positive and negative) prizes among the tickets is *random*. Miller appears to believe, however, that it is genuine only if the sum of the prizes is *zero*—a very different condition. This is nonsense, for the concept of lottery implies no particular sum, positive or negative. A more insidious fallacy is then committed in applying the false concept of lottery as a possible norm for the market. It is possible to hold that the distribution of prizes in the market is random. To stipulate that they have a zero sum is, on the contrary, to require an absurdity which contradicts the essential, *wealth-creating nature* of the market without which it would lose its whole point and would not exist. Gains and losses cannot possibly cancel out either interpersonally or intertemporally, but must be greater than zero both over all the players and over time as long as prizes breed more prizes—that is, in an economy where the productivity of capital (or, less metaphysically, the interest rate) is positive.

There seems to be a more than somewhat Freudian reason why a market socialist equates a properly ordered socialist market economy to a non-positive-sum game: for only in a world where no gain is permanent, let alone cumulative, can equal opportunity make sense as an identifiable end capable of being told apart from equality of results or "end-states." The slip of logic about lotteries reveals the self-destructive nature of the starting-gate "paradigm."

Suppose, first, that on the advent of market socialism an equal-opportunity placing of the contestants at the "entry point" has been accomplished by appropriate juggling with endowments, advantages, handicaps, discriminations, and head starts. The starting-gate is thus properly "patterned" and they now run the race. Anything they win is an advantage in the next race. However, since it is, by special stipulation, a "genuine lottery" excluding permanent and, *a fortiori*, cumulative advantage, either no one wins, or all win the same prize, or if one wins a bigger prize, he hastens to play double or quits and quickly loses it. Thus when they are past the finishing line, no one has an advantage, let alone a permanent and still less a cumulative one. Happily, therefore, the finishing line of the first race proves to be the right, correctly "patterned" starting-gate for the second race. The contestants again run it from an equal-opportunity position, presumably with the same result as the first race. So they can go on for any number of races. The equal-opportunity entry point, where each contestant is let loose on an even track, ensures that each finishing line is also a new entry-point of the same kind as the old. Each end-state faithfully reproduces the initial equal-opportunity position, and the just procedure duly generates a just outcome.

A POSITIVE-SUM GAME

Suppose next that the market economy is a positive-sum game. Gains and losses of a given participant do not tend to cancel out over time and, by the nature of market exchanges and the law of compound interest, the prizes of various kinds—differential earnings, profits, acquired skills, knowledge, goodwill—help win additional prizes. The contestants are again lined up at the "entry point" so as to enjoy equal opportunity. Now, however, any advantage is retained and becomes the source of further advantage. Whoever discovers marketable knowledge can accumulate capital, whoever gets hold of capital finds it easier to acquire knowledge, and so on in a cumulative process of "positive-sum" exchanges. Under such conditions, the "finishing line" of any one race will no longer serve as an equal-opportunity starting-gate for the following race. For each race, contest, or round, an equal-opportunity starting-gate has to be deliberately constructed all over again by stripping people of their acquired advantages, evening out differentials, arranging handicaps, awarding head starts, and so forth. Unhappily, and in contrast to the first scenario, this means that at each finishing line at the latest, distributive justice has to be administered to the participants before they are off again to the next round, according to "patterned" principles, to preserve a particular end-state of no net advantages at the new starting-gate. Aiming at equal opportunity *means* aiming *at an end-state* of which it happens to be a characteristic feature, that is, *where no one is ahead.*

If such is the case, however, one might as well not bother about equality of opportunity, for it turns out to be both analytically and operationally indistinguishable from equality of outcomes, and collapses into the latter.

The truth of the matter, of course, is that Ronald Dworkin's catchy, media-friendly metaphor of the "starting-gate" trips him up, and with him many of the lesser lights of the soft Left. If the world began at some starting-gate where the representative economic agent got going and ended some distance away at a finishing line where he had to stop, equal opportunity at the starting-gate might be a meaningful condition, independent of outcomes. It would be consistent with unequal outcomes at the finishing line, and would be operationally different from equality of end-states, for starting-gate and finishing line would be in two different places. But if the world continued beyond the putative finishing line, and the race went on or a new one began, the absurd zero-sum "genuine lottery" requirement would have to be satisfied for starting-gate equal opportunity to be preserved.

However, since there is no Day One and each starting-gate is the finishing line of the preceding round, while each finishing line is the starting-gate of the next one, we are dealing with an infinite regress of "races" or "lotteries." At the finish of each race, the participants are further removed from equal opportunity than at its start. People have parents who have transmitted advantages to them; they pursue careers, save money, win friends, and in turn transmit some of these advantages to their children. How often during a race, or after how many races, is equal opportunity to be restored by equalizing end-states? Can we leave it to a revolution or a lost war every thirty years or so? The sole logical market socialist answer, of course, is that to secure equal opportunity, we have to keep removing advantages all the time *as they accrue,* while confidently expecting that people will keep on accumulating them. We are invited to believe that they will not get wise to the fact that a "patterned" end-state principle is being busily applied to their income, wealth, education, or anything else that helps them win "races" or "lotteries," and makes for a competitive economy.

If we abandon the fiction of discrete rounds of finite length, and are facing a continuum of competitive economic activity instead, the distinction between equal opportunities and equal outcomes loses all meaning. Goodbye, then, to equal opportunity as an intelligible and at least metaphorically plausible policy goal; welcome to equal oppor-

tunity as an inoffensive and reassuring form of words that market socialists (and others) can use when they mean equal end-states or plain
equality. Vain as it may be, one can nonetheless express the wish that
people in general, would-be political philosophers in particular, would
learn to say what they mean.

III

By protesting too much, and promising too much, blueprints of
social organization have tended to discredit themselves and their
draughtsmen. Genuine socialism used to promise material progress,
equality, and freedom conceived as the end of alienation and subjection to blind economic mechanisms. It is of course true that it never
fulfilled any of these promises, let alone all three, and that it could
never have done so even if its earthly incarnations had not all been
dogged by bad luck in the geographical and historical "parameters"
that fell to their lot. I would nevertheless argue that had it offered a
trade-off of *more of two* desirable ends in exchange for *less of a third,*
it might have earned a degree of recognition for honesty. At least its
ultimate loss of credibility might have been less total. Striving for material progress, expecting ever greater hordes of machines served by
"work collectives" of progressively more mismotivated men to generate
abundance from misdirected resources, was a forlorn hope. Without
the fatal ambition to grow as rich and have as clever gadgets as capitalism, the socialist state might have come a little closer to redeeming
its promises of equality and liberation, for at least at first sight these
two are not mutually exclusive objectives in a simple, quasi-pastoral
economy stretched by no exacting demands.

Alternatively, the blueprint might have offered to the socialist élite
a strictly non-market, state capitalist system with an avowedly inegalitarian command economy running on quasi-slave labor; such a version
of socialism might make material progress of sorts, while also living
up to some albeit contorted ideal of liberation from the alienating relations of "production for exchange." It would of course have to shut
out, together with equality, all temptation of self-determination and
all basis for personal autonomy, and firmly refuse to seek popularity

by compromise; with these provisos, however, it could prove to be as credible an undertaking as it was unlovely. The *triple* promise of welfare, liberty, and equality, however, is too much and has so far always proved to be so, condemning all three to shameful defaults.

One could no doubt find *a priori* reasons why this could not have turned out otherwise, but in the face of the empirical evidence, that effort is hardly worth the trouble. Whether a less foolhardy or less insincere blueprint, promising a measure of equality and relative freedom from the compulsions of the market in a slack economic backwater, would have called forth more trust and tolerance, can of course only be guessed at, but the intellectual and moral fiasco would have been less humiliating.

"BUILDING SOCIALISM" VIA MARKETS?

Market socialism, for all its contrary protestations, shows every sign of setting out to march in genuine socialism's footsteps. Despite an occasional doubt, an *ad hoc* disclaimer, a shrewd, albeit momentary, awareness that one cannot always have it both ways:

> [t]he neo-liberal project of procedural justice cannot be made fully compatible with socialist ends (Plant, 74);
> the satisfaction of human needs through the equalisation of positive freedoms . . . will normally have an adverse effect on total income (Abell, 89),

the main drift of the market socialist project is that everything men of good will would like to do to society is feasible and painless; that "building socialism" does not commit us to the application of any particular and possibly objectionable tool of policy; that various market socialist objectives do not clash; that anything desirable that some existing type of modern social organization—capitalism, genuine socialism, social democracy—has accomplished, market socialism can accomplish at least as well, while managing to spare us the particular nastiness proper to each; in short, it too is undertaking *so much* that it would almost certainly fail in all.

It, too, makes a triple promise. *First,* under market socialism there would be substantial equality of material conditions among men, and it would be achieved not *against the grain* through the crude levelling of outcomes, but procedurally and *with the grain* through abolishing capitalist property rights, equalizing opportunity and positive freedom. *Second,* unlike in genuine socialism, individual choice would be given pride of place both in politics, by entrenching electoral democracy, and in economics, by conceding consumer sovereignty within a merely indicative framework of planning. *Third,* semi-automatic resource allocation by reliance on the market would ensure the material ease that can give us both the rising private consumption prized in capitalism, and the wherewithal for copious public provision of welfare.

"A DULL MUMBO-JUMBO"

Genuine socialism comes reciting a dull mumbo-jumbo, it is often hard work to decipher its propositions and proposals, and it carries the staggering handicap of having been tried in many places. For all the discredit practical failure has heaped upon it, however, it has the modest merit that each of its promises can be given a meaning, and that two out of the three may be mutually consistent. Market socialism has no such intellectual saving grace. The volume of essays that provoked the present paper is on the whole poorly and in places appallingly reasoned. It is astonishing to see on it the Clarendon Press imprint, reserved for works of original research and scholarship, and implying that it must have got past the Delegates. Yet the average market socialist tract is not much better argued, though perhaps less incongruous as to pretensions and performance. Plainly, advocates of a new kind of socialism have an implausible case to plead, and their chief fault is to imagine that it is a natural winner.

Genuine socialism shelters its reasoning within a private language where definitions and meanings adjust to the needs of the good cause. Social democracy carries little ballast by way of doctrine and is not in the habit of worrying about intellectual consistency. In the discourse of market socialism, however, favorite and pivotal concepts, "social ownership," "equality of opportunity," and "equal positive freedom" among them, prove under scrutiny to mean either nothing or something else altogether, often something that is in the same breath expressly disavowed.

The new type of "genuine-lottery" market, socialism's untried secret weapon, the guarantee of capitalist efficiency in an environment of "distributive justice" and "producer democracy," fares worst of all. It must get producers to compete in order to set roughly right prices and quantities, but must not be allowed to reward or punish them for it, for doing so is society's political prerogative. Reduced to a pretense without consequences, it is supposed to generate prices and shift resources, and "efficiently" at that, despite important kinds of exchanges being banned and others transformed into a charade for lack of real-life owners having real stakes to exchange.

Never did a political theory, in its eagerness to escape the liabilities of its predecessor, put forward so superficial an analysis and so many self-contradictions, as market socialism. Nor does any single market socialist promise, let alone two, never mind all three—an efficient market economy without capitalist ownership, equality through equal opportunity without imposing equal outcomes, and free choice without freedom of contract—look capable of being fulfilled, each being an open contradiction in terms, much like hot snow, wanton virgin, fat skeleton, round square.

Part Five

Freedom

15

Right, Wrong, and Economics

The preacher, invoking the love of God or the authority of religion, expounds moral precepts that help tell right from wrong. It is these signposts of morality that he exhorts us to follow whenever "self-interest" would point the other way. (Our preacher is all of one piece; he is not bothered by the ambiguities of the word "self-interest," and nor, as we shall see presently, is the economist when he steps up to the pulpit.) In tune with his fashionably open-minded flock, the preacher may dispense with God and authority altogether, and draw principles for identifying right and wrong from other sources: from "nature" with Aristotle, *a priori* with Kant, or in the manner of G. E. Moore, as matters knowable to our intuition. Whichever route he takes, his congregation can have no doubt about the object of the sermon. It is to make their conduct in life other, and worthier, than it would otherwise be.

To hear George Stigler tell it in his eponymous lectures on economics and ethics, *The Economist As Preacher*[1] has a very different object. He gets his ethical system "wherever [he] can find [it],"[2] namely in people's actual conduct. In fact, "he needs no ethical system to criticize error,"[3] which is what people commit when they pursue their ends inefficiently. If he adopts one that clashes with established behavioral

This paper was delivered at a Liberty Fund Colloquium on the work of George Stigler in Chicago in May 1995 and subsequently published in *Journal des Economistes et des Etudes Humaines*, 6, no. 4 (December 1995): 669–79; reprinted here with permission.

1. Stigler 1982.
2. Ibid., p. 19.
3. Ibid., p. 8.

norms, he will readily abandon it—a practice that "strongly argues for the acceptance of the community's values with whatever inconsistencies they contain."[4] Why the fact that something is usually done (i.e., that a minority ethical belief is usually abandoned) counts as a strong argument that some other thing *ought* usually to be done (i.e., that the majority belief should readily be accepted), is left unexplained, as if it went without saying.

The important thing the economist seeks above all to preach is that, whether an ethical system is internally consistent or not, people should pursue the ends incorporated in it consistently, applying their means to their ends efficiently, and not make silly mistakes. Individuals probably do not make many really silly ones in this sense, i.e., their choices are instrumentally rational. Stigler concedes that this guess of his is hard to test "because there is no accepted body of ethical beliefs"[5] against which to test it—a statement in surprising contradiction with his confident belief in the universality of the wealth-maximizing ethic. Collectivities, unlike individuals, do seem to make mistakes, choosing as they do policies that are inconsistent with their own stated purpose. In reality, the stated purpose is usually an alibi hiding the real one, and the policy is not as silly as it looks, for it serves some ulterior motive quite well.[6] Here, the Stigler who has fathomed the dark depths of the regulation of industry and commerce is advising Stigler on ethics. Both Stiglers seem to me seriously to underrate the force of sheer, obtuse, slogan-ridden stupidity in shaping the course of public affairs.

Admittedly, the economist's sermon is about efficiency *and* equity, too, but Stigler is largely satisfied that if efficiency is taken care of, eq-

4. Stigler 1982, p. 20. True to his own advice, Stigler is not shy of the odd inconsistency in his own ethics. In an essay castigating our tendency to look for our well-being to a meddlesome state, he claims that "our society is not dedicated to the principle that the good society consists of large herds of well-cared-for people." (Stigler 1961, 9). His own analysis, as far as I can see, shows what is obvious to the naked eye anyway, to wit that it is precisely this principle our society is dedicated to, and the opposite principle he praises, namely "the greatest possible individual responsibility and the freedom to meet it" (ibid.), clashes with the community's values and behavior. He is nevertheless not ready to change his ethical beliefs accordingly. For this, we owe him a full measure of gratitude.

5. Stigler 1982, 36.

6. Stigler 1982, 10.

uity will take care of itself, at least in the sense that "the distributional effects of the change in wealth . . . will be swamped by the change in aggregate wealth" and a significant increase in wealth will, as a general rule, also be a Pareto-improvement.[7] There is, reasonably enough, no comfort here for the pervasive belief, held by a small part of the economics profession and the vast majority of the rest of humanity, that "the rich get richer and the poor get poorer." We need have no qualms, on grounds of equity, about the wealth-maximizing ethic, unless we were to equate equity with equality—and there is no good reason for doing this, though there is always the bad one that many people do do it.

Granted that neither individuals nor groups need an inordinate amount of help from the pulpit to pursue their ends efficiently and equitably, there is still something very, very important the preacher can do for them. Stigler passes the opportunity by, though its potential is obvious once it is pointed out, as James Buchanan[8] has recently, and to my knowledge for the first time ever, done so. It is to preach an ethic which, if adopted by some people, generates positive externalities for all. In particular, the ethic of work and saving, as opposed to leisure and consumption, produces unrequited, windfall benefits for those who do not practice it. Hence, if they are rational maximizers, they should pay the preacher to preach it.

How does the economist's ethics come to be identified with efficiency, or the consistency of means with ends?—to such strong effect that the economist as preacher need only preach against the making of silly mistakes, of the sort that people as individuals are not very prone to make anyway? A necessary, though not sufficient, move is the separation of morality from ethics. If morality is understood as a set of deontological rules constraining our legitimate choices, hence constraining the ends we may choose to pursue, it must be held in limbo, outside ethical theory, for only so can ethics be confined to the pure means-ends argument of instrumental rationality, where practical reason is, in proper Humean fashion, the servant of "passions," of given ends about which *non est disputandum.* For the economist as preacher,

7. Stigler 1978/1984, 141.
8. Buchanan 1994.

as I propose to argue, there is only a black hole where others find non-consequentialist morals. This is a straightforward philosophical maneuver; it has significant consequences I intend to explore presently. Less straightforward, to my mind, is the almost surreptitious way in which the economist's ethic puts only prudential motives in the empty box of "given ends."

In the time it takes to get from *The Theory of Moral Sentiments* to the *Wealth of Nations,* the perfectly general and indefinitely diverse class of "given ends" gets amalgamated into a single synthetic one, "utility" or its visible *alter ego,* wealth. The economist used to take it[9] that all competing ends are commensurate. All their possible combinations are accordingly comparable, too, and each can be assigned a single number which causes it to be ranked either above, or below, or possibly at the same place as, other numbered combinations, giving rise to a single preference ordering. The hierarchical ordering of ends that have many properties (i.e., many "dimensions"), in terms of a single number (i.e., according to a single "dimension"), makes everything easy. It removes the disability that handicaps the scrupulous theorist who is conscious of the multiplicity of possible ends. For no law of nature decrees that rational men will usually accept tradeoffs of any of their ends against any other, i.e., that for everybody who economically fits means to ends, everything has a price. What has and what has not, and for whom, is an empirical question that cannot be prejudged. Failing positive assurance on this point, it is impossible to rank alternatives that neither dominate nor are dominated by one another, i.e., alternatives that offer more along one of their dimensions but less along another. (Where this non-domination condition wreaks havoc with traditional economic reasoning is, of course, in evaluating collective choices by trying to aggregate, in a single and complete ranking standing for the Common Good, the preference-

9. At any rate, he used to take it before being persuaded, notably by Little's *Critique* (Little 1950, 1973, 30) that a handful of axioms of choice suffice to explain behavior in the face of assured alternatives, and the proposition that "people can and do value all possible collections of goods in terms of some common measure" is not saying anything more, if it is saying anything at all. The same lesson was taught with regard to all alternatives, including uncertain or "risky" ones, by Neumann and Morgenstern, Savage, Harsanyi, and others.

rankings of the individuals composing the collectivity, and balancing the gainers' gains against the losers' losses. Welfare statements about Pareto-noncomparable states of affairs come to be seen as arbitrary, about Pareto-comparable ones as trivial—a thoroughly salutary result if it leads to the making of fewer welfare statements.)

The more economics grew into a general theory of choice—rather than just of choices where both means and ends lend themselves to "the measuring rod of money"—the less tenable it seemed to confine it to studying the pursuit of well-being, albeit of the fairly broad kind that includes regard for both the self and others, a measure of "proximity-altruism." Man after all can, and sometimes manifestly does, act under motives that are not conducive to anyone's well-being; and it is surely not irrational to pursue ends that are not prudential. Yet the more general and imprecise the content of the single, synthetic maximand that serves as the standard by which conduct passes for rational, the more tautological becomes the theory.[10] Subject only to consistency conditions (whose violation is often hard to detect), every deliberate choice is a rational choice and for that matter every non-deliberate one, too, for it deliberately avoids the cost of deliberation.[11]

Between the devil of a plurality of ends which may not be commensurate and permit only partial preference orderings, and the deep sea of a tautological "utility" that is meant to provide a synthetic common measure of the totality of motives that enter into choices, enabling the complete ordering of all alternatives along a common numerical scale, and is maximized by the definition of rational choice, it is perhaps understandable that in everyday discourse the economist keeps relapsing into the traditional usage where, if the "content" or the *causa causans* of utility is defined, it shows up as material wherewithal, wealth, sometimes equipped with such bells and whistles as the precautions the wise man takes to preserve (and enhance) his capacity to enjoy it, to help deal with his own myopia and weakness of will, to gain and hold the esteem of his fellows, to keep the social edifice

10. Stigler 1982, 36.

11. If radical proponents of "bounded rationality" and "transactions cost economics" take this for a malicious caricature of their position, they will have correctly divined my intent.

where he dwells in good repair, and so on. Thus embellished, the ethic of "wealth-maximization" is but a short step removed from prudential reason. It is, if I may be repetitive, far removed from morality if morality is a constraint on prudential reason, imposed by duties to do non-consequential, intrinsic right and to avoid intrinsic wrong. It is, of course, not removed at all from morality if the latter is derived, in a lamentably circular fashion, from the requirements of prudential conduct itself.

Stigler seems to delight in showing engagingly, wittily, with inexhaustible erudition and no-nonsense bluntness, that the most conventional of utilitarian positions is really all we have by way of universal ethics. The empirically discoverable utilitarian ethic is good enough as a normative code. No doubt deservedly, he makes a pitiful figure of fun of the Preacher as Economist ("[i]t cannot be denied that the economist's economic theory is better than everyone else's economic theory";[12] "flagrant inconsistency, usually stemming from that great source of inconsistency in intelligent men, a warm heart"[13]). He is all a civilized, rather agnostic yet conservative congregation could ask for: except around the rim of the black hole, he is thoroughly reassuring. His reassurance comes in two parts.

In the first place, he is persuaded that if people held, or at least professed, ethical principles that conflicted with their "self-interest" (as he chooses to call, for example, the appropriation of small sums of money manifestly destined for other people), self-interest would win "much of the time, most of the time."[14] Happily, however, people do not hold ethical beliefs that would often cause such conflicts.

For, in the second place, utility-maximization, manifesting itself as wealth-maximization, is the personal ethic most people adhere to. It is hardly surprising, then, that ethics and "self-interest" seldom clash.

Though he does not say so, by omission he suggests that pride, arrogance, charity, shame, envy, snobbism, a sense of justice, spite, emulation, posturing, class hatred, and the many other plausible motives

12. Stigler 1982, 130.
13. Ibid., 132.
14. Ibid., 25–26.

for human conduct that do not square with and may positively ob-
struct wealth-maximization, are negligible. Whether excluding them
from the maximand is a fair simplification is, of course, an empirical
question. Stigler is confident that "systematic and comprehensive testing"[15] would prove it correct. This reader begs to express mild doubt
both about the capacity of such testing to decide the question, and
about the answer it would furnish if it were able to decide it.

The fit between people's putative ethical code and wealth or income
maximization is, as we would expect from their definition, so close that
not only is conflict between them predictably rare, but it becomes questionable whether the two have any independent existence. Honesty
is the classic, and somewhat embarrassing, case in point. If we knew
that people are honest because they simply think it right that they
should, or because they owe it to their fondly embraced self-image, we
could rejoice at the sight of their disinterested virtue being unexpect-
edly rewarded by material success in the marketplace. But we do not
know why they are honest. What we do know, instead, is that honesty
is the best policy and it pays in the long run. Hence utility-maximizers
would have to be honest anyway, for prudential reasons. Is it, then,
that their moral principles correspond, by pure happenstance, to what
material success requires, or is it that they have none? Stigler, I suspect, would consider the question somewhat puerile, hardly worthy
and hardly capable of a response. His passing reference to it[16] leaves
the problem exactly where he found it.

And now to the rim of the black hole. A man takes a short cut
through the park every night on his way home, and one night in five
on the average, he is robbed of his trousers. This, for Stigler, is *indistinguishable*[17] from a voluntary transaction in which the same man
pays a toll of one-fifth of a pair of trousers for access to the short cut,
and which (assuming the toll-taker owns the short cut, an assumption Stigler does not make) is "honorable dealing" (ibid.). Do we then
gather that since trousers-robbing, where the victim has knowingly ex-

15. Ibid., 25.
16. Stigler 1982, 25.
17. Stigler 1982, 24.

posed himself to a statistically established risk of being debagged, is indistinguishable from a voluntary transaction, it *is* a voluntary transaction? If two phenomena are indistinguishable, they are the same phenomenon; logical positivists with the record of a George Stigler cannot mean anything less.

Going further than this is speculation rather than exegesis, but it is tempting to add that if a toll of one-fifth of a pair of trousers is demanded at the short cut, and our man takes the short cut fully prepared to pay it, the transaction is "honorable dealing," and never mind whether the toll-taker has title to the short cut, leases it from the owner, or is just squatting on it without the owner's consent. By the argument that buying passage through the short cut at the cost of one-fifth of a pair of trousers is a utility-enhancing voluntary transaction, it is presumably beside the point whether the robber was entitled to rob, or the toll-taker to take tolls.

A minor and a major objection arise, and the major one seems to me decisive.

Take the minor one first. Predictably losing one's trousers, and keeping them but paying a toll in lieu, are unlikely to be indistinguishable. If the trouser-robber, instead of lurking in the bushes, could choose to sit at a gate and collect a regular toll instead, he may well not charge a toll of one-fifth of a pair of trousers. If he thought the elasticity of demand for the short cut was greater than unity, he would expect to do better to charge less. If, in addition, the continuing existence of the trouser-robbing business looked more precarious than the toll-taking business, there could well be good reasons to "milk" the former while the going was good, and build the latter by a tariff even lower than that indicated by the short-run elasticity of demand. By extension of the same argument, the toll-keeper who had title or a secure lease could be expected to charge less than the squatter. The idea that an economist of Stigler's acuity and subtlety did not see this is too preposterous to entertain. If he chose to ignore the law-and-economics type effects that would make trouser-robbing distinguishable from toll-taking, it must have been in order not to blunt the point he thought he was making and was trying to drive home: that if both enhance utility to the same extent, the distinction between robbery and "honorable dealing" is metaphysical obfuscation.

However, Stigler has incompletely specified the institutional frame-work of his fable. This is the major objection to his thesis. If a vital missing piece is put in its proper place, it is immediately clear that the distinction between his two transactions, far from being metaphysical, is plain to the most austere logical positivist, and to you and me too; and this, to my mind, decides the case. Who, in this fable, is entitled to what? If the short cut is owned by nobody, or if title to it is limited by a general right-of-way, our man has the liberty to pass through it un-hindered, just as he has the liberty to perform any other action that is within his feasible set (the economist's "budget constraint") and is not preempted by another's duly acquired prior right. Hindering him is a violation of his liberty and if the hindrance is more than trivial, it is a tort. Forcibly taking off his trousers is robbery, charging him a toll is extortion. By a universal convention that varies but little across cul-tures and over the ages, neither is recognized as "honorable dealing," and they are perfectly distinguishable, too, from one another. If, on the other hand, the short cut is owned by someone and is not subject to an easement, and our man passes through it, he is not exercising a liberty; he is violating the owner's right by trespassing.

Suppose, next, that the owner allows passage against payment of a toll, and our man, to save the toll, takes a different, perhaps less con-venient short cut. At this short cut, robbers lurk and he runs a known (and small) risk of losing his trousers. For argument's sake, take it that the expected utility of passing by the robber-infested short cut, how-ever, is still greater than of the safe passage through the toll gate. By voluntarily letting himself be involuntarily undressed, our man has made a utility-maximizing transaction which has all "the ethical attrac-tiveness of voluntary exchange."[18]

The plain man, sitting in the congregation the economist is preach-ing to, who felt so comfortable and reassured by the beginnings of the sermon, is by now thoroughly bewildered. For him, the transaction in-volves coercion and looks, ethically and otherwise, quite unattractive.

Stigler, in full flight under the ample power of his logic, will have none of this. He insists that punishing illicit parking by a fine of $6 — and charging $6 — for parking space are either both coercive, or neither

18. Stigler 1982, 22.

is: making an action subject to a sanction coerces no more and no less than a relative price change that makes the action more expensive.[19] Coercion is admittedly a difficult concept, and some attempted definitions of it, including Hayek's (with which Stigler takes issue in the essay cited), are not very successful. However, for Stigler, no definition of it, nor of freedom, *can* be successful, because the very concept presupposes some moral code, and he thinks any such code is moot:

> Is not the coercion of one person by another immoral? This is a path I shall not follow, simply because I deny the existence of a widely accepted, coherent code in which noncoercion is an irresistible corollary. The assertion of moral values, in the absence of such a code, is either a disguised expression of personal preferences or a refusal to continue the analysis of a problem.[20]

It is baffling why he refuses to take any notice of the very moral code whose alleged lack is turned into an empirical justifier of narrow, minimalist ethics; a code which, except for some exotic nooks and crannies of the known world, its essentials universally accepted, not particularly incoherent, a living refutation of moral relativism, and in which noncoercion is indubitably a corollary. The code is not a comprehensive moral law directing all possible human action. It deals only with actions affecting the person and property of others, and not all of those at that. It has fuzzy edges that blur the status of acts *versus* omissions, the distinction between negative externalities and harms properly speaking, questions of intent, negligence, and accident, and the respective places of restitution and retribution. On these and other, even finer points, acceptance is not uniform cross-culturally and even within the same culture.

For all that, however, the code is remarkable in two respects. First, while it is largely silent on what ought to be done, it is probably as full and clear a system of stipulations of what must *not* be done as it is possible for mankind to agree on and by and large to respect. Second, while it is no doubt possible to impute to every one of its rules a consequentialist (particularly a rule-utilitarian) explanation and to

19. Stigler 1978/1984, 139.
20. *Op. cit.,* 141.

make a good case that it was adopted for a (functional) reason, men for many centuries have recognized and applied the rules without seeking such explanations. They do not often ask themselves whether compliance with a particular rule has good consequences in a given case or in general.[21] The person who needs convincing that killing or maiming another is wrong because the victim deserves to live, and needs the use of his limbs, or *because* if killing and maiming were not deemed categorically wrong, anyone might turn around and kill or maim him, is a rare bird most of us would regard with some mistrust if not distaste. The person who thinks stealing is wrong *because* secure property is an instrument of efficient resource allocation, and is also needed for social stability, is less rare but no more admirable. For the ordinary member of Stigler's congregation (and perhaps unbeknown to him) killing, maiming, stealing, damaging property, and defaulting on agreed reciprocal commitments, are wrong without having to be wrong torts in the original meaning[22] of the word, before a large part of torts was swallowed up by the criminal statute and another large part in the law of property and contract.

The moral code of torts functions through an immensely old, immensely widespread and influential convention, by which most people most of the time coordinate their conduct upon tort rules serving as norms. The convention needs to be supported by various second-order or satellite conventions to sanction transgressions of the various norms. (It used to be a convention that when someone cried "stop thief" all had to run and catch the thief.) Progressively, states took over the enforcement function, and most of the satellite conventions (ostracism, mutual help, vigilante action, local and voluntary adjudication) fell into desuetude. The primary convention, however, manifestly remains implanted in people's moral consciousness, and to assert the contrary, as I read Stigler to do in the passage above, is hard to comprehend. The common understanding of tort rules that people have, enables them to tell, except for the borderline cases that seem inseparable from any

21. Scanlon 1982, 108–9.

22. The original meaning is very broad. It includes being in error, being (morally or legally) in the wrong, or wrongfully inflicting harm. It is derived from the Latin *torquere,* i.e., to wring, to twist; arm-twisting is direct enough.

rule, not only what is wrong and must not be done, but by elimina-tion also what morally is licit—without having to be above reproach, let alone positively commendable. One implication of this common understanding of what is licit is that everybody has a fairly clear idea which part of his own and other people's sets of feasible choices are admissible subsets: this is how everyone has some moral grasp of the liberties of each, that is their *feasible* actions that are *not torts,* and can either be *freely chosen,* or are *obligations* to be carried out as the conse-quence of the rights granted to *others* in voluntary *contracts.*

Once again, it need not be claimed that the tort convention is a com-plete, all-embracing moral guide to all that ought and ought not to be done in all circumstances. Stigler may well be right that no such uni-versal code is (or could be) agreed. But he is not looking for *that* kind of code, and it is not of that kind of code that he denies the existence: he is merely looking, oddly enough in vain, for one that has "noncoercion as its irresistible corollary."

In making his case by pointing to the sameness of a $6 parking fee and a $6 parking fine, both diminishing wealth and neither impinging more, or less, on liberty than the other, Stigler has, probably unwit-tingly, defined coercion right out of his example. This is so because most of his congregation, while firmly holding on to the convention against torts, would consider that neither the fine nor the fee are co-ercive, since the city ordinances under which presumably both were imposed were "legal," and from the moral point of view not tortious.

Let us open up the example, to admit tort. Let there be only two alternatives if you want to park. One is to ask me to let you use my re-served parking space. The other is that you park in the road along my garden wall. In the former case, I let you park for a fee of $6. In the latter case, I let you know that as soon as your back is turned, I will tow your car away, or slash a tire or two, unless you pay me a fine of $6. I do not own the road outside my garden wall and nor does anyone else. You are free to park there. I have destroyed this option of yours by (credibly) attaching to it the threat of tortious acts (towing your car away, slashing the tire), *coercing* you to take the second-best option of paying for what ought to have been a *liberty.* In the case of the former alternative, however, you never had a corresponding first-best option, a liberty to park in the space reserved for my car. Paying me $6 (or, in dire need, $60) for its use was your first-best option. Though each transaction was avoidable (one was a close substitute of the other), was entered into voluntarily, and both had the same effect on your wealth, they did not have the same effect on your liberty; and my interference with your liberty to park in the road passes for coercion by virtue of its being "an irresistible corollary" of the moral norms incorporated in the convention against torts.

It is, I trust, not a sure sign of hopeless obtuseness to be at a loss why Stigler denies all this. Must he insist that the alleged effects on our liberty *are* effects on our wealth, neither more nor less, since both describe the same diminution by $6 of our remaining options, if they describe anything,[23] and are indistinguishable from one another? He votes, with dogged conviction, for the much disputed merger of the concept of "liberty" with the concept of the "power to do." This is not the place to go into the whys and wherefores of their sadly counter-productive merger. In fact, no place is the place; least said about it, soonest it might be mended. Clearly, however, there is something missing in Stigler's ethics, or in what he seems to be taking for the ethics of the economist. It is due to the missing piece that he is determined to get by without distinguishing between a pair of ideas for which ordinary language has never hesitated to employ two different words, "right" and "wrong." It is the missing piece that leads this superb economist to let his logic confound us and to argue that another pair of concepts for which ordinary language always uses two different words, "wealth" and "liberty," are really the same.

23. Stigler 1978/1984.

16

The Paretian Liberal, His Liberties and His Contracts

WITH HARTMUT KLIEMT

1. Introduction

The debate about the putative impossibility of a Paretian liberal has been going on since 1970. Looking back, the impression is one of a mixture of clear formal argument and often confused interpretations. Confusion arose, in particular, from a failure to distinguish conceptionally between the relevantly different phenomena of "liberties" and "rights." As we hope to show subsequently, the alleged paradoxes of liberalism lose their paradoxical character if one realizes that liberties differ from rights in the following way: We are at *liberty* to do something if we are under no constraint or obligation[1] to act otherwise, we

By Anthony de Jasay and Hartmut Kliemt. Reprinted with permission from *Analyse und Kritik,* 18 (1996): 126–47.

The authors owe a particular debt to James M. Buchanan for his detailed comments and constructive criticism. One of the authors has also benefited from discussing some of the issues raised here with Amartya Sen. Friedrich Breyer, who does not agree with the thrust of the paper, nevertheless sent us some useful suggestions for "corrections of errors." The usual disclaimers apply with added force.

1. We use "obligation" as the negative corollary of another's right. It is owed to the right-holder. A "duty" is not necessarily owed to anyone; however, if I owe a duty to someone, I do not do so as a matter of his right. He may, of course, have a non-enforceable moral claim to it. It seems best to preserve a distinction between the consequences of legal claims (and call them obligations) and the commands of morals (and call them duties). It makes good sense to say it is your

have a *right* only insofar as others have certain obligations towards us to act in ways demanded by us.

If person *A* has the liberty to decide whether to wear a green or a red dress and if person *B* has the same liberty to choose which dress suits her, *B*, neither of the two has a right to demand that a certain dress be worn by the other. Correspondingly, failing specific evidence to the contrary, neither of the two has any obligation to wear either kind of dress, nor is either of the two under an obligation to choose one color rather than another, even if their choices are not agreeable to each other. Each is at liberty to choose how to act. Individuals may, however, be willing to trade their respective liberties of choosing the color of their own dresses and thus to create rights and obligations.

Assume that a mutually agreeable trade confers on one person the right to choose the other person's color of dress, green or red. As a result of contracting, the latter is under an obligation to wear a dress of the color specified by the former, i.e., the right's holder. Assume also that the holder of the right has retained her liberty to choose the color of her own dress. Then, after the first individual has traded away her liberty, the second individual as holder of the right will be entitled to choose a *state of affairs* or to make a *social* choice. She may choose the color *both* of her own dress *and* that of the other. Therefore she has full control over which state of a set of social states—each defined by a combination of the colors of the two ladies' dresses—will be chosen.

It is impossible, though, that two individuals should have full control over the same pair of states of affairs. If person *A* has the right to choose one from a pair of social states, then person *B* cannot have a right to choose with respect to the same pair. Both cannot simultaneously have a *right* to decide which *combination* of dress colors of two individuals will form the state of the world. Nor could one have the *right* to choose either of two social states which both specify the colors of both dresses so long as the other still retains the *liberty* of choosing her dress.

Subsequently we shall illustrate our claim that the alleged paradox of liberalism loses its bite if one makes the distinction between how

---

duty to fulfil your obligation. "You have an obligation to do your duty," if it means anything, means something altogether different.

liberties and rights function. In a first step we shall present that distinction in a somewhat more formal manner (2). If the alleged liberal paradox should rest on such an obvious confusion as we claim, it must be explained how it could emerge and be taken seriously at all. After proposing our account of that matter (3) we try to present a more traditional and, as we feel, more adequate liberal view of the role of liberties, rights, and Paretian values (4). Some concluding remarks follow (5).

2. The Non-Paradoxical Paradox of Liberalism

2.1. FEASIBLE, PRE-EMPTED, AND ADMISSIBLE CHOICES

We take all social states rendered possible by nature as the given *feasible set*. A subset of the feasible set (e.g., reading lewd books, or buying them tax-free) cannot be chosen because of collective prohibitions ("do not read lewd books") or collective commands ("pay a pornography tax"). This then is the *pre-empted subset*. Its complement is the *admissible subset*, which includes everything that is feasible and not prohibited. (For our purposes, we may ignore the possibility of choosing alternatives in violation of prohibitions and commands.)

Prohibitions and commands are by their general nature collective choices (made *for* a collectivity either *by* a dictator or *by* a sub-collectivity or even the whole collectivity), leaving the choice between residual alternatives, if there are any left, to individuals. Evidently, there may be no residual. Short of this, the collectivity may choose not to choose, and to restrict its own domain of choice by a substantive meta-rule (constitutional provision), which specifies what is put into the public domain of collective or political decision-making and what shall be decided non-politically by individuals in their several capacities. (A procedural constitutional rule, as distinct from a substantive one, instead of delineating private and public domain lays down *how* a collective choice from a domain of alternatives is to be reached—e.g., by aggregating votes.)

The preceding way of dividing the feasible set into public and private treats collective choices as basic. Therefore, on the most fundamental level of decision-making, individual rights and liberties cannot impose any constraints on the collective choice of the proper realm of collective as opposed to private decision-making. We need a kind of Archimedean point preceding any collective decision if on that level constraints on collective choice are assumed to exist. Without some initial exogenous division between pre-empted and admissible, there may be no liberties to start with.

One such potential determinant, exogenous to the present, is history, which has bequeathed social convention to the present. Convention rules out certain alternatives for being *torts,* in the broad and ancient sense of the word, that is offenses against person and property subject to retribution and restitution. The concept is not very sharp-edged but it captures quite well our common intuitions about respecting other individuals as persons who are entitled to make certain choices. — In any event, we must start from somewhere. We will therefore begin our discussion under the assumption that the admissible sub-set, i.e., the initial area of liberties, is exogenously determined.

2.2. LIBERTIES, RIGHTS, AND OBLIGATIONS

Whether or not we accept that there can be any individual liberties and rights preceding any form of collective choice, the admissible sub-set of an individual's feasible choices consists of liberties, rights, and obligations towards other individuals. The individual exercises a liberty when performing an admissible act A that does not violate another's right. He exercises a right R when his doing so obliges another to perform an act bringing about a "state" r corresponding to R. Finally, he fulfills an obligation when performing an act bringing about r to which another is exercising a right R (for the determination of rights, cf. infra.).

A driver is free (has the liberty) to drive his motor car on the road in a manner that causes no tort or a high risk thereof to other users of the road. Every other driver has the same liberty, notwithstanding that the simultaneous use of their liberties by everyone would bring traffic on the road to a standstill. This is to say that the exercise of liberties may be incompatible. The exercise of one of a pair of incompatible liberties is not a violation of the other. It is an adverse externality. A liberty is only violated by a tort, an inadmissible act.

More specifically, consider again the example of two women each of whom is at liberty to choose the color of her dress. Each of the two, who for convenience are christened 1 and 2, may decide to wear a green, g_i, or a red, r_i, $i = 1, 2$, dress respectively. We take it that for both of the women each of the two decisions is admissible and neither of the women has a right limiting or controlling the choice of the other. Given these premises the ensuing interaction may be represented by the following game form:

2

		r_2	g_2
	r_1	r_1, r_2	r_1, g_2
1			
	g_1	g_1, r_2	g_1, r_2

All of the results represented in this game form are admissible. They emerge as individuals exercise their liberties. Exercising a liberty is equivalent to the choice of a row, in the case of player 1, or a column, in the case of player 2. Individuals' liberties are to be identified with their strategy sets (*rows or columns*) in the game form rather than with the social states (*cells*) brought about by the *joint* exercise of their liberties.[2]

If only liberties to choose the color of one's dress—but no rights with respect to another wearing one color or the other—exist, each individual is free to choose among the alternatives over which she has a liberty. The other individual has no legitimate complaint as far as this is concerned. Neither has either of the individuals, using her respective liberties—normatively speaking—any claim over the choices of the other. Each can choose her own actions within the realm of her liberties. Neither can choose a social state. Whatever comes out of their separate choices will be the social outcome.

---

2. We feel that Sugden 1985; 1993; 1994, and Gaertner, Pattanaik, and Suzumura 1992 are basically right when suggesting that game forms are the appropriate tool for analyzing the alleged liberal paradox. However, contrary to their views we think that the distinction between rows/columns and cells should be reflected in a terminological distinction between liberties and rights. Consequently, unlike the precedingly mentioned authors, we identify individuals' strategy sets with liberties rather than with rights. This difference may seem merely terminological but in view of the fundamentally different roles of liberties and rights it is of some systematic importance, too, to make this distinction.

On the other hand, imagine that lady 2 has given up her liberty to choose the color of her dress. She has accepted the obligation to comply with lady 1's wishes as far as the color of her (2's) dress is concerned. Lady 1 has acquired the *right* to choose a *social state* (from a *set of social states*). She is entitled to choose among whole states of affairs since she is at liberty to choose her own dress *and* has the right to impose the color of 2's dress. Contrary to this case, individuals, in exercising merely their *liberties,* can *never* bring about a collective result single-handedly.[3] Their *liberties allow for the simultaneous exclusion of sets of results* from the collective choice set but never for the choice or exclusion of a *single* alternative from a set of alternatives. Thus, minimal liberalism in Sen's sense—that is, the capacity to choose *one state of at least one pair of social states*—is *not* implied by "game form liberalism" based on the assignment of liberties rather than rights. Therefore, contrary to Sen's claims, his arguments do not apply to what might be called liberal individualism.

Essentially the same point has been made by James M. Buchanan twenty years ago (printed for the first time in this issue). Since it was strongly criticized in Buchanan's original presentation it may be helpful to look at it in some more formal detail in the light of our basic conceptual distinction between liberties and rights.

2.3. SOCIAL CHOICES BY EXCLUSION

In the above game form, so long as no rights exist, there is neither an individual choice nor a social choice of a cell. There is simply *no* choice of a cell. On the other hand, each person, in exercising her liberties, insures that the social state finally emergent must fall within the subset defined by her choice. Exercising their liberties individuals end up in a cell. But the cell is not chosen by any individual.

The liberties of individual 1 may be represented by the set of *sets* $D_1 = \{\{(r_1,r_2), (r_1,g_2)\}, \{(g_1,r_2), (g_1,g_2)\}\}$ while the liberties of individual 2 may be represented by the set of *sets* $D_2 = \{\{(r_1,r_2), (g_1,r_2)\}, \{(r_1,g_2),$

---

3. As shall become clear below there can be at most one individual that could single-handedly choose among social states. If all other choices are made already, one individual can choose between social states by exercising his liberties.

$(g_1,g_2)\}\}$. As can be checked immediately $\forall x \in D_1, \forall y \in D_2 : x \cap y \neq \emptyset$. Thus individuals 1 and 2 can simultaneously exercise their liberties in any way they like without precluding the emergence of a well-defined collective result in a situation characterized by the above game form.

However, if we postulate rights rather than liberties there is no guarantee that within the realm of the normatively admissible a well-defined collective result exists. This may be illustrated by Alan Gibbard's well-known example of Zubeida and Rehana (1974, also quoted in Sen 1976/1982a, 312–13) who are going to choose the color of their dresses. Each of the ladies can very well have the liberty to choose green or red. However, if Zubeida had the *right* both to choose between red and green, and to wear the same color as Rehana, Rehana would have an *obligation* to choose red when Zubeida chose red (and green when the latter chose green). Rehana could not have the liberty to choose her own color. This would be pre-empted by Zubeida's right. One's right would negate that of the other and, for that matter, the liberty of the other. Both women's "rights" could not simultaneously stand. No two contradictory *rights* can both stand.

Referring to the preceding game form this situation can again be illustrated in a very simple way. Recall that the liberties in that situation were

$D_1 = \{\{(r_1,r_2)\}, \{(r_1,g_2)\}, \{(g_1,r_2)\}, \{(g_1,g_2)\}\}$ and
$D_2 = \{\{(r_1,r_2), (g_1,r_2), (r_1,g_2), (g_1,g_2)\}\}$ with
$\forall x \in D_1, \forall y \in D_2 : x \cap y = x,$
that is lady 2 has neither a liberty nor a right to choose.

Now, the latter construction may seem unfair to Gibbard. He does not assume the existence of a decision right over *all* pairs of alternatives for one individual. It may seem therefore that such a dictatorial competence over all alternatives is over-extending Gibbard's use of the notion of a right. However, even under the most charitable interpretation of the approach a variant of the preceding argument would still apply.

Consider the following game tree in which player 2 is granted the "right" to decide between *pairs of states of affairs* contingent on the choice of the other. With this "contingent right" player 2 cannot require player 1 to choose in a specific way. As a second mover she can merely decide which of the social states will emerge *after* the first mover 1 has chosen her dress.

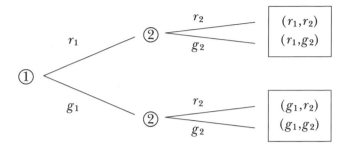

The corresponding decision "rights" then are

$$D_1 = \{\{(r_1,r_2), (r_1,g_2)\}, \{(g_1,r_2), (g_1,g_2)\}\}$$
$$D_2 = \{((r_1,r_2), (r_1, g_2)), ((g_1,r_2), (g_1,g_2))\}.$$

That is, the first can choose among sets while the second, contingent on the set chosen by the first, can choose among states of affairs. The decision rights do not let *both* choose *among states of affairs*. That is, they are *not*

$$D_1 = \{((r_1,r_2), (g_1,r_2)), ((r_1,g_2), (g_1,g_2))\}$$
$$D_2 = \{((r_1,r_2), (r_1,g_2)), ((g_1,r_2), (g_1,g_2))\}.$$

Thus, if "contingent rights" are construed appropriately not both individuals can hold "rights" such that an empty choice set emerges. The basic claim of those who think that there is a paradox of liberalism vanishes, since this claim amounts to nothing but the thesis that certain sets of axioms imply that an empty choice set emerges for some profile(s) of individual preferences.[4]—It is obvious that the same argument holds good for the symmetric case in which 2 is the first mover.

Moreover, if the game form of the corresponding—"simultaneous move"—imperfect information game is presented in its extensive vari-

---

4. With respect to the issue of Pareto optimality, Thompson and Faith 1981 prove that changing the information conditions such that a hierarchy of decision rights leading to what they call "truly perfect information" emerges, implies Pareto efficiency in any game.

ant basically the same argument still applies. Informationally, both moves take place simultaneously. Since none of the players can have any knowledge of what the other chose, none can intentionally choose a social state. Each can make her own choice of an action but then must "wait" for the result that is going to *emerge*.

Of course, in a non-informational sense there may be a time sequence between the players' moves. The second mover in time, though being ignorant of the choices of the first mover in time, may know that as a matter of fact by making her choice of a class she actually chooses between two states. But even if we would assume that this kind of a choice fully captures what we mean by a "choice of social states" it is clear that the argument that at most one player can be in a position to decide single-handedly between some *pair of states* of affairs still applies. For, the first mover is in the same position as before. Given the assumption about the time sequence in the "imperfect information tree" she must make her choice before the other player chooses and thus she can choose only between classes of states of affairs. For her this is not merely a matter of knowledge. From the point of view of the *first mover* the state of affairs will emerge only after the second mover has made her choices.[5]

In the case of the two girls choosing their dresses, Rehana can be normatively entitled to choose between two states of dressing only if she is entitled to require that Zubeida dresses the way Rehana chooses and Zubeida is obliged to comply. Thus, obviously, Zubeida cannot be at liberty to choose how she will dress if Rehana has a right to choose between a pair of completely specified social states. Thus, to

---

5. Replying to Bernholz 1974, who protests the confusion between choosing entire social states and their individual "features," Sen states: "Given the rest of the world, . . . Jack's choice between sleeping on his back and . . . on his belly is a choice over two 'social states.'" (Sen 1976; 1982a, 304; his italics). However, even if we grant that speaking of a choice of social states in a state of ignorance about what one is choosing is meaningful the argument that at most one individual can do what Sen assumes still applies. One should not confuse hypothetical considerations that treat the choices of others as given—in that sense all can simultaneously treat the choices of all others as hypothetically fixed—with the choices of all others actually being made and fixed. Sen's concept of a right to choose assumes the latter rather than the former!

reiterate, for entirely trivial reasons any of the individuals can choose a social state from a pair of social states only if she is—normatively speaking—in the position of a dictator entitled to determine all dimensions of the emerging state of the world.[6] This is no paradox but rather follows immediately from the underlying construction of "rights to choose."

To generalize, after recognizing the elementary distinction between rights, i.e., the choice of cells on the one hand, and liberties, i.e., the choice of columns or rows on the other, it is obvious that an individual *i* could virtually choose between two states of affairs—cells—only if all other individuals *j ≠ i*, from a set of individuals *N*, were under an obligation to choose according to her "orders." Individual *i* must be normatively entitled to tell them how they must choose. They cannot have any liberty left to choose against *i*'s wishes. If they choose otherwise they violate an obligation towards *i*. Individual *i* is in the position of a puppet master who can lead all other individuals by the strings of their normative obligations to follow suit if she asks them to do their parts in picking a specific cell.

Obviously, the adherent of liberal individualism would have to reject such a construction. He does not feel that letting individuals take turns in playing the role of the puppet master expresses liberal values. The adherent of liberal individualism is primarily interested in what we in this paper call liberties. Rights, or what we choose to call such in this paper, are in his view a contingent consequence of liberties: a person *A* creates a right for person *B* by assuming an obligation to perform a particular act if *B* requires him to do so. *B* cannot have the right to this performance if *A* *preserves* his liberty to perform or not to perform the act. The free choice between *preserving* and *surrendering* liberties is a defining feature of the liberal creed, and of a liberal theory of rights.

We do not claim a monopoly of correct usage when we call one particular relation between persons and acts "liberty," the other "right." What we claim is that they are fundamentally different relations; call-

---

6. We shall henceforth neglect the special case of a last mover who as a matter of fact is making the "last choice" in a sequence of choices. Obviously our basic argument that *at most* one individual can be in the position to choose between states of affairs would apply in that case as well.

ing them by the same name is to ignore the difference. If there is an excuse for doing so, it can only be the view that all such relations, i.e., both our liberties and our rights, are privileges conferred on individuals by collective social choice. However, even on this view they would be relevantly different, as a glance at the game form representation clearly reveals. What is puzzling, and needs explanation, is how so many eminent social choice theorists could fail to make the obvious distinction between the *phenomena* to which we refer as rights and liberties respectively and consequently could think that their collective choice concept of a right could capture intuitive individualist liberal notions of freedom of decision.

3. Rights as "Softeners" of Social Choice

Sen does not accept the Nozickean view that "rights" are simply constraints imposing restrictions on the realm of collective choice. As a genuine social choice theorist, Sen models individual choices as acts of participation in an overall social choice. He therefore tries to build "rights" into the collective choice mechanism itself: in translating individual orderings into a common social ordering, *society* must rank any alternatives over which individual i has a "right" as i ranks them, and any alternatives over which j has a "right," as j ranks them.

Let us reconstruct what that could mean by transforming the previously discussed example of a game form into a very simple *voting* game. The game form was defined by the set of players k, $k \in K = \{1, 2\}$ and the set of strategy profiles $Z = \{(z_1, z_2) \mid z_k \in \{g_k, r_k\}, k \in K\}$ which at the same time determined the set of possible states of the world characterized by the possible combinations of green or red dress colors of the two individuals. Now, let

$$Z^* := \{((Z_{11}, Z_{12}), (Z_{21}, Z_{22})) \mid Z_{k1} \in \{G_1, R_1\}, Z_{k2} \in \{G_2, R_2\}, k \in K\},$$

where capital letters stand for individuals' *voting* rather than for their dressing strategies. Thus "Z_{kj}" must now be read as individual k *votes* in favor of bringing about a state of the world in which individual j *acts* according to "z_j." Note, though, that according to this construction j

is no longer entitled to *choose* z_j. All choices are made collectively or socially since the state of the world is determined in a voting process. To put it slightly otherwise: when dressing, individuals are merely acting in the way corresponding to z_j but the choice of their act has been made *for* them on the level of voting. (Think of the collective body as a "puppet master" who is deciding by majority vote on the script for a "dressing performance.")

Whenever there is no unanimity the obvious question is whose wishes should prevail. For instance, individual 1 might vote (G_1, R_2) and individual 2 votes (G_1, G_2), etc. An obvious way out is giving dictatorial competence to one individual. Accordingly the next matrix shows what it would mean that 2 has dictatorial competence. In this matrix, whatever 2 chooses "for the collectivity" (by casting his vote according to one of the four pairs of "capital letter alternatives" in the top row of the matrix) is executed as the social choice and individuals merely act as "puppets on a string" when bringing about the socially determined result (one of the lower case alternatives forming the "inner" sub-matrix). By wearing a dress of the correct color they execute collective commands issued by the dictator.

"2" is dictator

		2			
		(G_1,G_2)	(R_1,G_2)	(G_1,R_2)	(R_1,R_2)
	(G_1,G_2)	(g_1,g_2)	(r_1,g_2)	(g_1,r_2)	(r_1,r_2)
	(R_1,G_2)	(g_1,g_2)	(r_1,g_2)	(g_1,r_2)	(r_1,r_2)
1	(G_1,R_2)	(g_1,g_2)	(r_1,g_2)	(g_1,r_2)	(r_1,r_2)
	(R_1,R_2)	(g_1,g_2)	(r_1,g_2)	(g_1,r_2)	(r_1,r_2)

To avoid dictatorship, individuals must change the voting mechanism. Individual 1 should not merely participate as a "dummy." His vote should have real weight. If the mechanism is "softened" so that every individual can determine one issue by making his vote effective for that issue we get the following matrix of the voting game:

1 and 2 can each decide one issue by their vote

1 \ 2	(G_1,G_2)	(R_1,G_2)	(G_1,R_2)	(R_1,R_2)	
(G_1,G_2)	(g_1,g_2)	(g_1,g_2)	(g_1,r_2)	(g_1,r_2)	
(R_1,G_2)	(r_1,g_2)	(r_1,g_2)	(r_1,r_2)	(r_1,r_2)	*
(G_1,R_2)	(g_1,g_2)	(g_1,g_2)	(g_1,r_2)	(g_1,r_2)	*
(R_1,R_2)	(r_1,g_2)	(r_1,g_2)	(r_1,r_2)	(r_1,r_2)	
		*	*		

If we reduce the latter matrix to the starred rows and columns by leaving out the duplicated results we get the game form Γ:

1 \ 2	G_2	R_2
G_1	g_1,g_2	g_1,r_2
R_1	r_1,g_2	r_1,r_2

This game form looks strikingly similar to the one presented before. The fact that the collective choice mechanism is "softened" by granting individuals a decisive vote in determining the collective command to be executed by them should not deceive us into believing, though, that the voting rights protect the individuals' *liberty* of dressing as they please. They do not. The formal "similarity" between the voting game form and the liberal game form conceals that the change from lower case to capital letters in denoting strategy choices makes all the difference in the world.[7]

7. Ignoring the distinction between lower case and capital letters in examples like the foregoing ones may provide an answer to Gibbard's query in 1982, 597f.: "These liberal paradoxes carry, with them, an air of sophistry: they must in some way be creating problems that do not really exist. . . . To talk about paradoxes, then, is to explore the role of one kind of mathematics in thought about social

As long as individuals chose "small letter actions" directly they were entitled to choose the color of their own dresses separately. They had liberties rather than participatory rights in a voting process. Whereas now they have a vote in a collective choice. They can choose to vote in a certain way and by this bring it about that the collectivity issues the command that they dress in their preferred way. Still, when dressing, they merely execute a collective command but do not choose how to dress. The action of dressing now amounts to the execution of a command rather than to exercising a liberty.[8]

"Rights," in the sense Sen uses that term, are elements of a collective command structure. They serve the function of keeping collective choice reasonably close to what could be accepted under the value premises of Paretian welfare economics.[9] Thus, even though he presents it as an attack on the Pareto principle, basically the same Paretian-Wicksellian aim of "softening" collective choice that was driving Buchanan and Tullock in their *Calculus of Consent* (1962) seems to be behind Sen's enterprise.[10]

Since the game form of the voting game and the reduced liberal game form of the preceding example look almost identical, one might be tempted to conclude that Sen's construction amounts to the same thing as the liberal game form. This similarity explains why so many people could think that the social choice theorists' representation of liberties as *participatory* rights in a social choice mechanism could capture what liberal individualism is all about. However, it is clearly inadequate to reconstruct the intuitive notion of what we call liberties in

---

norms and organization. What is it about the mathematical apparatus of social choice theory that apparently so misapplies to questions of liberty?"

8. Even if individual liberties were to be viewed as ultimately chosen in a collective act of constitutional choice they would be different from participatory voting rights and, for that matter, obligations to behave according to collective commands.

9. Bringing the Pareto principle into play on top of such "rights" as Sen does amounts to pursuing the same aim in two different ways. And, from this point of view, it is not surprising that inconsistency emerges.

10. As far as the latter enterprise is concerned game theoretic analyses like Breyer and Gardner 1980 that focus on Pareto-dominated equilibria in the presence of "rights" may be most fruitful.

this paper as special "voting rights."[11] Explicating the concept of a liberal "right" in terms of individual entitlements to make social choices for a collectivity does not capture adequate notions of "rights" or, for that matter, "liberties."

4. A Liberal View of the Liberal Constitution

We could be content to let it rest at that. Yet the adherent of the social choice approach may still insist that even if individuals are entitled to make their "private" choices within the scope of their admissible actions a collective result or social state will eventually emerge. Since "the rules of the game" are collectively determined—at least they can be collectively changed under some rule of rule change—society cannot avoid responsibility for collective results—at least the responsibility of not changing the rules. In this sense the collectivity acting as a whole or through its agents, may be regarded as being responsible for the initial delineation of liberties, of what kinds of contracts are going to be enforced, of what kinds of behavior will be treated as torts, and so on.

4.1. FREEDOM OF CONTRACT

Sen thinks that there are certain decisions that are intrinsically private. These decisions should be left to the individuals in their private capacities. And, as far as this is concerned, he claims to be in good company since ". . . most social philosophies accept certain personal or group rights" (what the present paper insists on calling liberties). "The fact that unqualified use of the Pareto principle potentially threatens all such rights gives the conflict an extraordinarily wide scope." (Sen 1976/1982a, 316) Indeed, as one could have guessed, the problem—if there is one—must go beyond lewd books, pink walls, sleeping on one's belly, and other "personal things" (297). "If we believe [in unrestricted domain and almost any form of the Pareto principle] the society cannot permit *even minimal liberalism.* Society cannot let more than one

11. In any event, if we use the construction of special voting rights in the way proposed here, the choice set will not be empty and thus the paradox is avoided.

individual be free to read what they like, sleep the way they prefer, dress as they care to, etc. irrespective of the preferences of others . . ." (Sen 1970a, 157; our italics). However, if there is unrestricted domain and *P*, Pareto optimality, and *L*, minimal liberalism, are the universal rules comprising the social choice mechanism, do they not apply to all pairs of alternatives in the critical preference configuration, regardless of their particular content? Why is the competence of *L* restricted to "personal" matters? And where do personal matters stop[12] and "impersonal" ones begin? Are matters of livelihood, work, property "personal," to be "protected" by *L*? If not, why not? The intended effect in Sen's theory of distinguishing between what is under an individual's control (that another may covet), and what he covets but can only get by giving up what he controls, is that subjecting the *former* to *L* (the dictates of freedom?) and *both* to *P* is capable of producing the impossibility result. The conflict is rooted in who controls what. At least in its formal logic it is not content-dependent. It would be arbitrary to make it so.

A substantive flaw of Sen's thesis (though he is in good and numerous company), seems to lie in his attempt to discriminate between rights (and of course liberties) according to their content. There are "personal matters," "a sphere of privacy," "an area of autonomy" in which an individual is to be sovereign, "free to decide," and the related preferences of others are "meddlesome," intrusive. There are, presumably, other matters of which this is not true. But if the individual's sphere of privacy, or area of autonomy, covers the set of his liberties and rights that must not be violated, has he any *others* that are not part of the set, and falling outside the protected area, may be violated?

If there are *no* liberties and rights that may be violated, so that no one can be made to do something against his will, which seems to be an inherent supposition of the "soft" social theory that uses Pareto-superiority as a criterion of "better," then none is *outside* the "sphere of privacy" or "area of autonomy." For what characterizes the latter is

12. We find no place in Sen where he would seek to define the area of privacy or "personal matter," but his examples suggest that he sees it as fairly narrow. Yet this may be doing him an injustice: for his objective, of course, is to show that even a puny area cannot be spared by the invasive Pareto principle. But then a larger area can *a fortiori* not be spared.

not that its content is particularly "private" (whatever that means, for aren't all individual liberties and rights "private"?) but that it is *the* set of a person's liberties and rights, over which he alone disposes. Expressions like "private sphere," that have no very precise meaning if understood as a particular ("private") class of objects of our options, are found to mean, more rigorously, the sum of an individual's admissible actions. Their "area" or "sphere" is better defined, negatively, by what the rights of *others,* and tort law, leave over. And, from a liberal point of view the freedom of contracting away what is in one's private sphere seems naturally included in the set of an individual's admissible actions.

From this point of view it seems doubtful to envisage the Pareto principle as operating *outside* the "private sphere" of liberties and rights. The Pareto principle operates *through* the medium of liberties and rights, since individuals can only choose what they are, by virtue of their liberties and rights, free to choose.

This has some relevance for the real nature of the alleged conflict between *P* and *L*. Sen depicts it as one between the Pareto principle and "rights." On a close look, it is a conflict between preserving some (any) liberty as dictated by *L,* and converting it into an obligation by selling others rights over it, as dictated by *P,* because the trade is mutually agreeable. But if *L* acts as an interdiction to trade certain liberties, can it be interpreted as "freedom to decide"?[13] We think not. Still, even though it is arbitrary to refer to interdictions of trade as "protections of the freedom to decide" it may still be justified for some reason to inter-

---

13. Jesuitically, we may say that an interdiction to trade preserves freedom, in that once you have traded an object away, you are no longer free to decide what should happen to it. It is possible (though we think unlikely) that Sen means his "minimal libertarianism" to be freedom-protecting in this sense: we are only free to choose until we do choose, and lose a liberty irrevocably if we choose irrevocably. While Sen's own position on this has at least a certain casuistic merit, its more widespread popular interpretation, where liberties are supposed to be suppressed by force in the name of Pareto-optimality, seems incomprehensible. Thus, one of his critics thunders: "It is, then, undeniable [*sic*] that if we propose a criterion for a good state of affairs like Pareto-optimality, then farewell legal rights" (Barry 1986, 94).

dict such trades. There can be indirect external effects of the trade of liberties that lead to Pareto-inferior results. That may hold true even with respect to such classical political liberties as "freedom of speech." Even somebody who has no interest at all to make use of such liberties himself may have good reason to hope that others would make good use of them and thus may want to enforce an interdiction to trade away such liberties. On the level of constitutional choice individuals might therefore want to render inalienable certain of each other's liberties and thus to restrict freedom of contract.

Of course, using traditional terminology one would speak of "inalienable rights" in this context. What is at issue here is not a mere quibble over words, though. It is rather the fundamental normative question whether the collectivity as a whole may or ought to interfere with the trade of liberties at all and if so in what way?

Forbidding certain contractual exchanges of liberties by making them inalienable is one thing; imposing trades on unwilling parties is another. The Pareto rule in the liberal paradox is dimly perceived by some as collective choice forcibly sacrificing liberties to get Pareto-improvements—the obverse of Rousseau's "forcing people to be free." P is thus confusedly interpreted as a social imperative to trade off a liberty "at a profit," i.e., as an interdiction to preserve it. It is supposed to imply that "the guarantee of individual liberty [must be] revoked" (Sen 1976/1982a, 313).

This view seems quite strange indeed. For, if it were the case that a particular distribution of liberties and rights is an obstacle to Pareto-optimality, the obstacle would either be overcome by trade, i.e., voluntary conversions of some liberties into obligations (hence new rights for others) and voluntary interpersonal transfers of some existing rights, or not.[14] If not, there must be obstacles stopping these mutually agreeable transactions. For all we know, there may be mutually acceptable means of removing such obstacles—we cannot prejudge that. But

14. Herbert L. Hart, discussing legal powers that some scholars call "norms of competence," quotes A. Ross's observation in the latter's *On Law and Justice:* "The norm of competence itself does not say that the competent person is obligated to exercise his competence" (Hart 1961, 238).

the means cannot possibly include the *violation* of "legal" liberties and rights, given that the parties would not want to be so violated—or so we may presume.

The freedom of contract is the engine of improving social states under "soft" social choice. A liberty can be contractually converted into an obligation, in exchange for value received (or to be received as of right). An employment contract, involving the conversion of certain liberties (to work or to play, to work for Jones or for Smith, etc.) into obligations to work as directed in exchange for rights to payments or other benefits, is a mundane example. More generally, one can regard every use of the freedom of contract as a *renunciation* or "consumption" of a liberty: for contracting parties, the acceptance of reciprocal obligations involves the abandonment of the pre-contract option they had to adopt a different course of action, a different commitment, a different allocation of their resources.

Of course, some liberties cannot advantageously be converted into obligations-cum-rights, because they have no exchange value. Many of Sen's illustrations of "minimal liberalism" have this character: whether I read naughty books or not, sleep on my back or my belly, have pink walls or white, is not only (as he stresses) my strictly personal business, but (*pace* both Sen and his critics) it is difficult to see anyone else making it his business to the extent of *compensating me for allowing it to become his business.* Our reciprocal preferences simply do not make room for potential gains from trade. These liberties of mine may never be worth as much to anyone else as they are to me. They are destined to remain my liberties.

The preceding line of argument does not restrict "collective choice" or the state to a completely passive role as far as contracting is concerned. Where the structure of trade is not self-enforcing the question of contract enforcement typically arises. In particular one may ask whether and when the state should act as an enforcer of freely chosen contracts. This may be an issue of constitutional choice.

4.2. ENFORCEMENT OF CONTRACTS

It is a commonplace that an unexecuted contract is a "game" of prisoners' dilemma. If potential gains from trade fail to be realized (the contract is not concluded, or concluded but not executed), we may say that the game was solved in a Pareto-inferior manner. Consider the matrix below

$$j$$

	s	r
q	q,s	q,r
p	p,s	p,r

i (labels rows q and p)

with the preference order $ps >_i qs >_i pr >_i qr$ for player i
and the preference order $qr >_j qs >_j pr >_j ps$ for player j.

Like every other potential contract, the interaction we are considering can be reduced, in a first approximation, to one of two ideal types. One is the non-cooperative game, where credible commitments are ruled out. In this setting dominated strategies should never be chosen and thus both players should use their non-dominated strategies. In a more psychological vein we could elaborate on this in the following way: Whether i chooses p or q, the dominant strategy of j is to choose r. Even if he offered to contribute s, a rational i would have to assume that j rationally will default and in fact do r. Given his correct perception of j's best strategy, i has no hope of qs being "available," hence no hope that he could bring that result about by his own contribution and thus no reason to contribute q to the joint result. He must opt for p if only for the "maximin" reason of escaping qr. The rational solution of this game is therefore pr, as in the simple one-shot prisoners' dilemma.

The other ideal type is cooperative: i offers q conditional on j producing s. The equilibrium solution is qs (which will satisfy P), if the contract providing for i performing q, and j performing s, is binding, or rather believed to be so. Other things being equal, the latter will be the case if it is "enforceable."

However, the binary alternative "commitments are/are not enforceable" is too crude even for a first approximation. A broad continuum of varying degrees of subjectively perceived credibility—in turn a function of enforceability—would serve better. But no continuum could be stretched to accommodate some of the cases that Sen puts in the foreground. How could Prude's promise to read even the lewdest passages of the lewd book in the privacy of his study, or Jack's promise to sleep on his back behind the closed door of his bedroom, be credible to *any* degree to someone who had to *pay* for this promise with a promise of his own?

Clearly, such undertakings cannot form either side of an arm's-length transaction. They might be credible as between persons linked by ties of affection and trust; but then they would not normally take the form of trades, commitments fulfilled *for a consideration*. Promises to feel, to think, or to believe something, promises to perform unwitnessed acts leaving no trace, are worth *no* consideration, since it is impossible to monitor, prove, or disprove their performance; and where there is no consideration, there is no contract. Sen knows this perfectly well, and puts it beautifully when having the gentle policeman call on Prude to inquire about his reading the good book (Sen 1982b; 1986, 227–a), though it is the very raison d'être of such contracts, rather than their dubious or socially objectionable enforcement, that he should have questioned. Why, then, did he pose the conflict between keeping a liberty and selling it in a Pareto-improving contract, in terms of objects that simply cannot be contracted for? — so that the question of the Pareto-improving solution cannot even arise? *L* will then prevail every time, as there is no contest with *P*. "How do you sell your freedom of thought?" is not, in this context, a mere rhetorical question.

It is obvious here that it may be unnecessary to protect such liberties against being traded away. For those who want these liberties to prevail the best constitutional policy may simply be following a maxim of "hands off." However, liberties and rights that enter into reciprocal preferences, and are sensible objects of arm's-length exchanges, may pose a genuine problem. The question that we ought to pursue a little further is whether contracting should be facilitated or not by public enforcement.

The standard means of making the cooperative solution of the prisoners' dilemma available to the parties is to refer to the historically accurate fact that in our type of civilization most contracts that suffer from no formal vices are enforced by the political authority. The effect of believing this is to stabilize the *qs* solution against the temptations of the default strategy that is dominant yet Pareto-inferior. Thus are people, so to speak, forced to be better off.

Can one, however, still describe the resulting qs solution as satisfying P? For it might be objected that qs is Pareto-optimal only if it is freely chosen, but not if it is weighed down by coercion (however latent); the two are not commensurate, nor is a freely chosen pr commensurate with the coerced qs. To defeat this objection, it would have to be argued that the coercion needed to transform qs into an available option is already allowed for in both individuals' preference orderings. It is not qs they prefer to pr, but "qs *cum* coercion to deter default."

Sen is anxious to establish (1986, 225–27) that the parties may not even wish to negotiate a contract (for qs) because their non-utility reasons in favor of preserving their relevant liberty outweigh the extra utility they would gain by converting it into an obligation. If utility is used in a narrow sense, that leaves room for non-utility reasons to induce choices; this is plainly something one is free to assume. The impossibility in that case is resolved by an assumption that makes L counter-preferentially stronger than P; the parties will conform to it, and the choice dictated by L will be the social choice. If, however, preference is to be taken broadly to encompass everything that influences choice, and "preferred" is to mean the choice waiting to be made if given the chance, counter-preferential choice is beyond the pale of theory; qs then yields a surplus of the entity, whether we call it utility or something else, that is supposed to motivate choice, and we are not free to assume that the parties have no wish to seek it.

This surplus yielded by contract performance can be indifferently identified as one of three things: it is the *reward* for bearing *default risk,* it is a resource available for arrangements to *deter defaults,* or it is a resource for *buying insurance* against it. Nothing permits us to assert and no good argument favors the supposition that insurance can only be bought from the political authority (which would justify its taxing power as an alternative way of collecting premiums), or that it will be bought at all. The economist would expect to find a tendency for the contracting party to be indifferent, with respect to his marginal contract, between carrying the risk and insuring it. He would also expect the mix between risks assumed and premia to be such as to help bring about this equilibrium.

Coping with default risk does not necessarily, or only, mean providing the wherewithal for an enforcement mechanism, whether a do-it-yourself or a bought-in variety. It may also mean modulating the very need for enforcement by adapting the terms of contracts to the desired level of risk. Half-executory contracts are, cet. par., riskier than either "spot" or fully executory, "forward" ones. Simultaneous performances, each fully contingent on the other, have a self-enforcing property. Refusing to enter into half-executory contracts with certain parties under certain circumstances is tantamount to paying for reduced default risk by forgoing uncertain gains. Avoiding to deal with unknown parties in cases where performance is hard to define and easy to contest is another obvious way of acting directly on the level of risk, rather than dealing with a given level of it. A multitude of adjustment, protective, and risk-avoidance devices, positive incentives for reputation-building in the reliable discharge of obligations, and the many informal extra-judicial sanctions of default, constitute a net that upholds contracts. It may be stronger or weaker, and more or less finely meshed. It is costly to knot and to maintain. Part of the cost is intangible if not altogether conjectural, since it consists of forgone advantages, missed dealings, and contracts entered into that would pass for sub-optimal in a world without default risk.

There is an obvious kinship between the costs that, if incurred, help enforce contracts, provide substitutes for enforcement, and mitigate the consequences of its inadequacies, and two other famous classes of costs: those incurred to secure property rights, i.e., "exclusion costs," and those that are entailed in their transfer from less to more highly valued uses, i.e., "transactions costs." All three classes are admittedly hard to define, elusive, all too often the result of imputation verging on tautology. They are, so to speak, obstacles that are invisible to the spectator, who only sees the horse that balks but not the fence that made it balk.

Unfortunately, however, the older, and supposedly better understood, pre-Coase and pre-Demsetz cost categories, such as production costs and transport costs, are similarly tainted by imputation and metaphysics. Yet, tainted or not, both science and life need concepts and categories of cost, and nothing more "objective" is likely to serve any better than the ones we have. The relatively new-fangled and somewhat shadowy triad of exclusion, transactions, and enforcement costs[15] goes some way towards explaining why asset markets discriminate, some goods become public and others private, many negative externalities are tolerated, and why some ostensibly Pareto-superior moves do not take place.

A commonsense resolution of the alleged paradox of the Paretian liberal is implicit in these considerations and is ready to be read off. If a choice mechanism combines two contingently contradictory rules — as, in Sen's construction, *L* interdicting the negotiation of rights and liberties, and *P* mandating them — a meta-rule can "socially" justify the individual choices that are necessarily made in violation of one rule or the other. It is hard to think of a more neutral, less discretionary meta-rule than the submission of possible rival outcomes, rival social states obeying rival rules, to the test of costs. Costs are grassroots *arguments against* an outcome. As near as one can tell, they determine whether the game of the Paretian liberal is solved by contract, or by the failure to contract. Both make perfect sense, given the "argument against." This is, it seems, as it should be; for why should we expect a uniform issue?

5. *Concluding Remark*

A right in Sen's framework amounts to being in a position to choose at least between two cells of the matrix of a game form. Sen's frequent claim, that his minimal liberalism as entitlement to choose between at

15. In his "The Problem of Externality" Dahlman 1979, 217, treats enforcement costs as part of transactions costs, and attributes the same view to Coase 1960. He goes on to argue that enforcement costs, like every other transaction cost, are in reality information costs: "enforcement costs are incurred because there is lack of knowledge as to whether one (or both) of the parties involved in the agreement will violate his part of the bargain." (218) This is circular reasoning. A party may keep his bargain if there is enforcement, and violate it if there is not. Apart from the ethical and historical ceteris paribus, the probability of violation is best captured as a decreasing function of the enforcement costs being incurred. To say that they would not have to be incurred if we knew that neither party was going to violate a bargain, is true enough but no less circular and no more helpful.

least one pair of states of affairs is implied by such concepts as for instance Gibbard's "issue liberalism," is correct. But, as we have shown, it is incorrect that the entitlement to choose between *classes* of social states, i.e., having a liberty, has the same implication. Having a liberty does definitely *not imply* the right to choose between at least two social states (i.e., liberal individualism as reconstructed here does *not* imply minimal liberalism in Sen's sense).

If this is true, the paradox of liberalism is no paradox at all. The impossibility results, though formally correct, do not capture the essence of liberal individualism since such a view of the world is based on a fundamental distinction between liberties and rights. Still, Sen's arguments as well as the general discussion of the alleged paradox of liberalism raise important and interesting issues of inalienability of liberties, rights, and enforcement of contracts in a free society. Even though the first three sections of our paper were critical of Sen and even though in section 4 we outlined a vision of the mutually compatible roles of liberties, rights, and Paretian policies that quite contradicts Sen's views, it is a great accomplishment of Sen's to put these issues again where they belong: at center stage of modern welfare economics.

17

The Bitter Medicine
of Freedom

From the romantic age of political philosophy, many stirring images have come down to us. Some depict a people wrenching its freedom from the clutches of oppressors, native or foreign. Others show the lone individual fighting for his spiritual autonomy and material independence against totalitarian encroachment. Whatever the truth of these images in the past, their relevance for the present is fading. The issue of freedom in our civilization is changing its character. It is not so much despots, dictators, or totalitarian creeds that menace it. In essence, we do.

It is far from evident that democratic control of government is usually conducive to the preservation of liberal practices and values, let alone to their enhancement. Anti-liberal ideologies gain and retain credence inasmuch as they suit our inclinations, legitimize our interests, and warrant our policies. We love the rhetoric of freedom-talk and indulge in it beyond the call of sobriety and good taste, but it is open to serious doubt that we actually like the substantive content of freedom. On the whole we do not act as if we did. I shall presently be arguing that it is an austere substance, not unlike bitter medicine that we do not naturally relish—though it can become an acquired taste for the exceptional individual—but take only when the need presses. My object is to show that contrary to the sweetness-and-light views of freedom,

Reprinted with permission from *The Balance of Freedom: Political Economy, Law, and Learning*, edited by Roger Michener (St. Paul, Minn.: Professors World Peace Academy, 1995), 31–60.

it is this more austere view that best explains why we keep praising it while in our politics we are busily engaged in shrinking its domain.

Taking Freedom Easy and In Vain

Countless notions of greater or lesser woolliness attach to freedom, and a full review of its alternative definitions would be tedious. The very limited sample I choose to look at, however, seems to me representative of the main live political currents of the age. The context of each is non-Robinsonian, in that it deals with a person's freedom as constituted by the options and constraints of his social life. The subject, in other words, is not the individual facing his Creator, nor the solitary player in the game against Nature, but the person acting with or against other persons. The freedom in question is a property of one's conduct in relation to the conduct of others, rather than an affirmation of free will, "inner" freedom, or some other proposition about the causation of human actions or the state of men's minds.

The rudiments of the liberal definition identify a free person as one who faces no man-made obstacles to choosing according to his preferences, provided only that his doing so does not cause a tort to another person. This idea of freedom takes preference and choice conceptually for granted, does not worry about how preference can be recognized unless it is revealed by choice, nor does it seek to make statements about the nature of the self. It is practical political freedom. This, however, means something far more general than conventional "political liberty," i.e., the freedom of each to affect collective decisions to some albeit minimal extent through a regulated political process, and normally understood to consist of the freedoms of speech, assembly, press, and election. Instead, it is political in the broader sense that it results from the political process, depending as it does on collectively imposed institutional restrictions of greater or lesser stringency on the opportunity set open to choice. As Frank Knight put it, it is coercion and not freedom that needs defining.[1]

By extension of this view, the corollary of freedom is said to be

1. F. H. Knight 1943, 75.

the reduction of coercion "as much as is possible"[2]; in the same vein, it is independence from the "arbitrary will" of another.[3] Giving the matter an ethical dimension, freedom is represented as a state of affairs that permits one to choose any feasible option provided that his doing so does not harm another person.[4] Loosely related to the principles of *non-coercion, independence,* and *no-harm* is the Kantian principle of "equal liberty." It appears to refer to a state of affairs where one person's options are not subjected to a man-made restriction to which those of any other person are not also subjected. This formulation, however, is incomplete. Needless to say, neither Kant nor those, notably Herbert Spencer, who followed him in employing this form of words, meant that the "extent" or "quantity" of freedom in a state of affairs was irrelevant and only its "distribution" needed to be of a certain kind—i.e., "equal." If such a distribution were the sole criterion, it would not matter how much or how little there was to be had, as long as everybody had as much or as little as everybody else. That freedom demanded to be both "maximized" and "distributed equally" was made explicit by Rawls in his adaptation of Kant's principle.[5]

In these versions, freedom appears as a unitary concept. It may or may not be capable of variation by degrees. Hayek suggests more than once that it is indivisible; it is either present or absent; we either have it or we do not; we either choose freely or we are coerced. The "size" of the feasible, uncoerced opportunity set does not affect the issue, nor does coercion vary in extent or intensity.[6]

Liberals of the orthodox tradition, for whom it is a property of the relation between individual preference and choice—a relation devoid of obstacles erected by politics except where such obstacles serve to shelter the freedom of others—do not as a rule recognize a plurality

2. F. A. Hayek 1960, 11, 21.

3. Hayek, *op. cit.,* 11.

4. Cf. the 1791 *Declaration of the Rights of Man;* also J. S. Mill 1848, Ch. 2.

5. "The most extensive basic liberty compatible with a similar liberty for others," Rawls 1972, 60. Liberty, then, is to be increased as long as its further increase does not require some to have less of it than others; equality of freedom is a constraint on its maximization. This is implicit in the formula but is not spelled out by Rawls.

6. Hayek, *op. cit.,* 13.

of freedoms. The plural usage, on the other hand, is fairly typical of heterodox, "redistributor" liberals who deal in numerous freedoms to accede to desirable states or activities, designated as "positive," as well as in "freedom from" hunger, want, insecurity, and other undesirable conditions. Dewey's freedom as "power to do" also belongs to this category, where diverse "freedoms" represent power to do diverse things. It is not hard to appreciate that these heterodox freedom concepts are in essence rhetorical proxies standing for diverse goods, some tangible and others intangible, that are perfectly recognizable under their everyday names and need not be described indirectly in the guise of "freedoms." Freedom from hunger is an oblique statement about food being a good, and about a condition in which one is not deprived of it; it can be turned into a general norm under which none must be deprived of it. Similarly, freedom of worship conveys, positively, that it is good for each to be able to profess his own faith, and normatively that none must be deprived of access to this good. Employing freedom-speak in discussing various goods can at best underline the importance we attach to them; at worst, it confuses issues of autonomy and coercion with issues of wealth and welfare. The term freedom in the classical sense seeks to express—whether successfully or not—the unhindered transformation of preference into action, the ability of each to do as he sees fit. "Freedom to" and "freedom from," on the other hand, seem to refer to the extent to which options to act are available to satisfy individual or even "social" preferences.

In a spectacular logical leap which speaks well of his insight if not of his talents of lucid explanation, Marx "unmasks" the liberal foundation of freedom: "The practical application of the right of man to freedom is the right of man to private property."[7]

Antagonistic to liberal inspiration, he turns to wholly different categories to construct a concept of freedom. The Marxist concept has nothing—or nothing explicit—to do with the passage, unobstructed or not, from individual preference to chosen action, a passage of which private property is the privileged vehicle. The corollary of Marxist freedom is not the absence of coercion of the individual by his fellow men through the political authority, but escape from the realm of material

7. Marx 1843, 1975, 229.

necessity, from the tyranny of things.[8] Its subject is not the individual, but mankind.[9] Self-realization—"rehumanization"—of the latter from the "reified" social relations of "commodity production" *is* the state of freedom.

To the extent that this thickly metaphoric language is intelligible, it seems to mean that humanity is free when, no longer subjected to the unconscious and impersonal force of things, which is Marx's code name for the automatism of a market economy, it collectively masters its own fate by deliberate, rational planning. The passage from the realm of necessity to that of freedom is both the cause of, and is caused by, the passage from the realm of scarcity to that of plenty.

Vacuity and Moral Truism

One common feature shines luminously through these various concepts, definitions, and normative principles of freedom. Each as it stands is a moral truism, impossible to dispute or reject because each is defined, if at all, in terms of indisputable superiority. Each, moreover, is defined in terms of conditions whose fulfillment cannot be empirically ascertained—when is coercion at its "possible minimum"?—when is man not subject to the "tyranny of things"? The proposition that a state of affairs is free is rendered "irrefutable," "unfalsifiable." Each, finally, expresses a condition which, if it prevails, one can enjoy without incurring any costs in exchange. Consequently, the question of trade-offs does not arise and it would be lunatic to say, with regard to any one of the rival concepts, that on balance one would rather not have it. Renunciation of freedom, so defined, would not bring any compensating benefit either to the self or to others, nor reduce any attendant sacrifice or disadvantage. Unlike values we buy by giving up some comparable value, it is always better to get and keep such freedom than to give it up.

No great analytical effort is needed to see that freedom concepts have this apple-pie-and-motherhood feature when they are vacuous,

---

8. Marx 1844, 1975, *passim.*
9. More precisely, the species, the *Gattungswesen.*

their stated conditions being impossible either to violate or to fulfill. They make no identifiable demand on anyone and lack any content one could disagree with. That coercion should be reduced "as much as possible" is, *pace* Hayek, a vacuous precept unless integrated into a stringent and clear doctrine of "necessary coercion."[10] Only then would the precept get any definite meaning, for only then would it be referring to some recognizable standard or measure of how far it is "possible" to reduce coercion, and only then could it identify the actual level of coercion as higher than necessary. Otherwise, any level could be as compatible with freedom as any other, and the most shamelessly intrusive dictators of this world would all be recognized as libertarians doing the best they could to avoid unnecessary coercion.

Immunity from the "arbitrary will" of another is similarly empty, for the will of another is judged arbitrary or not, according to the reasons the judge imputes to it. If another's decision rests on identifiable reasons, it may be unwelcome to me because it restricts my ability to act as I would, but I can only have a good claim to immunity from it in the name of my freedom if I have a valid argument to rule out those reasons. Bad reasons leave the decision unjustified, and absence of reasons makes it arbitrary—surely a relatively rare case. Manifestly, however, the crux of the problem is that the claim to immunity from the will of another stands or falls with somebody's judgement of the reasons for the latter; and lest his judgement itself be arbitrary, it must be guided by an independent system of laws, customs, moral principles, and whatever else goes into the determination of a person's liberties in his dealings with others. Immunity from the "arbitrary" will of another seems to mean no more than that one's liberties must be respected; its use to define freedom is simply a recourse to a tautologous

10. Whether there is any satisfactory doctrine of necessary coercion is a vast, open question, which I have tried to address at length elsewhere. Hayek, at all events, has not provided one; the coercion he considers justified because necessary to raise the means for providing useful public goods and services, including a social "safety net," is completely open-ended. It excludes as unnecessary the coercion involved in raising the means for useless public goods and services, or those that, though useful, could better be provided by private enterprise. This leaves a quasi-infinity of occasions for necessary coercion, or at least for coercion that can never be proven unnecessary by the loose Hayek criteria.

identity between it and the non-violation of liberties—whatever they are—whereas a meaningful definition should be capable to serve as a determinant, or more loosely as an argument about what those liberties ought to be. However, the rule that in a state of freedom nobody should be subject to the arbitrary will of another, does not commit anybody to anything beyond respecting well-defined rules of tort. It may in fact be that the immunity concept of freedom and the normative rule it provides is even more trivial than that, for it could be held that in these matters liberties are well-defined only if they are codified, and the rule then boils down to the banality that in a state of freedom nobody should break the law.

The harm principle turns out, on inspection, to lack specific content for much the same reason as the immunity principle. Under it, the political authority in a state of freedom does not prevent—or "artificially" raise the cost of—acts that are harmless to others; it does not allow anyone to interfere with the harmless acts of others; and prevents and sanctions harmful acts. However, there is no very evident binary division of acts into a harmful and a harmless class.[11] Some of our acts may possibly be beneficial or at worse indifferent to everybody else, though it would no doubt be hard to make sure that this was the case. As regards these acts, there is a clear enough reason why we should be left free to commit them. But this does not take liberty very far. For there is a vast number of other acts that are harmful to somebody to some degree, having as they do some unwelcome effect on somebody's interests, ranging in a continuous spectrum from the merely annoying to the gravely prejudicial.

This must be so for a variety of reasons, the simplest one being that in any realm of scarcity—scarce goods, crowded *Lebensraum,* limited markets, competitive examinations, rival careers, exclusive friendship, possessive love—one person's chosen course of action preempts and prejudges the choices of others, sometimes helpfully but mostly adversely. The place and the prize one gets is not available to runners-up, no matter how badly they want or "need" it. Where does "harm" to them begin? Common sense tells us that, depending on circumstances, there are acts you must be free to engage in even though they harm my

11. Cf., however, the approach adopted by Feinberg 1984.

interests, hurt my feelings, or expose me to risk. How to tell these acts from those which are to be prevented? Define them, and you have defined the rights that may be *exercised*— "positive" freedom—and must not be *violated*— "negative" freedom—the two kinds appearing as two perspectives of one and the same system of "rights." The harm principle is vacuous prior to a system of liberties and rights, while posterior to it all it does say is that the holders of liberties and rights are not to be deprived of them either by the state or by anybody else. Concisely, the harm principle affirms no more than that liberties are liberties and rights are rights.

The Kantian equal liberty, whether or not equipped with a maximizing clause, is baffling in its lack of guidance about what exactly is, or ought to be made, equal—and subject to equality, maximal. It appears, at first blush, to have to do with the distribution among individuals of something finite, quantifiable, and variable, analogous to a stretch devoid of obstacles, a level surface, a private space, a protected sphere. If this were a possible interpretation and freedom were a quantifiable dimension—or dimensions—of states of affairs, it would make perfect sense to say that one person disposed of more of it than another—a test of equality—or could have more if another had less—a test that problems of distribution are technically soluble—and that if there were more of it altogether, at least some—and subject to solving problems of distribution, all—could have more, which may also mean that by giving some more of it, it can be maximized—a test that maximization is a practical objective. The difficulty is that the analogy between unobstructed length, surface, or space, and freedom, is just that, an analogy and no more. There seems to be no apparent way in which freedom could be quantified. I suggest that the statement that two persons are "equally free" has the same cognitive status as that they are "equally happy" or "equally handsome"; these are statements of somebody's judgment from the evidence, but the same evidence could have induced somebody else to pass a different judgment, and it is impossible conclusively to settle, from the evidence alone, which of two contradictory judgments is more nearly right. There is no agreed arbitrator, nor is a last-resort test built into the practice of these subjective comparisons for settling contrary judgments and perceptions. On the view that interpersonal comparisons of such states of mind conditions as utility, happiness, or satisfaction are a category-mistake to begin with, and that the freedom of one person, being as it is bound up with subjective perceptions, is similarly incomparable to the freedom of another, the whole practice of seeking their levels or the extent of differences between them may be logically suspect anyway. In its normative version, "equal freedom" is no more stringent than Dworkin's "equal concern and respect," the central plank in his democratic ethics, rightly dismissed by Raz with the deadpan finding that it "seems to mean that everyone has a right to concern and respect."[12] Like "equal respect," the norm of "equal freedom" is unexceptionable, due in no small measure to its non-committal vagueness: practically *any* feasible state of affairs can be claimed, without fear of rebuttal, to be satisfying such norms.[13]

If it is reasonable to read the Marxist concept of freedom as emancipation from the regime of "reified relations" and mastery over one's material destiny, and then to translate this into less exalted English as the abolition of commodity and labor markets, the concept is extravagant but not vacuous. "Abolition of the market" and "resource allocation by the political authority" have sufficiently precise factual content that can be empirically recognized as being or not being the case. Unlike "arbitrary will," "minimum necessary coercion," or "equal liberty," they are ascertainable features of a given social state of affairs: they either obtain or they do not. A Ministry of Planning and Rationing cannot very well be "deconstructed" and shown to be "really" a market in thin disguise. Where Marxist freedom nevertheless convicts itself of vacuousness and moral truism is in tirelessly transforming and qualify-

12. Raz 1986, 220.

13. One of Rawls's two versions of equal liberty, that consisting of an integrated, coherent "system . . . defining rights and duties" (*op. cit.,* 202) seems to me clearly open to this charge. In the other version, the system is said to consist of a number of distinct "basic liberties" (*op. cit.,* 302) of "equal citizenship." They are the conventional political freedoms ensuring democratic representation and equality before the law, and they are not vacuous. They seem to me, however, too confined in their effects and therefore inadequate to pass for a "principle of liberty." For one, they offer too few safeguards to minorities against the will of the majority. For another, they provide no defense of property, nor of privacy. Such "basic liberties" leave the respective domains of individual and collective choice wholly indeterminate.

ing descriptive statements, till they cease to describe anything that is ascertainable. "Servitude" is not to the conditions of the market, but to its "blind caprice," its "irrationality"; absence of central resource allocation is a "chaotic, self-destructive" system; "the product is master of the producer"; "man, too, may be a commodity" and as such becomes "a plaything of chance."[14] Production under socialist planning is not in obedience to the instructions of the political authority—a testable statement—but "according to need"—an irrefutable vacuity. Any situation, whatever its characteristic empirical data, can be qualified as harmonious or a tooth-and-claw jungle war; any resource allocation can safely be called socially optimal or condemned as "bureaucratic," hence failing to produce "according to needs." There is the compulsion to agree to the moral truism that rational, conscious social deliberation is more conducive to the freedom of mankind than irrational, unconscious thrashing about in the dark; but as we can never tell which is which, the agreement is easy; freedom's name is taken in vain and does not commit anyone to anything.

The Freedom That Hurts

The rough underside of freedom is responsibility for oneself. The fewer the institutional obstacles an individual faces in choosing acts to fit his preferences, the more his life is what he makes it, and the less excuse he has for what he has made of it. The looser the man-made constraints upon him, the less he can count on others being constrained to spare his interests and help him in need. The corollary of an individual's discretion to contribute to or coldly ignore the purposes of the community is that he has no good claims upon it to advance his purposes. It may be that immunity from the "arbitrary will" of others is coextensive with freedom, but so is dependence on one's own talents, efforts, and luck. As Toynbee put it, the "road from slavery to freedom is also the road from security to insecurity of maintenance."

The agreeable corollary of my right is the duty of others to respect

14. F. Engels 1891, 1968, 680–81.

it; less agreeably, *their* right entails *my* duty. Freedom, if it has ascertainable content, turns out to have attendant costs, and, if freedom has degrees, the greater it is, probably the higher is its opportunity cost. Trade-offs between freedom and other goods are manifest facts of social life, though it may be embarrassing to admit to our better selves how often we take advantage of them. By no means is it evident that men want all the freedom that tyrannical or "bureaucratic" political systems deny them.

The less nebulous and the more matter-of-fact is the content of freedom, the more obtrusive become its costs. Nowhere is this so clear as in the matter of the most contested safeguard of freely chosen individual action, that is private property. Freedom of contract, privacy, and private property rights are mutually entailed. Complete respect for either member of the triad would exclude taxation. Even when it has no deliberate redistributive function, taxation simultaneously violates privacy, property rights, and the freedom of contract as the taxpayer loses the faculty to dispose of part of his resources by voluntary contract, and must permit the political authority to dispose of it by command. A reconciliation between the freedom of contract—and by implication, private property and taxation—is offered by social contract theory, whose assumptions lead to taxation, as well as political obedience in general, being recognized as if it were voluntarily undertaken.

There is a tendency, cutting across the political spectrum from left to right, to see private property as divisible into several distinct and independent rights.[15] While this position is certainly tenable, its consequence is to encourage the view that restrictions on transfers of ownership, rent, dividend and price controls, the regulation of corporate control, etc., are consistent with the integrity of private property. If the latter is to be regarded as a "bundle" consisting of a number of separable rights, any one of these measures leaves all other rights within the bundle inviolate; yet any one of them is a violation of the freedom of contract. No ambiguity about their mutual entailment arises when property is conceived as an integral, indivisible right.

15. Cf. Alchian and Demsetz 1973, 18.

Adherence to any maximizing principle of freedom[16] *prima facie* implies non-violation of the freedom of contract, for it would be extravagant to maintain that its restriction, whatever its purportedly beneficial effects on, say, efficiency or income distribution, somehow leaves intact, let alone contributes to maximize, freedom in general. Moreover, if freedom is really about the unobstructed faculty of every sane adult person to be the judge of his own interest, acting as he sees fit and "doing what he desires,"[17] freedom of contract must be its irreducible hard core. To argue in the same breath for maximized (and "equal") freedom in general and restricted freedom of contract, seems to me to presuppose that we judge *unilateral* and potentially "Pareto-inferior" acts not requiring the consent of a contracting party by a liberal standard, bilateral and presumably "Pareto-superior" ones, depending on willing reciprocity of two or more parties, by a more severe one. Yet this is surely applying the standards the wrong way round. If a double standard were admissible, and necessary to sort out actions that *should* from those that should *not* be interfered with, the easier one should be applied to contracts since, unlike unilateral acts, they have passed a prior test of mutual consent by the parties most directly concerned. The chosen action of one person that is not contingent on the agreed cooperation of another and may leave the latter worse off, can hardly have a better claim to the social *laissez passer* of freedom from legalized obstruction, than the proposed action that must, for its realization, first obtain the agreement and fit in with the matching proposed action of a potential contracting party.

Insistence on freedom of contract and on its corollaries, property and privacy, is a hard position that attracts only a minority constituency of doctrinaires on the one hand, old-fogey-nostalgics of a better past that never really was, on the other. Such a constituency is naturally suspect. Its stand offends the moral reflexes of a broad public; for it is yet another moral truism that fair prices, fair rents, fair wages and conditions of employment, fair trade, fair competition are incontrovertibly better and worthier of approval than prices, rents, wages, etc.,

16. ". . . an equal right to the most extensive total system of equal basic liberties"; Rawls, *op. cit.,* 302.

17. J. S. Mill 1848, Ch. 5.

that have merely been agreed in a bargain without being necessarily fair. Anyone who contests this may be putting an ulterior motive above justice, and the onus of proving the contrary is on him.

A somewhat more clever argument that does not directly beg the question of fairness holds that even if a bargain between willing parties at some point on their contract curve is "in itself" better than failing to agree and staying off the curve, some points are nevertheless better than others for one party, worse for the other. In two-person or two-group face-to-face dealings, the actual point they agree on is partly a matter of their relative bargaining power, which must in turn depend on the distribution of wealth, will, skill, and so forth. Untrammelled freedom of contract subject only to no force and fraud thus gives "a moral blessing to the inequalities of wealth,"[18] and, for that matter, of abilities and other advantages. Commitment to it is a commitment *both* to a maximizing principle of freedom and to non-interference with a given distribution of natural and acquired assets.

An attempt to escape from this commitment, with which many feel ill at ease and vulnerable, is to promote the idea that there could be an initial distribution of advantages that would act as a "level playing field." Once this special distribution is achieved—by redistribution of acquired and transferable assets, such as wealth, and by compensatory measures of "positive discrimination" in education to offset natural and non-transferable advantages, such as talent and intelligence— freedom of contract becomes not only compatible with justice but is the very means to it. It produces "pure procedural justice," in the same way as a game played by the rules on a level playing field by definition produces a just result. This particular distribution-cum-compensatory-discrimination amounts to a state of equal opportunity for all. Under equality of opportunity, freedom of contract gives rise to outcomes that need not be overridden in the interest of justice. Equality of opportunity, freedom of contract, and just outcomes constitute a triadic relation such that any two entail the third. In terms of causation, the first two jointly constitute the procedure whose outcome is distributive justice.

This attempt at squaring freedom with justice must clear two hur-

18. Atiyah 1979, 337.

dles, the first substantive, the second analytical. The substantive hurdle concerns the practical possibility of levelling the playing-field, instead of perversely making it more uneven in the attempt. I do not intend to discuss this problem (except to note that it is a genuine one), and could not resolve it if I did. The second hurdle consists in the argument for procedural justice proving to depend on self-contradictory reasoning. A distribution of resources and advantages is both an end-state and a starting position leading to a new distribution. The object of a particular initial distribution D, offering equal opportunities, is to have the freedom of contract to produce just outcomes. However, whatever outcome D′ it did produce will differ from the initial equal-opportunity distribution D; some people will have gotten ahead of the position—in terms of wealth, skills, reputation, place in the social net-work—assigned to them in the equal-opportunity distribution, others will have lagged behind it. (Countless handicap races have been run on the world's race courses but despite the best efforts of expert handi-cappers, there is to my knowledge no record of a single race ever pro-ducing a dead heat of *all* the runners.) We need not decide whether this is an empirical law or a logical necessity. Such will be the just out-come of the first round; however, this just end-state represents a new distribution D′ of assets and advantages that, unlike the initial D, no longer offers equal opportunities for the second round. Equality of op-portunity must be restored by redistribution, positive discrimination, and so forth. The just end-state D′ generated by equal opportunities and freedom of contract in the first round offers the participants un-equal opportunities for the second round, and must be overridden to secure the justice of the end-state to be generated in it, and so on to the third and all subsequent rounds to the end of time.

The contradiction in the reasoning of many liberals who want to embrace a plurality of values, seek the reconciliation of freedom and justice, and find in equality of opportunity combined with freedom of contract the joint necessary and sufficient conditions of a proce-dural type of social justice, resides in this: 1) a particular end-state distribution D, and only D, is consistent with equality of opportunity, 2) equality of opportunity combined with freedom of contract engen-ders non-D, and only non-D, 3) D is not compatible with procedural distributive justice, 4) therefore equality of opportunity, freedom of contract, and procedural distributive justice are not mutually compatible.

The reader will remark that if equality of opportunity is not itself a final value, but has only instrumental value in bringing about a certain valuable end-state, yet that kind of end-state must continually be overridden because it is inconsistent with the maintenance of equality of opportunity, the instrumental value of the latter is fleeting and self-destructive. If it is to be commended, it must be on its own merits as a final value, and not for its instrumental capacity to bring about procedural justice in distribution. If no equivalent procedure suggests itself, the attempt at procedural distributive justice must be considered a failure, the justice or otherwise of a distribution must be ascertained in some other manner, such as by listening to the moral consensus of public opinion, and the just distribution either given up as too costly and awkward to achieve, or enforced by direct measures that *ipso facto* violate the freedom of contract and the corollary rights of property and privacy.

Twist it as we may, the dilemma will not go away. The hard sort of freedom that is more than moral truism and non-committal, costless piety, forbids the exercise of social choice over questions of "who gets what." Yet that is the crucial domain over which voters, groups, classes, and their coalitions generally aspire, and often succeed, to turn the power of the political authority to their advantage. More freedom is less scope for collective choice and vice versa; there is a trade-off which democratic society has used these past hundred years or so to whittle down freedom sometimes overtly, sometimes surreptitiously, and the most often fairly unconsciously. The process of whittling down has been promoted and justified by a more plausible and seductive ideology than anything classical liberals could muster.

No Hard Choices

The ideology of the expanding domain of social choice used to have, and probably has not lost, the ambition of showing how this is compatible with the avoidance of hard choices, notably the preservation of freedom. Two key theses serve as its twin pillars.

The first, put briefly, concerns the reliance on reason. It seems to affirm that, whether embodied in the knowledge of a technocratic elite or in the consensual wisdom born of democratic debate, reason is the only guide we should follow, and, in a more exacting and activist version, we should never fail to follow. Reason is in most circumstances able to detect faults in the functioning of economic and social arrangements, and can prescribe the likely remedy. This thesis is common to doctrines as disparate as Benthamite utilitarianism, Saint Simonian, Marxist or just *ad hoc* socialism, Fabian compromise, "constructivist" system-building, and Popperite trial-and-error social engineering. They are consequentialist doctrines, willing the means if they will the end: they fear no taboos and stop at no barriers of a non-reasoned and metaphysical nature.

All hold, albeit implicitly, that government whose vocation it is to elicit and execute social choices, is a uniquely potent tool which it is wasteful and inefficient not to employ to capacity for bringing about feasible improvements. Government, and it alone, can correct the deformities of markets. It can deal with unwanted externalities and regulate the conduct of private enterprise when the divergence of private and social costs and returns misguides it by false signals. Forgoing society's political power to improve results in these respects, and indeed in any others, is irrational and obscurantist.

Without actually being a series of truisms, the easy plausibility of this thesis makes it near-invincible in public debate. Counter-arguments, if directed against "excessive interference" and "bureaucratic busybodyness," are irrefutable but ineffective, since meliorist measures dictated by reason are never *meant* to be excessive or bureaucratic. A general plea to leave well alone is, to all intents and purposes, a defeatist or uncaring stance against trying to do better. Each policy, each measure is defended piecemeal by reason, on its separate merits. The perhaps unintended sum of winning piecemeal arguments for doing this and that, is a win for government intervention as a general practice. The twin of the thesis about reason is about justice. The former aims at allocative efficiency, the latter at the right distribution of the product. The dual structure of the domain of social choice suggested by this division of aims implies that logically and temporally production comes first, distribution follows second. Things are produced, as Mill believed, according to "the laws of economics," and once they are there, become available for distribution according to some other law or precept. Such has been the position of Christian Socialists since high medieval times, and such is that of redistributor liberals from Mill and T. H. Green to Rawls. Distributions caused by the hazard of heredity, heritage, and history may be freely altered, subject only to limits set by expediency, by social choice which is sovereign over the matter. They ought to be altered, to conform to some moral standard, because they are morally arbitrary.

The charge of moral arbitrariness, if it is upheld, means no more than it says, namely that rewards are not, or not wholly, determined by the moral features of a social state of affairs: the morally arbitrary distribution fails to fulfill the positive prediction that people's incomes, etc., depend on their deserts, as well as the normative postulate that they ought to depend on them. However, a cognitive diagnosis of arbitrariness might be applied to a distribution not only from the moral, but also from the economic, legal, social, or historical points of view. A morally arbitrary distribution fails to conform to a moral theory; arbitrariness, however, may also obtain with respect to economic, legal, or historical theories of distribution as well. If the actual distribution is partly determined by genetic endowments and their development, character, education, wealth, and chance, which seems to me a sensible hypothesis, it has, from the point of view of any theory which does not properly account for these factors, an ineradicable property of un-caused randomness, or to use the value-loaded synonym, "arbitrariness." Thus, we can say that, in terms of the marginal productivity theory of factor rewards, the distribution of factor incomes in the Soviet Union is arbitrary. That, however, does not in itself condemn it. Arbitrariness is an obstacle to explaining or predicting, and it is also the absence of reasons for upholding or commending a particular distribution, but it is not a reason for changing it.[19] Some further, positive argument is needed to make the case that an arbitrary distribution

19. For a different argument about moral arbitrariness, cf. Nozick 1974, 213–26.

ought to be purged of its random features and transformed into one that fully obeys some ordering principle drawn from a moral (or some other) theory.

It would be too easy if the ideology which, for its completeness, needed a theory of distributive justice, could validate the latter by the mere claim, however well founded, that the actual distribution was arbitrary. The theory needs the support of axioms that must be independent, difficult to reject, and adequate. However, what axioms will bear the weight of a theory that must justify the subjection of who-gets-what questions to the political authority? Neither moral desert[20] nor the various versions of egalitarianism are difficult enough to reject.

Moral desert lacks independence, in that what is judged as morally deserved, obviously depends on an (at least implicit) moral theory guiding such judgments. Only prior agreement on such a theory, and notably on its implications for distributive justice, can secure agreed judgments of moral desert. They are indeterminate without the support of the theory, hence cannot serve as its antecedents.

Unlike moral desert, egalitarianism is at least not circular, and can be, though it rarely is, non-vacuous, i.e., its necessary conditions can be so defined that whether they are fulfilled or not becomes an empirical question. However, little else is left to be said for it. As an instrumental value, it used to be bolstered by consequentialist arguments, e.g., maximization of utility from a given total income, better satisfaction of "real needs," or reduced pain of envy, that no longer enjoy much intellectual credit. As an ultimate, non-instrumental value that need not be argued for, it retains the emotional appeal it always had and probably always will have; paradoxically, however, the clearer it becomes that the appeal is essentially emotional, the more its effect fades.

On the whole, like certain seductive mining prospects that have been sadly spoiled by the drilling of core samples, distributive justice loses some of its glitter in analysis. "A distribution ought to be just" is a plausible requirement. "A just distribution ought to corre-

---

20. There can, in any case, be no differential moral desert if all differential performance is due to some differential advantage (talent, education, character, etc.), and all such advantages are themselves undeserved. Cf. Sandels 1982, 88. Moral desert then collapses into equality, and becomes redundant.

spond to moral deserts," or "a just distribution ought to be equal" are a good deal easier to contradict. Moreover, attempts to put such norms into practice have not helped either, ranging as they did from the disappointing when they were ineffective, to the disastrous when they were effective. Sir Stafford Cripps, Olaf Palme, and Willy Brandt have done much to make redistributive compromises unappealing. Pol Pot and Nicolae Ceauscescu have done as much for the uncompromising variety.

A more ingenious strategy proceeds by revising the order of the arguments. The usual sequence is to propose that, 1) the existing distribution is arbitrary, 2) only non-arbitrary distributions can be just, 3) a just distribution conforms to an appropriate ordering principle, 4) social choice legitimately mandates the government to realize this conformity. Instead of this roundabout route to the sovereignty of social choice over distribution, it is more efficient directly to propose that the assets, endowments, and other advantages that make the existing distribution what it is, are not rightfully owned by the persons to whom they are in various ways attached, but are the property of their community,[21] and it is up to the community to decide the disposal of the fruits of its property. Genetic qualities, wealth, acquired knowledge, and organization all belong to society as a whole and are *eo ipso* subject to social choice, without any need for a legitimation drawn from controversial requirements of justice, and a debatable mandate for actually imposing them.

Distributions "chosen by society" may or may not be just. They are *ipso facto* just only in case the moral axioms that are used to define the justice or otherwise of a distribution, are taken to be the same as those that help, by fixing the choice rule, to identify an alternative as the "socially chosen" one. This means, broadly speaking, that if in a given political society the "chosen" alternative is some resultant of the wishes of its members, if every member's wish "counts for one and no more than one," and the majority wish prevails, then the "just" distribution is identified by the same rule in the same way. "Just" then means "chosen by society," found to be such by a democratic process of search and consultation, or, more loosely, conforming to the moral consensus. It

21. G. A. Cohen in Paul, Miller, Paul, and Ahrens 1986.

is just that a person should be allowed to keep what he has if, and only if, more people than not think that he should. This is perhaps a brutal and unsympathetic statement of what the sovereignty of social choice implies, but it is by no means a caricature of it.

The real difference between the two ideological strategies for extending the domain of social choice consists in this: if assets, in the broad sense which includes wealth, skill, and character, belong to individuals in a "capitalist free-for-all," there is a *prima facie* implication that it is their right to dispose of the resulting income, both "earned" and "unearned." Society, however, speaking by the medium of the "social choice rule" might declare such an income distribution unjust, refuse to countenance it, and proceed to its redistribution. In doing so, it would contradict itself, for it could not in the same breath both respect and violate a given set of property rights with the attendant freedom of contract. Its solution, adopted, as Hayek called them in the *Road to Serfdom,* by "socialists of all parties" except the genuine ones, is to chop up property rights into a variety of separate rights, recognize and attach some to certain classes of asset or asset-holder, and detach others, depending on the origin, type, or size of the asset or advantage in question, finally declaring its unshaken respect for the resulting mishmash. Ownership of property and the right to use, sell, bequeath, rent, or consume it thus become disjointed, fitting together as *ad hoc* "social choices" decree. In conjunction with this solution, society or its government can affirm allegiance to any innocuous notion of freedom, and for good measure even give it "lexicographic priority," that requires the non-violation of rights in general without committing itself to specific and potentially inconvenient rights, and to the freedom of contract in particular.

Genuine socialists, probably no longer a very numerous or happy class, face no such contradiction between private rights and the ambition for social choice to override them, and need not have recourse to the ambiguities of redistributor liberals. With property vested in society, it is "social choice" that by rights distributes incomes, positions, and ranks in the first place; it does not need to redistribute what it has distributed, hence it does not come into conflict with any right it may have recognized to begin with; the problem of the freedom of contract does not even arise.

One way or the other, as long as freedom is allowed to be "soft," nebulous, innocuous, costless, and as long as the claim that it is being respected and its conditions are fulfilled, remains "unfalsifiable" because the conditions are vacuous and commit to little, there are no hard choices. Allocative efficiency and social justice can be pursued in conjunction with the "greatest possible" and most "equal" freedom. We can have it all. By contrast, the painful trade-offs imposed by laying down "hard," specific, falsifiable conditions of freedom can be made to stand out clearly. Privacy, private property, and freedom of contract strike at the heart of "social choice," removing as they do from its domain many of the most valuable opportunities any decisive subset of society would use for imposing on the superset the choices and solutions it prefers, considers right or just, or expects to profit from.

Non-violation of privacy, private property, and freedom of contract involves massive self-denial. It demands a large measure of renunciation of the use of political processes for advancing certain interests in conflict with others. Instead of getting their way, majorities may have to bargain and buy it by contractual means. It also involves negation of plausible and well-developed ideologies that would justify the use of political power to promote one's selfish or unselfish ends in the name of allocative efficiency or social justice.[22] Small wonder, then, that these principles of freedom are systematically violated or talked out of existence. The contrary would be surprising in a civilization with a good deal of political sophistication, skills of adversarial argument, and no inconvenient taboos; a civilization like our own.

Undeserved Luck

The problem is not how to explain why enlightened men do not noticeably like the more-than-rhetorical freedom that imposes upon

22. Since "talk is cheap" and language will adapt to anything, one can override principles of freedom to advance one's interest in the name of freedom. When in 1776, in one of the failed attempts of the century to make French society more efficient and mobile, Turgot tried to put through a program of fairly extensive deregulation, the "duly constituted" corporations defended and saved regulation as a system of "real freedom," necessary for the public good.

them self-denial, renunciation, responsibility, and duty. It is to account for the far stranger fact that, perhaps for the first time in a hundred-odd years, this freedom most of us do not really like is nevertheless holding its own. It seems actually to have gained in some important countries of the political West, and has ceased to retreat in most others. From an abysmal starting level, it is clearly in the ascendant in the societies of the political "East," that had set out really to build socialism and have found that they have inadvertently joined the Third World in the process. Why should the relentless expansion of the domain of collective choice, which has all the logic of political power behind it, now be checked and reversed in so many different places?

Each of these societies has its particular case history; each is no doubt rich in particular lessons. This is not the occasion to survey their more bizarre episodes and their high and low moments. As always, however, each case history has much in common with every other. The chief common feature, to my mind, is that the cumulative imposition by "social choice" of reasoned solutions to an infinity of problems in production and distribution, efficiency and justice, has gradually built up perverse effects, whose total weight finally sufficed to convert the afflicted society to the bitter medicine of freedom.

It is important to admit and indeed to underline that the attempted solutions were reasoned. The caprice of the tyrant played little part in modern attempts at social problem-solving. In each instance, some sort of rational case could be constructed for them. Nothing is easier than to state with hindsight that the case for solution A was "obviously" false and owed its adoption to the stupidity or wickedness of politicians. Nothing is more dangerous than to follow up this train of thought with the all too frequent suggestion that because A was so obviously wrong, B ought to have been chosen. This is the sort of argument that would always justify one more try[23] and would give rise to an endless chain of measures, instead of to the decisive abandonment of tinkering. Often we reason as if alternative measures and policies came with

23. In a large flock of geese, the most precious ones started to languish and die one by one. The wise rabbi was asked to find a remedy. As each of his suggestions was put into practice, more geese died. When the wretched gooseherd finally reported the demise of his last bird, the rabbi, much annoyed, exclaimed: "What a shame, I had so many good ideas left!"

labels describing the likely effects of each, and perhaps also the "objective" probability that a particular effect will manifest itself. If this were so, the social choice of policies would be a choice between sets of specified consequences, or their probability distributions. Better policies would therefore on the whole tend to be chosen in preference to worse ones. Logically the power of the political authority to put chosen policies into practice would be beneficial at least in the long run, over large numbers of measures; collective choice equipped with such coercive power would have a good chance of yielding better results than the sum of individual choices that has lacked such power; and the enlargement of the collective domain at the expense of "hard" freedom would augment the scope for better results. Power, chance, and scope would jointly work for progress, and speed us towards the meliorist ideal.

In reality, the labels the policies carry specify only the narrow band of their effects that have reasonably good visibility. Only hindsight shows that there always is, in addition, a broader and fuzzier band of consequences whose *ex ante* predictability must have been very low, very conjectural, or simply non-existent. Whether this is so because our knowledge about these matters is inadequate though capable of improvement, or because they are inherently unknowable, is perhaps immaterial at any period in time for the consequentialist evaluation of a policy. There may, in addition, be effects that are reasonably predictable but so slow to mature that they get heavily discounted at the inception of a measure—discounting, of course, is a legitimate and indeed a mandatory operation in the rational calculus—and only begin seriously to hurt when the measure that has caused them is as good as forgotten together with the men who had chosen it.

I propose to call unwelcome consequences "perverse" in a broad sense, not only when they are the direct opposite of the main aim of a policy (e.g., a redistributive measure intended to decrease inequality which in fact increases it; a policy of import substitution which makes exports shrink more than imports; government sponsorship of research that actually retards technological progress; and so forth) but also when, acting over a more diffuse area, indirectly or in unexpected directions, they impose costs and reduce benefits so as to leave society worse off than if a given policy had not been adopted. I am aware that condemning a measure on this ground may be question-begging for two reasons. First, the imputation to it of particular unwelcome effects may be too conjectural when the supposed causation is indirect. It may be that lavish spending on arms over the last decade has for round-about reasons weakened the war-making ability and fighting prowess of both the great powers, but how can the diagnosis of cause and effect be made conclusive? Second, a judgment that society is on balance worse off when certain things, say inflation or child delinquency, have gone wrong but others, say care for the old or water pollution, have gone right, is forever fated to depend on how homogenous weights are to be assigned to heterogenous variables; give greater weight to the ones which have gone right, and you find society better off.

Nevertheless, there are well within our memory unmitigated disasters, utter failures, and glaring disproportions between outlay and return, where a distinct policy is so clearly the prime suspect in producing perverse effects that it is bad faith or intellectual preciosity to argue the incompleteness of the proof. The collectivization of land and the attendant pursuit of "economies of scale" in agriculture and, for that matter, in manufacturing too, is now almost unanimously recognized as an act of self-mutilation that has done irreparable damage to the Soviet Union. Strengthening the powers, disciplinary cohesion, and legal immunities of trade unions, and taking them into the corporatist conspiracy of the Macmillan, Wilson, and Heath years is now, albeit less unanimously, seen as a major cause of the "English disease." The policy of forcibly diverting investment from the rest of Italy to its Mezzogiorno has not only cost the country dear in direct and indirect ways—that transferring benefits from one part of society to another is not costless is after all quite consistent with the fond supposition that the exercise nevertheless has a "positive sum"—but may not even have been of real net benefit to the Mezzogiorno.

There are less localized examples of once respected policies that are now highly suspect of perverse effects. Progressive taxation is one: even its natural advocates have learnt to say that it must not be "too" progressive. Free, universal, nonselective formal education, no "streaming," no elitism, diplomas for all, open access for all to universities crowned by the principle of one man-one Ph.D., is another. We are discovering that it hinders the education of those who could profit from it and wastes the time of the rest, breeds student unrest and disappointment, and buys these personal and social blessings at a near-crippling cost to the community's finances. Public policies of welfare and public guarantees (including compulsory insurance) against risks and wants of various kinds in both "mixed" and avowedly "socialist" economies, are coming to be suspected of generating unwelcome behavioral changes: sluggishness to respond to incentives and opportunities, poor resistance to adverse conditions, a weakening of the "work ethic," free riding, irresponsibility for oneself and one's offspring, a falling personal propensity to save, over-consumption and waste of freely provided public goods; these costs, and the long-run damage they do to society's capacity to function, and to the character and virtue of its members, are beginning to weigh heavily against the putative gain in welfare and social justice of which they are dimly perceived to be a by-product.

Not that disillusion, suspicion, and an "agonizing reappraisal" of their costs and benefits is actually leading to the wholesale rolling back of these policies. But their easy expansion has by and large been checked, and in some areas collective choice seems to be restraining itself to give way to the operation of "hard," non-vacuous freedom principles. Its remaining champions, by way of last-ditch defense, design fall-back positions holding out the same old promise that we can, after all, have it both ways. Though they have mostly given up talk about the Yugoslav Road, the Third Way, Indicative Planning, and Social Justice in a Free Society, and though such magic passwords to coercion as "prisoners' dilemma," "externality," and "community preference ordering" may with luck soon go the way of "the diminishing marginal utility of money" and "pump-priming for full employment," the intellectual advocacy of using the power of collective decisions to make a better world will never cease. There are still so many good ideas left! Assuredly, we have not heard the last of the prize inanity, market socialism.

When and where societies, and the decision-making coalitions of interests within them, renounce to use their force for allocating resources and rewards, and take the bitter medicine of freedom instead, they do so because their meliorist solutions that would violate freedom are proving too costly in perverse effects. Contrast this with the diametrically opposite position of actually liking freedom, even if it proved costly in material sacrifice. As Roepke[24] has movingly put it:

> I would stand for a free economic order even if it implied material sacrifice and if socialism gave the certain prospect of material increase. It is our undeserved luck that the exact opposite is true.

It is undeserved luck indeed. Where would we be now if socialism were affordable and whittling freedom down were not as expensive as we are finding it to be?

24. Roepke 1959, 232.

Works Cited

Alchian, A., and H. Demsetz. (1973) The Property Rights Paradigm. *Journal of Economic History* 33.

Anderson, T., and P. J. Hill. (1979) An American Experiment in Anarcho-Capitalism: The *Not So Wild* Wild West. *Journal of Libertarian Studies* 3.

Atiyah, P. S. (1979) *The Rise and Fall of the Freedom of Contract*. Oxford: Oxford University Press.

Axelrod, Robert. (1984) *The Evolution of Cooperation*. New York: Basic Books.

Barry, B. (1986) Lady Chatterley's Lover and Doctor Fischer's Bomb Party. In J. Elster and A. Hylland, eds., *Foundations of Social Choice Theory*. Cambridge: Cambridge University Press. Revised version in B. Barry (1989), *Liberty and Justice*, Oxford, Oxford University Press.

———. (1991) *Liberty and Justice*. Oxford: Oxford University Press.

———. (1994) Justice, Freedom, and Basic Income. In H. Siebert, ed., *The Ethical Foundations of the Market Economy*. Tubingen: J. C. B. Mohr/Paul Siebeck.

———. (1995) *A Treatise on Social Justice*. Vol. 2, *Justice as Impartiality*. Oxford: Oxford University Press.

Baumol, W. J. (1952) *Welfare Economics and the Theory of the State*. Cambridge, Mass.: Harvard University Press.

Benson, B. L. (1989) The Spontaneous Evolution of Commercial Law. *Southern Economic Journal* 55.

———. (1990) *The Enterprise of Law: Justice Without the State*. San Francisco: Pacific Research Institute for Public Policy.

Bergman, M., and J. T. Lane. (1990) Public Policy in the Principal-Agent Framework. *Journal of Theoretical Politics* 2, no. 3.

Bergson, A. (1948) Socialist Economics. In H. S. Ellis, ed., *A Survey of Contemporary Economics*. Homewood, Ill.: American Economics Association.

———. (1967) Market Socialism Revisited. *Journal of Political Economy* 75, no. 5.

Berlin, I. (1978) *Concepts and Categories*. London: Hogarth Press.

Bernholz, P. (1974) Is a Paretian Liberal Really Impossible? *Public Choice* 19: 99–107.

Breyer, F. (1977) The Liberal Paradox. Decisiveness over Issues and Domain Restrictions. *Zeitschrift für Nationalökonomie* 37: 45–60.

Breyer, F., and R. Gardner. (1980) Liberal Paradox, Game Equilibrium, and Gibbard Optimum. *Public Choice* 35: 469–81.

Buchanan, J. M. (1965) An Economic Theory of Clubs. *Economica* 32.

———. (1968) *The Demand and Supply of Public Goods.* Chicago: Rand-McNally.

———. (1975) *The Limits of Liberty.* Chicago and London: University of Chicago Press.

———. (1994) *Ethics and Economic Progress.* Norman: University of Oklahoma Press.

Buchanan, J. M., and G. Tullock. (1962) *The Calculus of Consent.* Ann Arbor: University of Michigan Press.

Coase, R. H. (1960) The Problem of Social Cost. *Journal of Law and Economics* 3: 1–15.

———. (1974) The Lighthouse in Economics. *Journal of Law and Economics* 17, no. 2: 357–76.

———. (1988) *The Firm, the Market, and the Law.* Chicago: University of Chicago Press.

Cowen, Tyler, ed. (1988) *The Theory of Market Failure.* Fairfax, Va.: George Mason University Press.

Dahlman, C. J. (1979) The Problem of Externality. *Journal of Law and Economics* 22: 141–62. Repr. in Cowen 1988.

Demsetz, Harold. (1964) The Exchange and Enforcement of Property Rights. *Journal of Law and Economics* 7. Repr. in Cowen 1988.

———. (1970) Private Production of Public Goods. *Journal of Law and Economics* 13, no. 2: 293–306.

Ellickson, R. C. (1991) *Order Without Law: How Neighbors Settle Disputes.* Cambridge, Mass.: Harvard University Press.

Engels, F. (1891) The Origin of the Family, Private Property and the State. In K. Marx and F. Engels, *Selected Writings,* 1968.

Feinberg, J. (1984) *Harm to Others.* Oxford: Oxford University Press.

Friedman, D. (1978) *The Machinery of Freedom: Guide to a Radical Capitalism.* New Rochelle, N.Y.: Arlington House.

Gaertner, W., P. K. Pattanaik, and K. Suzumura. (1992) Individual Rights Revisited. *Economica* 59: 161–78.

Gauthier, D. (1986) *Morals by Agreement.* Oxford: Oxford University Press.

Gauthier, D., and R. Sugden, eds. (1993) *Rationality, Justice and the Social Contract.* Hemel Hempstead: Harvester Wheatsheaf.

Gibbard, A. (1974) A Pareto-Consistent Libertarian Claim. *Journal of Economic Theory* 7: 388–410.

———. (1982) Rights and the Theory of Social Choice. In L. Cohen et al., eds., *Logic, Methodology and Philosophy of Science* vol. 6. Amsterdam, 595–605.

Gray, J. (1992) *The Moral Foundations of Market Institutions.* London: IEA Health and Welfare Unit.

Griffin, J. (1986) *Well-Being.* Oxford: Clarendon Press.

Hahn, F., ed. (1989) *The Economics of Missing Markets, Information and Games.* Oxford: Clarendon Press.

Hampton, J. S. (1987) The Free Rider Problem in the Production of Collective Goods. *Economics and Philosophy* 3, no. 2: 245–73.

———. (1990) *Hobbes and the Social Contract Tradition.* Cambridge: Cambridge University Press.

Harsanyi, J. C. (1977) *Rational Behavior and Bargaining Equilibrium in Games and Social Situations.* Cambridge: Cambridge University Press.

Hart, H. L. A. (1961) *The Concept of Law.* Oxford: Clarendon Press.

———. (1983) *Essays in Jurisprudence and Philosophy.* Oxford: Clarendon Press; New York: Oxford University Press.

Hayek, F. A., ed. (1935) *Collectivist Economic Planning.* London: George Routledge and Sons.

———. (1960) *The Constitution of Liberty.* Chicago: University of Chicago Press.

———. (1973–1979) *Law, Legislation and Liberty* (3 volumes). Chicago: University of Chicago Press.

———. (1978) *New Studies in Philosophy, Politics, Economics and the History of Ideas.* London: Routledge Kegan Paul.

Heiner, R. A. (1996) Exogenous Versus Endogenous Information: A General Theory of Nash Equilibrium. *Public Choice* (forthcoming).

Hobbes, T. (1651) *Leviathan.* Harmondsworth: Penguin Books, 1968.

Jasay, A. de. (1985) *The State.* Oxford: Basil Blackwell.

———. (1989) *Social Contract, Free Ride: A Study of the Public Goods Problem.* Oxford: Clarendon Press.

Kliemt, H., and B. Lahno. (1992) Social Contract, Free Ride. *Constitutional Political Economy* 3, no. 2: 267–71.

Knight, F. H. (1943) The Meaning of Freedom. In C. M. Perry, ed., *The Philosophy of American Democracy.* Chicago: University of Chicago Press.

Lange, O. (1936) On the Economic Theory of Socialism I–II. *Review of Economic Studies* 4 (October): 1.

———. (1937) On the Economic Theory of Socialism I–II. *Review of Economic Studies* 4 (February): 2.

Leoni, B. (1961/1972) *Freedom and the Law.* Los Angeles: Nash Publishing.

Lewis, D. (1979) Prisoners' Dilemma Is a Newcomb Problem. *Philosophy and Public Affairs* 8, no. 3: 235–40.

Libecap, G. D. (1992) The Rise of the Chicago Packers and the Origins of Meat Inspection and Antitrust. *Economic Inquiry* 30 (April): 218–24.

Little, I. M. D. (1950/1973) *Critique of Welfare Economics.* Oxford: Clarendon Press. Repr. as Oxford Paperback.

———. (1952) Social Choice and Individual Values. *Journal of Political Economy* 60: 422–32.

Loan, A. (1991/1992) Institutional Bases of the Spontaneous Order: Surety and Assurance. *Humane Studies Review* 7, no. 1.

Love, J. R. (1991) *Antiquity and Capitalism: Max Weber and the Sociological Foundations of Roman Civilization.* New York: Routledge.

MacFarlane, A. (1979) *The Origins of English Individualism.* Cambridge: Cambridge University Press.

Maddison, A. (1991) *Dynamic Forces in Capitalist Development.* Oxford: Oxford University Press.

Maine, H. (1885, 1976) *Popular Government.* Indianapolis: Liberty Fund.

Marx, K. [1843] The Jewish Question. Economic and Philosophical Manuscripts. In *Early Writings,* 1975.

McPherson, T. (1967) *Political Obligation.* London: Routledge & Kegan Paul.

Mill, J. S. (1848) *Principles of Political Economy.*

Mises, L. von (1966) *Human Action* (2nd ed.). Chicago: Chicago University Press.

Musgrave, R. A. (1939) The Voluntary Exchange Theory of Public Economy. *Quarterly Journal of Economics* 53.

———. (1959) *The Theory of Public Finance.* New York: McGraw-Hill.

Nozick, R. (1973) Distributive Justice. *Philosophy & Public Affairs* 3: 45–126.

———. (1974) *Anarchy, State, and Utopia.* New York: Basic Books.

———. (1993) *The Nature of Rationality.* Princeton: Princeton University Press.

Oakeshott, M. (1962) *Rationalism in Politics.* London: Methuen.

Olson, Mancur, Jr. (1965) *The Logic of Collective Action.* Cambridge, Mass.: Harvard University Press.

Ostrom, Elinor. (1990) *Governing the Commons.* Cambridge and New York: Cambridge University Press.

Paqué, K.-H. (1986) *Philantropie und Steuerpolitik,* Tubingen: J. C. B. Mohr/Paul Siebeck.

Pareto, V. (1909) *Manuel d'economie politique.* Lausanne.

Paul, E. F., F. D. Miller Jr., J. Paul, and J. Ahrens, eds. (1986) *Marxism and Liberalism.* New York: Social Philosophy and Policy Center.

Popper, K. R. (1963) *The Open Society and Its Enemies.* Princeton: Princeton University Press.

Posner, R. A. (1993) Leftist Legal Formalism. *Critical Review* 6: 4.

Radnitzky, G. (1933) Wie marktkonform ist die Soziale Marktwirtschaft? *Schweizerische Monatshefte* 73: 6.

Rawls, J. (1971) *A Theory of Justice.* Cambridge, Mass.: Belknap Press.

Raz, J. (1986) *The Morality of Freedom.* Oxford: Oxford University Press.

Ricardo, D. (1817) *Principles of Political Economy and Taxation.* London.

Roepke, W. (1959) The Economic Necessity of Freedom. *Modern Age.* Reprinted with a foreword by E. J. Feulner Jr., *The President's Essay,* Washington, D.C.: Heritage Foundation, 1988.

Sabourian, H. (1989) Repeated Games: A Survey. In F. Hahn, *The Economics of Missing Markets, Information and Games.* Oxford: Clarendon Press.

Samuelson, Paul A. (1954) The Pure Theory of Public Expenditure. *Review of Economics and Statistics* 36.

Sandels, M. J. (1982) *Liberalism and the Limits of Justice*. Cambridge: Cambridge University Press.

Scanlon, T. M. (1982) Contractualism and Utilitarianism. In A. Sen and B. Williams, eds., *Utilitarianism and Beyond*. Cambridge: Cambridge University Press.

Sen, A. K. (1970a) *Collective Choice and Social Welfare*. Edinborough.

———. (1970b) The Impossibility of a Paretian Liberal. *Journal of Political Economy* 78: 152–57.

———. (1970c) Interpersonal Aggregation and Partial Comparability. *Econometrica* 38: 393–409. Repr. in Sen 1982a.

———. (1976) Liberty, Unanimity and Rights. *Economica* 43: 217–45. Repr. in Sen 1982a.

———. (1982a) *Choice, Welfare and Measurement*. Oxford: Blackwell.

———. (1982b) Liberty as Control: An Appraisal. *Midwest Studies in Philosophy* 7: 207–21.

———. (1983) Liberty and Social Choice. *Journal of Philosophy* 80: 5–28.

———. (1986) Foundations of Social Choice Theory: An Epilogue. In J. Elster and A. Hylland (eds.), *Foundations of Social Choice Theory*. Cambridge: Cambridge University Press.

Starbatty, J., et al. (1993) *Adjektivlose oder Soziale Marktwirtschaft*. Bonn: Ludwig Erhard Stiftung.

Stigler, G. (1961) Private Vice and Public Vertue. *Journal of Law and Economics* (October): 1–11.

———. (1978/1984) Wealth, and Possibly Liberty. *Journal of Legal Studies* 7, no. 2. Repr. in Stigler 1984.

———. (1982) *The Economist as Preacher*. Chicago: University of Chicago Press.

———. (1984) *The Intellectual and the Marketplace*. Cambridge, Mass.: Harvard University Press.

Strauss, L. (1953) *Natural Right and History*. Chicago: University of Chicago Press.

Streit, M. (1994) Comment on Robert Sugden "The Theory of Rights." In H. Siebert, ed., *The Ethical Foundations of the Market Economy*. Tübingen: Mohr.

Sugden, R. (1985) Liberty, Preference, and Choice. *Economics and Philosophy* 1/2: 213–29.

———. (1991/2) Suckers, Free Riders and Public Goods. *Humane Studies Review* 7.

———. (1993) Rights: Why Do They Matter and to Whom. *Constitutional Political Economy* 4: 127–52.

———. (1994) The Theory of Rights. In H. Siebert, ed., *The Ethical Foundations of the Market Economy*. Tübingen: Mohr.

Taylor, Michael. (1976) *Anarchy and Cooperation*. London and New York: Wiley.

———. (1987) *The Possibility of Cooperation*. Cambridge: Cambridge University Press.

Thompson, E. A., and R. Faith. (1981) A Pure Theory of Strategic Behavior and Social Institutions. *American Economic Review* 71: 366–79.

Trakman, L. (1983) *The Law Merchant: The Evolution of Commercial Law*. Littleton, Colo.: Rothman & Co.

Ullman-Margalit, E. (1977) *The Emergence of Norms*. Oxford: Oxford University Press.

Vaughn, K. I. (1981) Introduction. In T. J. B. Hoff (1949, 1981), *Economic Calculation in the Socialist Society*. Indianapolis: Liberty Fund.

Wagner, R. E. (1989) *To Promote the General Welfare*. San Francisco: Pacific Research Institute for Public Policy.

Walzer, M. (1983/1985) *Spheres of Justice*. Oxford: Blackwell.

Wicksell, K. (1896) *Finanztheoretische Untersuchungen*. Jena: Gustav Fischer.

Index

The typeface used for this book is ITC New Baskerville, which was created
for the International Typeface Corporation and is based on the types of the
English type founder and printer John Baskerville (1706–75). Baskerville is the
quintessential transitional face: it retains the bracketed and oblique serifs of
old-style faces such as Caslon and Garamond, but in its increased lowercase
height, lighter color, and enhanced contrast between thick and thin strokes,
it presages modern faces.

The display type is set in Didot.

Printed on paper that is acid-free and meets the requirements of the American
National Standard for Permanence of Paper for Printed Library Materials,
z39.48-1992. ∞

Book design by Richard Hendel, Chapel Hill, North Carolina
Composition by Tseng Information Systems, Durham, North Carolina
Printed by Edwards Brothers, Inc., Ann Arbor, Michigan, and bound by
Dekker Bookbinding, Grand Rapids, Michigan